365 Day
AIR
FRYER
COOKBOOK

550 Mouth-Watering Air Fryer Recipes for Your Friends and Family with 365-Day Hand-Picked Meal Plan

Travis K. Weaver

TABLE OF CONTENTS

DESCRIPTION

By now, you must have heard of an air fryer, right? If not, then this is the time you get one. Getting started on air fryer recipes can be daunting for so many people, most notably because it is a new thing. It may also be because of other reasons. Whatever the rationale is, you've got to seal that deal!

It is time you get cooking with an air fryer, and you will be surprised at all the things you get to enjoy. One thing you will note about the air fryer is that you will cook all sorts of breaded meals that traditionally, you would have to bake or deep fry. How cool is that!

That said, these air fryer recipes promise you all the healthy dishes that will taste all crispy and fried. You will not be indulging in greasy foods that traditional deep fryers yield.

You may be thinking; "but how do you make them crispy without deep frying?" Well, an air fryer works by circulating scorching air that is mixed with tiny oil droplets. It is this that goes a long way in crisping up whatever it that you are cooking so that it is golden brown and mouth-watering.

Trust me; your foods will not only look yummy but will also taste better. Try our 550+ air fryer recipes and 365-Day meal plans, and you will never have to look back.

What are you still waiting for?

Start cooking already!

INTRODUCTION

An air fryer is inarguably one of the best kitchen devices that you can add to your kitchen for daily cooking use. It offers so much advantages which include the following:

Why Use It

Low-Fat Meals: Unarguably, the most essential benefit of the air fryer is its use of hot-air circulation to cook food ingredients from all angles, thereby eliminating the need for oil usage. This makes it possible for people on low fat diet to comfortably prepare delightfully healthy meals.

Healthier Foods& Environment: Airfryers are designed to function without fattening oils and to produce healthier foods with up to 80 percent less fat. This makes it easier to lose weight because you can still eat your fried dishes while conserving the calories and saturated fat. Making that switch to a healthier life is more achievable by using this appliance. Your home is also rid of the aroma that comes with deep fried foods that often stays around the atmosphere even several hours after deep frying.

Multipurpose Use: The airfryer enables you to multitask as it can prepare multiple dishes at once. It is your all-in-one appliance that can grill, bake, fry and roast those dishes that you love! You no longer need multiple appliances for various jobs. It is capable of doing other jobs separate appliances will do. It can grill meat, roast veggies and bake pastries. It serves as an effective substitution for your oven, deep fryer and stovetop.

Extremely Safe: Remember how extra careful you have to be when throwing chicken or some other ingredients into the deep fryer? You want to ensure that the hot oil does not spill and burn your skin since it's always very hot. With your airfryer, you wouldn't need to worry about brunt skin from hot oil spillage. It does all the frying and is completely safe. Nevertheless, use cooking gloves while repositioning your fryer to avoid hazards from the heat. Additionally, keep your air fryer out of children's reach.

Easy Clean Up: The Air Fryer leaves no grease and therefore no mess. Clean-up time is enjoyable

since there oils spills to clean on walls and floors, and no scrapping or scrubbing of pans. There is no need to spend time ensuring that everything is squeaky clean. The Air fryer parts are made of non-stick material which prevents food from sticking to surfaces, thereby making it hard to clean. These parts are easy to clean and maintain. They are removable and dishwasher-safe as well.

Save Valuable Time: People who are on tight schedules can make use of the speediness of the air fryer to make delicious meals. For instances, you can make French fries in less than 15 minutes and bake a cake within 25 minutes. Within minutes too, you can enjoy crispy chicken tenders or golden fries. If you are always on the go, the air fryer is just right for you because you will spend less time in the kitchen. It enables you to manage your hectic and busy daily life, making your day more manageable.

01. EASY EGG MUFFINS

Preparation Time: 25 Minutes
Servings: 4

Ingredients:

- 2 tbsp. olive oil
- 3 tbsp. milk
- 1 egg
- 3.5 oz. white flour
- 1 tbsp. baking powder
- 2 oz. parmesan; grated
- A splash of Worcestershire sauce

Directions:

1. In a bowl; mix egg with flour, oil, baking powder, milk, Worcestershire and parmesan; whisk well and divide into 4 silicon muffin cups.
2. Arrange cups in your air fryer's cooking basket; cover and cook at 392, °F, for 15 minutes. Serve warm for breakfast.

Nutrition Values: Calories: 251; Fat: 6; Fiber: 8; Carbs: 9; Protein: 3

02. BREAKFAST POTATOES

Preparation Time: 45 Minutes
Servings: 4

Ingredients:

- 2 tbsp. olive oil
- 3 potatoes; cubed
- 1 yellow onion; chopped.
- 1 red bell pepper; chopped
- 1 tsp. garlic powder
- 1 tsp. sweet paprika
- 1 tsp. onion powder
- Salt and black pepper to the taste

Directions:

1. Grease your air fryer's basket with olive oil; add potatoes, toss and season with salt and pepper.
2. Add onion, bell pepper, garlic powder, paprika and onion powder, toss well, cover and cook at 370 °F, for 30 minutes. Divide potatoes mix on plates and serve for breakfast.

Nutrition Values: Calories: 214; Fat: 6; Fiber: 8; Carbs: 15; Protein: 4

03. BREAKFAST HAM DISH

Preparation Time: 25 Minutes
Servings: 6

Ingredients:

- 6 cups French bread; cubed
- 4 oz. green chilies; chopped.
- 2 cups milk
- 5 eggs
- 1 tbsp. mustard
- 10 oz. ham; cubed
- 4 oz. cheddar cheese; shredded
- Salt and black pepper to the taste
- Cooking spray

Directions:

1. Heat up your air fryer at 350 °F and grease it with cooking spray.
2. In a bowl; mix eggs with milk, cheese, mustard, salt and pepper and stir.
3. Add bread cubes in your air fryer and mix with chilies and ham.
4. Add eggs mix; spread and cook for 15 minutes. Divide among plates and serve.

Nutrition Values: Calories: 200; Fat: 5; Fiber: 6; Carbs: 12; Protein: 14

04. BANANA OATMEAL CASSEROLE

Preparation Time: 30 Minutes
Servings: 8

Ingredients:

- 2 cups rolled oats
- 1 tsp. baking powder
- 1/2 cup chocolate chips
- 2/3 cup blueberries
- 1 banana; peeled and mashed

- 1/3 cup brown sugar
- 1 tsp. cinnamon powder
- 2 cups milk
- 1 eggs
- 2 tbsp. butter
- 1 tsp. vanilla extract
- Cooking spray

Directions:

1. In a bowl; mix sugar with baking powder, cinnamon, chocolate chips, blueberries and banana and stir.
2. In a separate bowl; mix eggs with vanilla extract and butter and stir.
3. Heat up your air fryer at 320 degrees F; grease with cooking spray and add oats on the bottom.
4. Add cinnamon mix and eggs mix; toss and cook for 20 minutes. Stir one more time, divide into bowls and serve for breakfast.

Nutrition Values: Calories: 300; Fat: 4; Fiber: 7; Carbs: 12; Protein: 10

05. TASTY POLENTA BITES

Preparation Time: 30 Minutes
Servings: 4

Ingredients:

For the polenta:
- 1 tbsp. butter
- 3 cups water
- 1 cup cornmeal
- Salt and black pepper to the taste

For the polenta bites:
- 2 tbsp. powdered sugar
- Cooking spray

Directions:

1. In a pan; mix water with cornmeal, butter, salt and pepper, stir, bring to a boil over medium heat; cook for 10 minutes, take off heat; whisk one more time and keep in the fridge until it's cold.
2. Scoop 1 tbsp. of polenta, shape a ball and place on a working surface.
3. Repeat with the rest of the polenta; arrange all the balls in the cooking basket of your air fryer, spray them with cooking spray; cover and cook at 380 °F, for 8

minutes. Arrange polenta bites on plates; sprinkle sugar all over and serve for breakfast.

Nutrition Values: Calories: 231; Fat: 7; Fiber: 8; Carbs: 12; Protein: 4

06. EGGS AND TOMATOES

Preparation Time: 15 Minutes
Servings: 4

Ingredients:

- 4 eggs
- 2 oz. milk
- 2 tbsp. parmesan; grated
- 8 cherry tomatoes; halved
- Salt and black pepper to the taste
- Cooking spray

Directions:

1. Grease your air fryer with cooking spray and heat it up at 200 degrees F.
2. In a bowl; mix eggs with cheese, milk, salt and pepper and whisk.
3. Add this mix to your air fryer and cook for 6 minutes. Add tomatoes; cook your scrambled eggs for 3 minutes, divide among plates and serve.

Nutrition Values: Calories: 200; Fat: 4; Fiber: 7; Carbs: 12; Protein: 3

07. FRIED SANDWICH

Preparation Time: 16 Minutes
Servings: 2

Ingredients:

- 2 English muffins; halved
- 2 bacon strips
- 2 eggs
- Salt and black pepper to the taste

Preparation:

1. Crack eggs in your air fryer, add bacon on top; cover and cook at 392 °F, for 6 minutes. Heat up your English muffin halves in your microwave for a few seconds; divide eggs on 2 halves, add bacon on top, season with salt and pepper; cover with the other 2 English muffins and serve for breakfast.

Nutrition Values: Calories: 261; Fat: 5; Fiber: 8; Carbs: 12; Protein: 4

08. BREAKFAST CASSEROLE

Preparation Time: 40 Minutes
Servings: 4

Ingredients:

- 3 tbsp. brown sugar
- 4 tbsp. butter
- 2 tbsp. white sugar
- 1/2 cup flour
- 1/2 tsp. cinnamon powder

For the casserole:

- 2 eggs
- 2 tbsp. white sugar
- 2 ½ cups white flour
- 1 tsp. baking soda
- 1 tsp. baking powder
- 2 eggs
- 1/2 cup milk
- 2 cups buttermilk
- 4 tbsp. butter
- 1 ⅔ cup blueberries
- Zest from 1 lemon; grated

Preparation:

1. In a bowl; mix eggs with 2 tbsp. white sugar, 2 ½ cups white flour, baking powder, baking soda, 2 eggs, milk, buttermilk, 4 tbsp. butter, lemon zest and blueberries; stir and pour into a pan that fits your air fryer.
2. In another bowls; mix 3 tbsp. brown sugar with 2 tbsp. white sugar, 4 tbsp. butter, 1/2 cup flour and cinnamon, stir until you obtain a crumble and spread over blueberries mix.
3. Place in preheated air fryer and bake at 300 °F, for 30 minutes. Divide among plates and serve for breakfast.

Nutrition Values: Calories: 214; Fat: 5; Fiber: 8; Carbs: 12; Protein: 5

09. CHEESE FRIED BAKE

Preparation Time: 30 Minutes
Servings: 4

Ingredients:

- 4 bacon slices; cooked and crumbled
- 2 cups milk
- 1 lb. breakfast sausage; casings removed and chopped.
- 2 eggs
- 2 ½ cups cheddar cheese; shredded
- 1/2 tsp. onion powder
- 3 tbsp. parsley; chopped.
- Salt and black pepper to the taste
- Cooking spray

Directions:

1. In a bowl; mix eggs with milk, cheese, onion powder, salt, pepper and parsley and whisk well.
2. Grease your air fryer with cooking spray; heat it up at 320 °F and add bacon and sausage.
3. Add eggs mix; spread and cook for 20 minutes. Divide among plates and serve.

Nutrition Values: Calories: 214; Fat: 5; Fiber: 8; Carbs: 12; Protein: 12

10. DELIGHTFUL EGGS CASSEROLE

Preparation Time: 35 Minutes
Servings: 6

Ingredients:

- 12 eggs
- 1 lb. turkey; ground
- 1 sweet potato; cubed
- 1 cup baby spinach
- 1 tbsp. olive oil
- 1/2 tsp. chili powder
- 2 tomatoes; chopped for serving
- Salt and black pepper to the taste

Directions:

1. In a bowl; mix eggs with salt, pepper, chili powder, potato, spinach, turkey and sweet potato and whisk well.
2. Heat up your air fryer at 350 degrees F; add oil and heat it up.
3. Add eggs mix, spread into your air fryer; cover and cook for 25 minutes. Divide among plates and serve for breakfast.

Nutrition Values: Calories: 300; Fat: 5; Fiber: 8; Carbs: 13; Protein: 6

11. MORNING EGG BOWLS

Preparation Time: 30 Minutes
Servings: 4

Ingredients:

- 4 eggs
- 4 dinner rolls; tops cut off and insides scooped out
- 4 tbsp. mixed chives and parsley
- 4 tbsp. parmesan; grated
- 4 tbsp. heavy cream
- Salt and black pepper to the taste

Preparation:

1. Arrange dinner rolls on a baking sheet and crack an egg in each.
2. Divide heavy cream, mixed herbs in each roll and season with salt and pepper.
3. Sprinkle parmesan on top of your rolls; place them in your air fryer and cook at 350 °F, for 20 minutes. Divide your bread bowls on plates and serve for breakfast.

Nutrition Values: Calories: 238; Fat: 4; Fiber: 7; Carbs: 14; Protein: 7

12. THYME POTATO BREAKFAST MIX

Preparation time: 5 minutes
Cooking time: 25 minutes
Servings: 4

Ingredients:

- 1½ pounds hash browns
- 1 red onion, chopped
- 2 teaspoons vegetable oil
- 1 red bell pepper, chopped
- Salt and black pepper to taste
- 1 teaspoon thyme, chopped
- 2 eggs

Directions:

1. Heat up your air fryer at 350 degrees F. Then add the oil and heat it up.
2. Add all other ingredients and cook for 25 minutes.

3. Divide between plates and serve

Nutrition Values: calories 241, fat 4, fiber 2, carbs 12, protein 11

13. CHICKEN AND SPINACH BREAKFAST CASSEROLE

Preparation time: 5 minutes
Cooking time: 25 minutes
Servings: 4

Ingredients:

- 1 pound chicken meat, ground
- 1 tablespoon olive oil
- ½ teaspoon sweet paprika
- 12 eggs, whisked
- 1 cup baby spinach
- Salt and black pepper to taste

Directions:

1. In a bowl, whisk the eggs with the salt, pepper, and paprika. Then add the spinach and chicken and mix well.
2. Heat up your air fryer at 350 degrees F; add the oil and allow it to heat up.
3. Add the chicken and spinach mix, cover, and cook for 25 minutes.
4. Divide between plates and serve hot.

Nutrition Values: calories 270, fat 11, fiber 8, carbs 14, protein 7

14. SAUSAGE BAKE

Preparation time: 5 minutes
Cooking time: 20 minutes
Servings: 4

Ingredients:

- 4 bacon slices, cooked and crumbled
- A drizzle of olive oil
- 2 cups coconut milk
- 2½ cups cheddar cheese, shredded
- 1 pound breakfast sausage, chopped
- 2 eggs
- Salt and black pepper to taste
- 3 tablespoons cilantro, chopped

Directions:

1. In a bowl, mix the eggs with milk, cheese, salt, pepper, and the cilantro, and whisk

well.

2. Grease your air fryer with the drizzle of oil, and heat it up at 320 degrees F.
3. Add the bacon, sausage, and the egg mixture, spread, and cook for 20 minutes.
4. Serve hot and enjoy!

Nutrition Values: calories 244, fat 11, fiber 8, carbs 15, protein 9

15. BREAKFAST CHICKEN BURRITO

Preparation time: 5 minutes
Cooking time: 10 minutes
Servings: 2

Ingredients:

- 4 chicken breast slices, cooked and shredded
- 1 green bell pepper, sliced
- 2 eggs, whisked
- 1 avocado, peeled, pitted and sliced
- 2 tablespoons mild salsa
- Salt and black pepper to taste
- 2 tablespoons cheddar cheese, grated
- 2 tortillas

Directions:

1. In a bowl, whisk the eggs with the salt and pepper, and pour them into a pan that fits your air fryer.
2. Put the pan in the air fryer's basket, cook for 5 minutes at 400 degrees, and transfer the mix to a plate.
3. Place the tortillas on a working surface, and between them divide the eggs, chicken, bell peppers, avocado, and the cheese; roll the burritos.
4. Line your air fryer with tin foil, add the burritos, and cook them at 300 degrees F for 3-4 minutes.
5. Serve for breakfast—or lunch, or dinner!

Nutrition Values: calories 329, fat 13, fiber 11, carbs 20, protein 8

16. FRUITY BREAKFAST CASSEROLE

Preparation time: 10 minutes
Cooking time: 20 minutes

Servings: 6

Ingredients:

- 2 cups old fashioned oats
- 1 teaspoon baking powder
- ⅓ cup sugar
- 1 teaspoon cinnamon powder
- 1 cup blueberries
- 1 banana, peeled and mashed
- 2 cups milk
- 2 eggs, whisked
- 2 tablespoons butter
- 1 teaspoon vanilla extract
- Cooking spray

Directions:

1. In a bowl, mix the sugar, baking powder, cinnamon, blueberries, banana, eggs, butter, and vanilla; whisk.
2. Heat up your air fryer at 320 degrees F, and grease with cooking spray.
3. Add the oats, the berries and banana mix; cover, and cook for 20 minutes.
4. Divide into bowls and serve.

Nutrition Values: calories 260, fat 4, fiber 7, carbs 9, protein 10

17. SMOKED BACON AND BREAD MIX

Preparation time: 10 minutes
Cooking time: 30 minutes
Servings: 6

Ingredients:

- 1 pound white bread, cubed
- 1 pound smoked bacon, cooked and chopped
- ¼ cup avocado oil
- 1 red onion, chopped
- 30 ounces canned tomatoes, chopped
- ½ pound cheddar cheese, shredded
- 2 tablespoons chives, chopped
- ½ pound Monterey jack cheese, shredded
- 2 tablespoons chicken stock
- Salt and black pepper to taste
- 8 eggs, whisked

Directions:

1. Add the oil to your air fryer and heat it up at 350 degrees F.
2. Add all other ingredients except the chives and cook for 30 minutes, shaking halfway.
3. Divide between plates and serve with chives sprinkled on top.

Nutrition Values: calories 211, fat 8, fiber 7, carbs 14, protein 3

18. CHEESY HASH BROWN MIX

Preparation time: 10 minutes
Cooking time: 20 minutes
Servings: 6

Ingredients:

- 1½ pounds hash browns
- 1 cup almond milk
- A drizzle of olive oil
- 6 bacon slices, chopped
- 8 ounces cream cheese, softened
- 1 yellow onion, chopped
- 1 cup cheddar cheese, shredded
- 6 spring onions, chopped
- Salt and black pepper to taste
- 6 eggs

Directions:

1. Heat up your air fryer with the oil at 350 degrees F.
2. In a bowl, mix all other ingredients except the spring onions, and whisk well.
3. Add this mixture to your air fryer, cover, and cook for 20 minutes.
4. Divide between plates, sprinkle the spring onions on top, and serve.

Nutrition Values: calories 231, fat 9, fiber 9, carbs 8, protein 12

19. ROASTED PEPPERS FRITTATA

Preparation time: 10 minutes
Cooking time: 20 minutes
Servings: 6

Ingredients:

- 6 ounces jarred roasted red bell peppers, chopped
- 12 eggs, whisked
- ½ cup parmesan cheese, grated
- 3 garlic cloves, minced
- 2 tablespoons parsley, chopped
- Salt and black pepper to taste
- 2 tablespoons chives, chopped
- 6 tablespoons ricotta cheese
- A drizzle of olive oil

Directions:

1. In a bowl, mix the bell peppers with the eggs, garlic, parsley, salt, pepper, chives, and ricotta; whisk well.
2. Heat up your air fryer at 300 degrees F, add the oil, and spread.
3. Add the egg mixture, spread, sprinkle the parmesan on top, and cook for 20 minutes.
4. Divide between plates and serve.

Nutrition Values: calories 262, fat 6, fiber 9, carbs 18, protein 8

20. BLACKBERRIES AND CORNFLAKES MIX

Preparation time: 5 minutes
Cooking time: 10 minutes
Servings: 4

Ingredients:

- 3 cups milk
- 1 tablespoon sugar
- 2 eggs, whisked
- ¼ teaspoon nutmeg, ground
- ¼ cup blackberries
- 4 tablespoons cream cheese, whipped
- 1½ cups corn flakes

Directions:

1. In a bowl, mix all ingredients and stir well.
2. Heat up your air fryer at 350 degrees F, add the corn flakes mixture, spread, and cook for 10 minutes.
3. Divide between plates, serve, and enjoy.

Nutrition Values: calories 180, fat 5, fiber 7, carbs 12, protein 5

21. SIMPLE SCRAMBLED EGGS

Preparation time: 5 minutes
Cooking time: 10 minutes
Servings: 4

Ingredients:

- 4 eggs, whisked
- A drizzle of olive oil
- Salt and black pepper to taste
- 1 red onion, chopped
- 2 teaspoons sweet paprika

Directions:

1. In a bowl, mix all ingredients and whisk.
2. Heat up your air fryer with the oil at 240 degrees F, add the eggs mixture, stir again, and cook for 10 minutes.
3. Serve right away.

Nutrition Values: calories 190, fat 7, fiber 7, carbs 12, protein 4

22. CREAMY MUSHROOM PIE

Preparation time: 10 minutes
Cooking time: 10 minutes
Servings: 4

Ingredients:

- 1 tablespoon olive oil
- 9-inch pie dough
- 6 white mushrooms, chopped
- 2 tablespoons bacon, cooked and crumbled
- 3 eggs
- 1 red onion, chopped
- ½ cup heavy cream
- Salt and black pepper to taste
- ½ teaspoon thyme, dried
- ¼ cup cheddar cheese, grated

Directions:

1. Roll the dough on a working surface, then press it on the bottom of a pie pan that fits your air fryer and grease with the oil.
2. In a bowl, mix all other ingredients except the cheese, stir well, and pour mixture into the pie pan.
3. Sprinkle the cheese on top, put the pan in the air fryer, and cook at 400 degrees F for 10 minutes.
4. Slice and serve.

Nutrition Values: calories 192, fat 6, fiber 6, carbs 14, protein 7

23. CARROTS AND CAULIFLOWER BREAKFAST MIX

Preparation time: 10 minutes
Cooking time: 20 minutes
Servings: 4

Ingredients:

- 1 cauliflower head, stems removed, florets separated, and steamed
- 3 carrots, chopped and steamed
- 2 ounces cheddar cheese, grated
- 3 eggs
- 2 ounces milk
- 2 teaspoons cilantro, chopped
- Salt and black pepper to taste

Directions:

1. In a bowl, mix the eggs with the milk, parsley, salt, and pepper; whisk.
2. Put the cauliflower and the carrots in your air fryer, add the egg mixture, and spread. Then sprinkle the cheese on top.
3. Cook at 350 degrees F for 20 minutes, divide between plates, and serve.

Nutrition Values: calories 194, fat 4, fiber 7, carbs 11, protein 6

24. DELICIOUS DOUGHNUTS

Preparation Time: 28 Minutes
Servings: 6

Ingredients:

- 1/2 cup sugar
- 2 ¼ cups white flour
- 1 tsp. cinnamon powder
- 2 egg yolks
- 1/3 cup caster sugar
- 4 tbsp. butter; soft
- 1 ½ tsp. baking powder
- 1/2 cup sour cream

Directions:

1. In a bowl; mix 2 tablespoon butter with simple sugar and egg yolks and whisk well
2. Add half of the sour cream and stir.
3. In another bowls; mix flour with baking powder, stir and also add to eggs mix
4. Stir well until you obtain a dough, transfer

it to a floured working surface; roll it out and cut big circles with smaller ones in the middle.

5. Brush doughnuts with the rest of the butter; heat up your air fryer at 360 degrees F; place doughnuts inside and cook them for 8 minutes

6. In a bowl; mix cinnamon with caster sugar and stir. Arrange doughnuts on plates and dip them in cinnamon and sugar before serving.

25. BLACKBERRIES AND CORNFLAKES

Preparation Time: 15 minutes
Servings: 4

Ingredients:

- 3 cups milk
- 1/4 cup blackberries
- 2 eggs; whisked
- 1 tbsp. sugar
- 1/4 tsp. nutmeg; ground
- 4 tbsp. cream cheese; whipped
- 1½ cups corn flakes

Directions:

1. In a bowl, mix all ingredients and stir well.
2. Heat up your air fryer at 350°F, add the corn flakes mixture, spread and cook for 10 minutes. Divide between plates, serve and enjoy

26. FRIED MUSHROOM

Preparation Time: 25 minutes
Servings: 4

Ingredients:

- 7 oz. spinach; torn
- 8 cherry tomatoes; halved
- 4 slices bacon; chopped.
- 4 eggs
- 8 white mushrooms; sliced
- 1 garlic clove; minced
- A drizzle of olive oil
- Salt and black pepper to taste

Directions:

1. In a pan greased with oil and that fits your air fryer, mix all ingredients except for the spinach; stir.

2. Put the pan in your air fryer and cook at 400°F for 15 minutes. Add the spinach, toss and cook for 5 minutes more. Divide between plates and serve

27. PANCAKES

Preparation Time: 30 minutes
Servings: 4

Ingredients:

- 1¾ cups white flour
- 1 cup apple; peeled, cored and chopped.
- 1¼ cups milk
- 1 egg; whisked
- 2 tbsp. sugar
- 2 tsp. baking powder
- 1/4 tsp. vanilla extract
- 2 tsp. cinnamon powder
- Cooking spray

Directions:

1. In a bowl, mix all ingredients -except cooking sprayand stir until you obtain a smooth batter
2. Grease your air fryer's pan with the cooking spray and pour in 1/4 of the batter; spread it into the pan.
3. Cover and cook at 360°F for 5 minutes, flipping it halfway
4. Repeat steps 2 and 3 with 1/4 of the batter 3 more times and then serve the pancakes right away.

28. CREAMY MUSHROOM PIE

Preparation Time: 20 minutes
Servings: 4

Ingredients:

- 6 white mushrooms; chopped.
- 3 eggs
- 1 red onion; chopped.
- 9-inch pie dough
- 1/4 cup cheddar cheese; grated
- 1/2 cup heavy cream
- 2 tbsp. bacon; cooked and crumbled
- 1 tbsp. olive oil

- 1/2 tsp. thyme; dried
- Salt and black pepper to taste

Directions:

1. Roll the dough on a working surface, then press it on the bottom of a pie pan that fits your air fryer and grease with the oil
2. In a bowl, mix all other ingredients except the cheese, stir well and pour mixture into the pie pan
3. Sprinkle the cheese on top, put the pan in the air fryer and cook at 400°F for 10 minutes. Slice and serve.

29. PEAR OATMEAL

Preparation Time: 17 minutes
Servings: 4

Ingredients:

- 1 cup milk
- 1/4 cups brown sugar
- 1/2 cup walnuts; chopped.
- 2 cups pear; peeled and chopped.
- 1 cup old fashioned oats
- 1/2 tsp. cinnamon powder
- 1 tbsp. butter; softened

Directions:

1. In a heat-proof bowl that fits your air fryer, mix all ingredients and stir well. Place in your fryer and cook at 360°F for 12 minutes. Divide into bowls and serve

30. HAM AND CHEESE PATTIES

Preparation Time: 20 minutes
Servings: 4

Ingredients:

- 8 ham slices; chopped.
- 4 handfuls mozzarella cheese; grated
- 1 puff pastry sheet
- 4 tsp. mustard

Directions:

2. Roll out puff pastry on a working surface and cut it in 12 squares. Divide cheese, ham and mustard on half of them, top with the other halves and seal the edges
3. Place all the patties in your air fryer's basket and cook at 370°F for 10 minutes.

Divide the patties between plates and serve

31. PEPPERS AND LETTUCE SALAD

Preparation Time: 15 minutes
Servings: 4

Ingredients:

- 2 oz. rocket leaves
- 4 red bell peppers
- 1 lettuce head; torn
- 2 tbsp. olive oil
- 1 tbsp. lime juice
- 3 tbsp. heavy cream
- Salt and black pepper to taste

Directions:

1. Place the bell peppers in your air fryer's basket and cook at 400°F for 10 minutes
2. Remove the peppers, peel, cut them into strips and put them in a bowl. Add all remaining ingredients, toss and serve

32. COD TORTILLA

Preparation Time: 27 minutes
Servings: 4

Ingredients:

- 4 cod fillets; skinless and boneless
- 4 tortillas
- 1 green bell pepper; chopped.
- 1 red onion; chopped.
- A drizzle of olive oil
- 1 cup corn
- 1/2 cup salsa
- 4 tbsp. parmesan cheese; grated
- A handful of baby spinach

Directions:

1. Put the fish fillets in your air fryer's basket, cook at 350°F for 6 minutes and transfer to a plate.
2. Heat up a pan with the oil over medium heat, add the bell peppers, onions and corn and stir
3. Sauté for 5 minutes and take off the heat. Arrange all the tortillas on a working surface and divide the cod, salsa, sautéed

veggies, spinach and parmesan evenly between the 4 tortillas; then wrap / roll them
4. Place the tortillas in your air fryer's basket and cook at 350°F for 6 minutes. Divide between plates, serve.

33. ARTICHOKE OMELET

Preparation Time: 20 minutes
Servings:

Ingredients:

- 3 artichoke hearts; canned, drained and chopped.
- 6 eggs; whisked
- 2 tbsp. avocado oil
- 1/2 tsp. oregano; dried
- Salt and black pepper to taste

Directions:

1. In a bowl, mix all ingredients except the oil; stir well. Add the oil to your air fryer's pan and heat it up at 320°F.
2. Add the egg mixture, cook for 15 minutes, divide between plates and serve

34. CARROT OATMEAL

Preparation Time: 20 minutes
Servings: 4

Ingredients:

- 1/2 cup steel cut oats
- 2 cups almond milk
- 1 cup carrots; shredded
- 2 tsp. sugar
- 1 tsp. cardamom; ground
- Cooking spray

Directions:

1. Spray your air fryer with cooking spray, add all ingredients, toss and cover. Cook at 365°F for 15 minutes. Divide into bowls and serve

35. CHICKEN BURRITO

Preparation Time: 15 minutes
Servings: 2

Ingredients:

- 4 chicken breast slices; cooked and shredded
- 2 tortillas
- 1 avocado; peeled, pitted and sliced
- 1 green bell pepper; sliced
- 2 eggs; whisked
- 2 tbsp. mild salsa
- 2 tbsp. cheddar cheese; grated
- Salt and black pepper to taste

Directions:

2. In a bowl, whisk the eggs with the salt and pepper and pour them into a pan that fits your air fryer. Put the pan in the air fryer's basket, cook for 5 minutes at 400°F and transfer the mix to a plate
3. Place the tortillas on a working surface and between them divide the eggs, chicken, bell peppers, avocado and the cheese; roll the burritos
4. Line your air fryer with tin foil, add the burritos and cook them at 300°F for 3-4 minutes. Serve for breakfast-or lunch, or dinner!

36. POTATO FRITTATA

Preparation Time: 25 minutes
Servings: 6

Ingredients:

- 1 lb. small potatoes; chopped.
- 1 oz. parmesan cheese; grated
- 1/2 cup heavy cream
- 2 red onions; chopped.
- 8 eggs; whisked
- 1 tbsp. olive oil
- Salt and black pepper to taste

Directions:

1. In a bowl, mix all ingredients except the potatoes and oil; stir well.
2. Heat up your air fryer's pan with the oil at 320°F. Add the potatoes, stir and cook for 5 minutes
3. Add the egg mixture, spread and cook for 15 minutes more. Divide the frittata between plates and serve

37. HERBED OMELET

Preparation Time: 20 minutes

Servings: 4

Ingredients:

- 6 eggs; whisked
- 2 tbsp. parmesan cheese; grated
- 4 tbsp. heavy cream
- 1 tbsp. parsley; chopped.
- 1 tbsp. tarragon; chopped.
- 2 tbsp. chives; chopped.
- Salt and black pepper to taste

Directions:

1. In a bowl, mix all ingredients except for the parmesan and whisk well. Pour this into a pan that fits your air fryer, place it in preheated fryer and cook at 350°F for 15 minutes
2. Divide the omelet between plates and serve with the parmesan sprinkled on top

38. CHEESE TOAST

Preparation Time: 13 minutes
Servings:2

Ingredients:

- 4 bread slices
- 4 cheddar cheese slices
- 4 tsp. butter; softened

Directions:

1. Spread the butter on each slice of bread. Place 2 cheese slices each on 2 bread slices, then top with the other 2 bread slices; cut each in half
2. Arrange the sandwiches in your air fryer's basket and cook at 370°F for 8 minutes. Serve hot and enjoy!

39. CARROTS AND CAULIFLOWER MIX

Preparation Time: 30 minutes
Servings: 4

Ingredients:

- 1 cauliflower head; stems removed, florets separated and steamed
- 2 oz. milk
- 2 oz. cheddar cheese; grated
- 3 carrots; chopped and steamed

- 3 eggs
- 2 tsp. cilantro; chopped.
- Salt and black pepper to taste

Directions:

1. In a bowl, mix the eggs with the milk, parsley, salt and pepper; whisk. Put the cauliflower and the carrots in your air fryer, add the egg mixture and spread. Then sprinkle the cheese on top
2. Cook at 350°F for 20 minutes, divide between plates and serve

40. VANILLA OATMEAL

Preparation Time: 22 minutes
Servings: 4

Ingredients:

- 1 cup steel cut oats
- 1 cup milk
- 2½ cups water
- 2 tsp. vanilla extract
- 2 tbsp. brown sugar

Directions:

1. In a pan that fits your air fryer, mix all ingredients and stir well. Place the pan in your air fryer and cook at 360°F for 17 minutes. Divide into bowls and serve

41. FISH TACOS BREAKFAST

Preparation Time: 23 Minutes
Servings: 4

Ingredients:

- 4 big tortillas
- 1 yellow onion; chopped
- 1 cup corn
- 1 red bell pepper; chopped
- 1/2 cup salsa
- 4 white fish fillets; skinless and boneless
- A handful mixed romaine lettuce; spinach and radicchio
- 4 tbsp. parmesan; grated

Directions:

1. Put fish fillets in your air fryer and cook at 350°F, for 6 minutes
2. Meanwhile; heat up a pan over medium

high heat, add bell pepper, onion and corn; stir and cook for 1 - 2 minutes

3. Arrange tortillas on a working surface, divide fish fillets, spread salsa over them; divide mixed veggies and mixed greens and spread parmesan on each at the end.

4. Roll your tacos; place them in preheated air fryer and cook at 350°F, for 6 minutes more. Divide fish tacos on plates and serve for breakfast

42. TUNA SANDWICHES

Preparation Time: 14 minutes
Servings: 4

Ingredients:

- 16 oz. canned tuna; drained
- 6 bread slices
- 6 provolone cheese slices
- 2 spring onions; chopped.
- 1/4 cup mayonnaise
- 2 tbsp. mustard
- 1 tbsp. lime juice
- 3 tbsp. butter; melted

Directions:

1. In a bowl, mix the tuna, mayo, lime juice, mustard and spring onions; stir until combined.

2. Spread the bread slices with the butter, place them in preheated air fryer and bake them at 350°F for 5 minutes

3. Spread tuna mix on half of the bread slices and top with the cheese and the other bread slices

4. Place the sandwiches in your air fryer's basket and cook for 4 minutes more. Divide between plates and serve.

43. TOFU AND BELL PEPPERS

Preparation Time: 15 minutes
Servings: 8

Ingredients:

- 3 oz. firm tofu; crumbled
- 1 green onion; chopped.
- 1 yellow bell pepper; cut into strips
- 1 orange bell pepper; cut into strips
- 1 green bell pepper; cut into strips

- 2 tbsp. parsley; chopped.
- Salt and black pepper to taste

Directions:

1. In a pan that fits your air fryer, place the bell pepper strips and mix

2. Then add all remaining ingredients, toss and place the pan in the air fryer. Cook at 400°F for 10 minutes. Divide between plates and serve

44. CHEERING CHICKEN SANDWICHES

Preparation Time: 20 Minutes
Servings: 4

Ingredients:

- 2 chicken breasts; skinless, boneless and cubed
- 1/2 cup Italian seasoning
- 1/2 tsp. thyme; dried
- 1 red onion; chopped.
- 1 red bell pepper; sliced
- 2 cups butter lettuce; torn
- 4 pita pockets
- 1 cup cherry tomatoes; halved
- 1 tbsp. olive oil

Directions:

1. In your air fryer, mix chicken with onion, bell pepper, Italian seasoning and oil; toss and cook at 380 °F, for 10 minutes. Transfer chicken mix to a bowl; add thyme, butter lettuce and cherry tomatoes, toss well; stuff pita pockets with this mix and serve for lunch.

Nutrition Values: Calories: 126; Fat: 4; Fiber: 8; Carbs: 14; Protein: 4

45. CHICKEN PIE RECIPE

Preparation Time: 29 Minutes
Servings: 4

Ingredients:

- 2 chicken thighs; boneless, skinless and cubed
- 1 carrot; chopped
- 1 tsp. Worcestershire sauce
- 1 tbsp. flour
- 1 tbsp. milk
- 2 puff pastry sheets
- 1 tbsp. butter; melted
- 1 yellow onion; chopped
- 2 potatoes; chopped
- 2 mushrooms; chopped
- 1 tsp. soy sauce
- Salt and black pepper to the taste
- 1 tsp. Italian seasoning
- 1/2 tsp. garlic powder

Directions:

1. Heat up a pan over medium high heat, add potatoes, carrots and onion; stir and cook for 2 minutes.
2. Add chicken and mushrooms, salt, soy sauce, pepper, Italian seasoning, garlic powder, Worcestershire sauce, flour and milk; stir really well and take off heat.
3. Place 1 puff pastry sheet on the bottom of your air fryer's pan and trim edge excess.
4. Add chicken mix, top with the other puff pastry sheet; trim excess as well and brush pie with butter.
5. Place in your air fryer and cook at 360 °F, for 6 minutes. Leave pie to cool down; slice and serve for breakfast.

Nutrition Values: Calories: 300; Fat: 5; Fiber: 7; Carbs: 14; Protein: 7

46. DILL AND SCALLOPS

Preparation Time: 15 Minutes
Servings: 4

Ingredients:

- 1 lb. sea scallops; debearded
- 1 tsp. dill; chopped.
- 2 tsp. olive oil
- 1 tbsp. lemon juice
- Salt and black pepper to the taste

Directions:

1. In your air fryer, mix scallops with dill, oil, salt, pepper and lemon juice; cover and cook at 360 °F, for 5 minutes. Discard unopened ones, divide scallops and dill sauce on plates and serve for lunch.

Nutrition Values: Calories: 152; Fat: 4; Fiber: 7; Carbs: 19; Protein: 4

47. CHEESY RAVIOLI AND MARINARA SAUCE

Preparation Time: 18 Minutes
Servings: 6

Ingredients:

- 20 oz. cheese ravioli
- 10 oz. marinara sauce
- 1/4 cup parmesan; grated
- 1 tbsp. olive oil
- 1 cup buttermilk
- 2 cups bread crumbs

Directions:

1. Put buttermilk in a bowl and breadcrumbs in another bowl.
2. Dip ravioli in buttermilk, then in breadcrumbs and place them in your air fryer on a baking sheet. Drizzle olive oil over them; cook at 400 °F, for 5 minutes; divide them on plates, sprinkle parmesan on top and serve for lunch

Nutrition Values: Calories: 270; Fat: 12; Fiber: 6; Carbs: 30; Protein: 15

48. CHEESE AND MACARONI

Preparation Time: 40 Minutes
Servings: 3

Ingredients:

- 1 ½ cups favorite macaroni
- 1/2 cup heavy cream
- 1/2 cup mozzarella cheese; shredded
- 1/4 cup parmesan; shredded
- 1 cup chicken stock
- 3/4 cup cheddar cheese; shredded
- Salt and black pepper to the taste
- Cooking spray

Directions:

1. Spray a pan with cooking spray; add macaroni, heavy cream, stock, cheddar cheese, mozzarella and parmesan but also salt and pepper; toss well, place pan in your air fryer's basket and cook for 30 minutes. Divide among plates and serve for lunch.

Nutrition Values: Calories: 341; Fat: 7; Fiber: 8; Carbs: 18; Protein: 4

49. ZUCCHINI AND TUNA TORTILLAS

Preparation Time: 20 Minutes
Servings: 4

Ingredients:

- 1 cup zucchini; shredded
- 1/3 cup mayonnaise
- 2 tbsp. mustard
- 4 corn tortillas
- 4 tbsp. butter; soft
- 6 oz. canned tuna; drained
- 1 cup cheddar cheese; grated

Directions:

1. Spread butter on tortillas; place them in your air fryer's basket and cook them at 400 °F, for 3 minutes.
2. Meanwhile; in a bowl, mix tuna with zucchini, mayo and mustard and stir.
3. Divide this mix on each tortilla, top with cheese, roll tortillas; place them in your air fryer's basket again and cook them at 400 °F, for 4 minutes more. Serve for lunch.

Nutrition Values: Calories: 162; Fat: 4; Fiber: 8; Carbs: 9; Protein: 4

50. BEEF MEATBALLS

Preparation Time: 25 Minutes
Servings: 4

Ingredients:

- 1/2 lb. beef; ground
- 1/2 tsp. garlic powder
- 1/2 tsp. onion powder
- 1/2 lb. Italian sausage; chopped.
- 1/2 cup cheddar cheese; grated
- Mashed potatoes for serving
- Salt and black pepper to the taste

Directions:

1. In a bowl; mix beef with sausage, garlic powder, onion powder, salt, pepper and cheese; stir well and shape 16 meatballs out of this mix.

2. Place meatballs in your air fryer and cook them at 370 °F, for 15 minutes. Serve your meatballs with some mashed potatoes on the side.

Nutrition Values: Calories: 333; Fat: 23; Fiber: 1; Carbs: 8; Protein: 20

51. FISH AND KETTLE CHIPS

Preparation Time: 22 Minutes
Servings: 2

Ingredients:

- 2 medium cod fillets; skinless and boneless
- 1/4 cup buttermilk
- 3 cups kettle chips; cooked
- Salt and black pepper to the taste

Directions:

1. In a bowl mix fish with salt, pepper and buttermilk; toss and leave aside for 5 minutes.
2. Put chips in your food processor, crush them and spread them on a plate.
3. Add fish and press well on all sides.
4. Transfer fish to your air fryer's basket and cook at 400 °F, for 12 minutes. Serve hot for lunch.

Nutrition Values: Calories: 271; Fat: 7; Fiber: 9; Carbs: 14; Protein: 4

52. EGG ROLLS

Preparation Time: 25 Minutes
Servings: 4

Ingredients:

- 1/2 cup mushrooms; chopped.
- 1/2 cup carrots; grated
- 1/2 cup zucchini; grated
- 8 egg roll wrappers
- 1 eggs; whisked
- 2 green onions; chopped.
- 2 tbsp. soy sauce
- 1 tbsp. cornstarch

Directions:

1. In a bowl; mix carrots with mushrooms, zucchini, green onions and soy sauce and stir well.

2. Arrange egg roll wrappers on a working surface; divide veggie mix on each and roll well.
3. In a bowl; mix cornstarch with egg, whisk well and brush eggs rolls with this mix.
4. Seal edges, place all rolls in your preheated air fryer and cook them at 370 °F, for 15 minutes. Arrange them on a platter and serve them for lunch.

Nutrition Values: Calories: 172; Fat: 6; Fiber: 6; Carbs: 8; Protein: 7

53. SPECIAL PANCAKE

Preparation Time: 20 Minutes
Servings: 2

Ingredients:

- 1 cup small shrimp; peeled and deveined
- 1 tbsp. butter
- 3 eggs; whisked
- 1/2 cup flour
- 1/2 cup milk
- 1 cup salsa

Directions:

1. Preheat your air fryer at 400 degrees F; add fryer's pan, add 1 tbsp. butter and melt it.
2. In a bowl; mix eggs with flour and milk, whisk well and pour into air fryer's pan, spread, cook at 350 degrees for 12 minutes and transfer to a plate. In a bowl; mix shrimp with salsa; stir and serve your pancake with this on the side.

Nutrition Values: Calories: 200; Fat: 6; Fiber: 8; Carbs: 12; Protein: 4

54. TURKISH STYLE KOFTAS

Preparation Time: 25 Minutes
Servings: 2

Ingredients:

- 2 tbsp. feta cheese; crumbled
- 1 leek; chopped
- 1 tbsp. parsley; chopped
- 1 tsp. garlic; minced
- 1/2 lb. lean beef; minced
- 1 tbsp. cumin; ground

- 1 tbsp. mint; chopped
- Salt and black pepper to the taste

Directions:

1. In a bowl; mix beef with leek, cheese, cumin, mint, parsley, garlic, salt and pepper; stir well, shape your koftas and place them on sticks.
2. Add koftas to your preheated air fryer at 360 °F and cook them for 15 minutes. Serve them with a side salad for lunch.

Nutrition Values: Calories: 281; Fat: 7; Fiber: 8; Carbs: 17; Protein: 6

55. CHICKEN WINGS

Preparation Time: 55 Minutes
Servings: 4

Ingredients:

- 3 lbs. chicken wings
- 3/4 cup potato starch
- 1 tsp. lemon juice
- 1/2 cup butter
- 1 tbsp. old bay seasoning
- Lemon wedges for serving

Directions:

1. In a bowl; mix starch with old bay seasoning and chicken wings and toss well.
2. Place chicken wings in your air fryer's basket and cook them at 360 °F, for 35 minutes shaking the fryer from time to time.
3. Increase temperature to 400 degrees F; cook chicken wings for 10 minutes more and divide them on plates.
4. Heat up a pan over medium heat; add butter and melt it.
5. Add lemon juice; stir well, take off heat and drizzle over chicken wings. Serve them for lunch with lemon wedges on the side.

Nutrition Values: Calories: 271; Fat: 6; Fiber: 8; Carbs: 18; Protein: 18

56. SUMMER SQUASH FRITTERS

Preparation Time: 17 Minutes
Servings: 4

Ingredients:

- 3 oz. cream cheese
- 1 egg; whisked
- 1/2 tsp. oregano; dried
- 1/3 cup carrot; grated
- 2/3 cup bread crumbs
- A pinch of salt and black pepper
- 1 yellow summer squash; grated
- 2 tbsp. olive oil

Directions:

1. In a bowl; mix cream cheese with salt, pepper, oregano, egg, breadcrumbs, carrot and squash and stir well.
2. Shape medium patties out of this mix and brush them with the oil.
3. Place squash patties in your air fryer and cook them at 400 °F, for 7 minutes. Serve them for lunch.

Nutrition Values: Calories: 200; Fat: 4; Fiber: 7; Carbs: 8; Protein: 6

57. FRESH STYLE CHICKEN

Preparation Time: 32 Minutes
Servings: 4

Ingredients:

- 2 chicken breasts; skinless, boneless and cubed
- 1/2 tsp. thyme; dried
- 10 oz. alfredo sauce
- 8 button mushrooms; sliced
- 1 red bell pepper; chopped
- 1 tbsp. olive oil
- 6 bread slices
- 2 tbsp. butter; soft

Directions:

1. In your air fryer, mix chicken with mushrooms, bell pepper and oil; toss to coat well and cook at 350 °F, for 15 minutes.
2. Transfer chicken mix to a bowl; add thyme and alfredo sauce, toss, return to air fryer and cook at 350 °F, for 4 minutes more.
3. Spread butter on bread slices; add it to the fryer, butter side up and cook for 4

minutes more. Arrange toasted bread slices on a platter; top each with chicken mix and serve for lunch.

Nutrition Values: Calories: 172; Fat: 4; Fiber: 9; Carbs: 12; Protein: 4

58. GREEK BAR B Q SANDWICHES

Preparation Time: 13 minutes
Servings: 3

Ingredients:

- Barbecue sauce-1/3 cup
- Bacon slices-8 -cooked and cut into thirds
- Pita pockets-2 -halved
- Honey-2 tbsps
- Lettuce-1-1/4 cups -torn
- Red bell peppers-2 -sliced
- Tomatoes-2 -sliced

Directions:

1. Take a bowl and mix the barbecue sauce with honey.
2. After whisking finely, brush the bacon and bell peppers with this mixture.
3. Insert the bacon and bell peppers in your air fryer.
4. Cook at 350 o F for 6 minutes. During cooking shake once.
5. Fill the pita pockets with the bacon and bell peppers mixture.
6. Add some tomatoes and lettuce in the end.
7. To serve, garnish with the rest of the barbecue sauce and honey. Enjoy!

Nutrition Values:

calories 206, fat 6, fiber 9, carbs 14, protein 5

59. UNIQUE PIE

Preparation Time: 22 minutes
Servings: 3

Ingredients:

- A large chicken breast -boneless, skinless and cubed
- Yellow onion-1 -chopped
- Soy sauce-1 tsp
- Salt and black pepper to taste

- Garlic powder-1/2 tsp
- White flour-1 tbsp
- Puff pastry sheets-2
- Carrot-1 -chopped
- White mushrooms-6 -chopped
- Italian seasoning-1 tsp
- Worcestershire sauce-1 tsp
- Milk-1 tbsp
- Olive oil-2 tbsps

Directions:

1. Warm up a pan with half of the oil over medium-high heat.
2. Mix the carrots with onions and stir.
3. Cook them for 2 minutes.
4. Add the chicken, mushrooms, salt, soy sauce, pepper, Italian seasoning, garlic powder, Worcestershire sauce, flour, and milk.
5. Mix them all really well and then remove from the heat.
6. Insert a puff pastry sheet on the bottom of your air fryer's pan.
7. Layer the chicken mix on it and top with another puff pastry sheet.
8. Oil the pastry with the rest of the oil finely.
9. Place the pan in the fryer to cook at 360 o F.
10. After 8 minutes of cooking, slice to serve and enjoy.

Nutrition Values:

calories 270, fat 5, fiber 7, carbs 14, protein 5

60. PIZZA LIKE ROLLS

Preparation Time: 43 minutes
Servings: 2

Ingredients:

- Olive oil-2 tsp
- Chicken breasts-2 -skinless, boneless and sliced
- Worcestershire sauce-1 tbsp
- Parmesan cheese-1-1/2 cups -grated
- Pizza dough-14 ounces
- Yellow onion-1 -sliced
- Tomato sauce-1/2 cup
- Salt and black pepper to taste

Directions:

1. Prepare your air fryer at 400 o F.
2. Throw in the onion and half of the olive oil in it to fry.
3. Cook for 8 minutes, shaking the fryer halfway.
4. Combine the chicken, Worcestershire sauce, salt and pepper and toss.
5. Fry for 8 more minutes, stirring once, then shift to a bowl.
6. On a working surface, roll the pizza dough and shape into a rectangle.
7. All over the dough, spread the cheese and then the chicken and onion mixture.
8. In the end, layer the tomato sauce to roll the dough.
9. Insert it in your air fryer's basket and brush the roll with the rest of the oil.
10. At 370 o F, cook for 14 minutes, flipping the roll halfway.
11. To serve, slice your roll.

Nutrition Values:

calories 270, fat 8, fiber 17, carbs 16, protein 6

61. CHINESE LUNCH

Preparation Time: 19 minutes
Servings: 5

Ingredients:

- Eggs-2
- Cornstarch-1 cup
- Chinese five spice-1/4 tsp
- Pork stew meat-2 pounds -cubed
- Salt and black pepper to taste
- Olive oil-3 tbsps
- Sesame oil-1 tsp

Directions:

1. Pick a bowl finely mix the Chinese spice, salt, pepper, and cornstarch.
2. Take another bowl to whisk the eggs and sesame oil very well.
3. Fold the pork cubes in the cornstarch mixture and then dip them in the egg mix.
4. Keep the pork cubes in your air fryer and then drizzle all over with the olive oil.
5. Cook at 360 o F for 12 minutes.
6. Share into the serving bowls with a side salad

Nutrition Values:

calories 270, fat 8, fiber 12, carbs 16, protein 5

62. WINGS IN OLD BAY STYLE

Preparation Time: 52 minutes
Servings: 3

Ingredients:

- Chicken wings-3 pounds
- Old Bay seasoning-1 tbsp
- Lemon juice-1 tsp
- Butter-1/2 cup -melted
- Potato starch-3/4 cup

Directions:

1. Pick up a bowl and mix the chicken wings with the starch and Old Bay seasoning.
2. Toss the mixture well once again and then place the pieces in your air fryer's basket.
3. Prepare at 360 o F for 35 minutes, shaking the fryer from time to time.
4. Raise the temperature to 400 o F while frying the chicken wings for 10 more minutes.
5. Present the wings between plates to serve.
6. Top with the melted butter mixed with the lemon juice drizzled all over.

Nutrition Values:

calories 261, fat 6, fiber 8, carbs 18, protein 13

63. DIJON SPECIAL HOT DOGS

Preparation Time: 15 minutes
Servings: 3

Ingredients:

- Hot dog buns-3
- Dijon mustard-1 tbsp
- Hot dogs-3
- Parmesan cheese-2 tbsps -grated

Directions:

1. Put the hot dogs in preheated air fryer to cook at 390 o F for 5 minutes.
2. Add the hot dogs into the buns.
3. Spread the mustard all over, and sprinkle with the Parmesan.
4. Fry the hot dogs at 390 o F for 3 more minutes.
5. Serve and enjoy!

Nutrition Values:

calories 251, fat 7, fiber 8, carbs 16, protein 7

64. LENTIL CAKE BITES

Preparation Time: 22minutes
Servings: 2

Ingredients:

- Canned yellow lentils-1 cup -drained
- Turmeric powder-1/2 tsp
- Hot chili pepper-1 -chopped
- Garam masala-1 tsp
- Ginger-1 tsp -grated
- Baking powder-1 tsp
- Olive oil-2 tsp
- Water-1/3 cup water
- Salt and black pepper to taste
- Cilantro-1/2 cup -chopped
- Garlic cloves-4 -minced
- Baby spinach-1-1/2 cups -chopped
- Yellow onion-3/4 cup -chopped

Directions:

1. Bring your blender and add all ingredients in it.
2. Blend the mixture very well and then shape into two medium cakes.
3. Keep the lentils cakes in your preheated air fryer at 400 o F.
4. Let it cook for 10 minutes. Leave for few seconds.
5. Serve the lentil cakes on plates and enjoy.

Nutrition Values:

calories 182, fat 2, fiber 8, carbs 16, protein 4

65. BEEFY BALLS WITH SAUCE

Preparation Time: 27 minutes
Servings: 3

Ingredients:

- Lean ground beef-1 pound
- Garlic cloves-2 -minced
- Panko breadcrumbs-1/4 cup
- Salt and black pepper to taste
- An egg yolk
- Olive oil-1 tbsp
- Red onion-1 -chopped

- Tomato sauce-16 ounces

Directions:

1. Pick a bowl and mix all the ingredients except for the tomato sauce and olive oil.
2. Mix well and then shape into medium-sized meatballs.
3. Oil the meatballs evenly and place them in your air fryer.
4. Cook at 400 o F for 10 minutes.
5. Warm up a pan over medium heat and pour the tomato sauce.
6. Heat it up for 2 minutes and then insert the meatballs.
7. Toss them a bit, and cook for 3 more minutes.
8. Dish out evenly the meatballs between plates and serve to eat.

Nutrition Values:

calories 270, fat 8, fiber 9, carbs 16, protein 4

66. MEATBALL SANDWICHES

Preparation Time: 34 minutes
Servings: 3

Ingredients:

- Baguettes-3 -sliced halfway
- Tomato sauce-7 ounces
- Egg-1 -whisked
- Parmesan cheese-2 tbsps -grated
- Olive oil-1 tbsp
- Fresh basil-1 tsp -chopped
- Beef-14 ounces -minced
- Yellow onion-1 -chopped
- Breadcrumbs-1 tbsp
- Oregano-1 tbsp -chopped
- Salt and black pepper to taste

Directions:

1. Take a bowl to mix all ingredients except the tomato sauce, oil, and baguettes.
2. After stirring well, shape into medium-sized meatballs.
3. Warm up your air fryer with the oil at 375 o F to add the meatballs.
4. Prepare them for 12 minutes, flipping them halfway.
5. Pour the tomato sauce and cook for 10 more minutes.

6. Dish out the meatballs with sauce on half of the baguette halves.
7. Finally top with the other baguette halves to serve.

Nutrition Values:

calories 280, fat 9, fiber 6, carbs 16, protein 15

67. KALE SALAD WITH COD FILLETS

Preparation Time: 22minutes
Servings: 2

Ingredients:

- Black cod fillets-2 -boneless
- Salt and black pepper to taste
- Grapes-1 cup -halved
- Pecans-1/2 cup
- Olive oil-2 tbsps + 1 tsp
- A fennel bulb -thinly sliced
- Kale leaves-3 cups -shredded
- Balsamic vinegar-2 tsp

Directions:

1. Season the fish with salt and pepper to place the fish in your air fryer's basket.
2. Drizzle a tsp of the olive oil over the fish to cook at 400 o F for 10 minutes.
3. Divide fish between plates.
4. Pick a bowl to mix the fennel, grapes, kale, pecans, vinegar, and 2 tbsps of oil.
5. After fine tossing, dish out.
6. Serve the salad next to the fish and enjoy.

Nutrition Values:

calories 240, fat 4, fiber 2, carbs 15, protein 12

68. SIMPLE TURKEY DISH

Preparation Time: 1 hour and 13 minutes
Servings: 7

Ingredients:

- Whole turkey breast-1
- Sweet paprika-1/2 tsp
- Salt and black pepper to taste
- Mustard-2 tbsps
- Olive oil-2 tsp
- Thyme-1 tsp -dried
- Butter-1 tbsp -melted

- Maple syrup-1/4 cup

Directions:

1. Use oil to brush over the turkey breast.
2. Marinate salt, pepper, paprika, and thyme and rub the seasoning well into the turkey breast.
3. Keep the turkey in your air fryer and cook at 350 o F for 25 minutes.
4. Turn the turkey breast and cook for 12 minutes more.
5. Again change the side and cook for another 12 minutes.
6. Take a bowl to whisk the butter, mustard, and maple syrup very well.
7. Brush the turkey breast with the maple syrup mixture.
8. Leave to cook for another 5 minutes.
9. Shift the meat to a cutting board and slice.
10. If desired, serve with a side salad.

Nutrition Values:

calories 230, fat 13, fiber 3, carbs 16, protein 11

69. COD BALLS LUNCH

Preparation Time: 24 minutes
Servings: 5

Ingredients:

- Fresh cilantro-3 tbsps -minced
- Yellow onion-1 -chopped
- Salt and black pepper to taste
- Garlic cloves-2 -minced
- Panko breadcrumbs-1/4 cup
- Cod-1 pound -skinless and chopped
- Egg-1
- Sweet paprika-1/2 tsp
- Oregano-1/2 tsp -ground
- A drizzle of olive oil

Directions:

1. Pick your food processor and clean to mix all ingredients except the oil.
2. After blending well, shape medium-sized meatballs out of this mix.
3. Insert the meatballs in your air fryer's basket.
4. Let them grease with oil, and cook at 320 o F for 12 minutes, shaking halfway.
5. Divide the meatballs between plates and,

if desired, serve with a side salad.

Nutrition Values:

calories 230, fat 9, fiber 3, carbs 10, protein 15

70. STEW-POTATO & BEEF

Preparation Time: 37 minutes
Servings: 5

Ingredients:

- Beef stew meat-2 pounds -cubed
- Gold potatoes-4 -cubed
- Beef stock-1 quart
- A handful of cilantro -chopped
- Carrot-1 -sliced
- Salt and black pepper to taste
- Smoked paprika-1/2 tsp
- Worcestershire sauce-4 tbsps

Directions:

1. Take a pan that fits your air fryer; mix all the ingredients well except the cilantro.
2. Keep it in your air fryer to cook at 375 o F.
3. After 25 minutes, divide into bowls.
4. Sprinkle the cilantro on top. Serve right away.

Nutrition Values:

calories 250, fat 8, fiber 1, carbs 20, protein 17

71. PASTA WITH SHRIMP

Preparation Time: 27 minutes
Servings: 5

Ingredients:

- Spaghetti-5 ounces -cooked
- Salt and black pepper to taste
- Butter-1 tbsp -melted
- Shrimp-8 ounces -peeled and de veined
- Garlic cloves-5 -minced
- Chili powder-1 tsp
- Olive oil-2 tbsp

Directions:

1. Add 1 tbsp of the oil, along with the butter, in your air fryer.
2. Preheat the air fryer at 350 o F and add the shrimp.
3. Cook for 10 minutes and then combine all

other ingredients, including the remaining a tbsp of oil,
4. Toss and cook for 5 minutes more.
5. Divide between plates, serve, and enjoy.

Nutrition Values:

calories 270, fat 7, fiber 4, carbs 15, protein 6

72. RAVIOLI LUNCH MEAL

Preparation Time: 12minutes
Servings: 5

Ingredients:

- Cheese ravioli-15 ounces
- Butter-1 tsp -melted
- Breadcrumbs-2 cups
- Buttermilk-1 cup
- Marinara sauce-10 ounces
- Cheddar cheese-1/4 cup -grated

Directions:

1. Pour the buttermilk in one bowl and add the breadcrumbs in another.
2. In buttermilk, dip ravioli, then in breadcrumbs.
3. Place the ravioli in your air fryer's basket and brush them with the melted butter.
4. Cook at 400 o F for 5 minutes and then divide the ravioli between plates.
5. Sprinkle the cheddar cheese on top, and serve.

Nutrition Values:

calories 260, fat 12, fiber 4, carbs 14, protein 11

73. CURRY MADE WITH COD

Preparation Time: 27 minutes
Servings: 5

Ingredients:

- Cod fillets-4 -skinless, boneless and cubed
- Curry paste-2 tsp
- Milk-1-1/2 cups -heated up
- Ginger-2 tsp -grated
- Cilantro-2 tbsps -chopped
- Salt and black pepper to taste

Directions:

1. Take a bowl and mix the milk, curry paste, ginger, salt, and pepper.

2. Place the fish in a pan that fits your air fryer, and then add the milk and curry mixture together.
3. After tossing the mixtures gently, place the pan in the fryer.
4. Cook at 400 o F for 15 minutes, shaking halfway.
5. Divide the curry into bowls, sprinkle the cilantro on top, and serve.

Nutrition Values:

calories 260, fat 8, fiber 3, carbs 13, protein 9

74. SPECIAL CASSEROLE FOR LUNCH

Preparation Time: 42 minutes
Servings: 7

Ingredients:

- Butter-2 tbsps -melted
- Cream cheese-12 ounces -softened
- Yogurt-1 cup
- Salt and black pepper to taste
- Curry powder-2 tsp
- Chicken meat-2 cups -cooked and cubed
- Scallions-4 -chopped
- Cilantro-1/4 cup -chopped
- Monterey jack cheese-6 ounces -grated
- Almonds-1/2 cup -sliced
- Chutney-1/2 cup

Directions:

1. Take a baking dish that fits your air fryer and add all ingredients except the Monterey jack cheese.
2. After mixing well, sprinkle the Monterey jack cheese all over chicken mixture.
3. Place the dish in your air fryer, and cook at 350 o F for 25 minutes.
4. Divide between plates and serve.

Nutrition Values:

calories 280, fat 10, fiber 2, carbs 24, protein 15

75. CREAMY POTATOES MEAL

Preparation Time: 29 minutes
Servings: 3

Ingredients:

- Gold potatoes-4 -cut into medium wedges
- Eggs-2
- Garlic powder-1 tsp
- Salt and black pepper to taste
- Sour cream-1/4 cup
- Sweet paprika-1-1/2 tsp
- Olive oil-1 tsp
- Cajun seasoning-1/2 tsp

Directions:

1. Pick a bowl and mix the eggs with the sour cream, paprika, garlic powder, Cajun seasoning, salt, and pepper.
2. After whisking well, take a pan that fits your air fryer.
3. Grease with the oil and arrange the potatoes on the bottom of the pan.
4. Spread the sour cream to mix all over.
5. Keep the pan in the fryer and cook at 370 o F for 17 minutes.
6. Divide between plates and serve.

Nutrition Values:

calories 290, fat 8, fiber 2, carbs 15, protein 7

76. CHINESE CABBAGE & BEEF BOWLS

Preparation Time: 22 minutes
Servings: 5

Ingredients:

- Sirloin steak-1/2 pound -cut into strips
- Soy sauce-1 tbsp
- Olive oil-1 tbsp
- Salt and black pepper to taste
- Green cabbage-2 cups -shredded
- Green onions-2 -chopped
- Yellow bell pepper-1 -chopped
- Garlic cloves-2 -minced

Directions:

1. Pick a pan that fits your air fryer and mix the cabbage, salt, pepper, and oil.
2. After tossing well, put the pan in your air fryer and cook at 370 o F for 4 minutes.
3. Combine the steak, green onions, bell peppers, soy sauce, and garlic.
4. Toss and cover to cook for another 6 minutes.

5. Divide into bowls and serve.

Nutrition Values:

calories 262, fat 9, fiber 8, carbs 14, protein 11

77. PUDDING WITH VEGGIES

Preparation Time: 43 minutes
Servings: 7

Ingredients:

- Butter-1 tbsp -softened
- Yellow onion-1 -chopped
- Corn-2 cups
- Celery-1/4 cup -chopped
- Thyme-1 tsp -chopped
- Red bell peppers-2 -chopped
- Garlic-2 tsp -minced
- Heavy cream-1/2 cup
- Salt and black pepper to taste
- Milk-1-1/2 cups
- Bread-3 cups -cubed
- Eggs-3 -whisked
- Cheddar cheese-4 tbsps -grated

Directions:

1. Butter to grease a baking dish that fits your air fryer.
2. Mix all other ingredients except the cheddar cheese.
3. After tossing well, sprinkle the cheese all over.
4. Place the dish in the fryer, and cook at 360 o F for 30 minutes.
5. Divide between plates, serve, and enjoy.

Nutrition Values:

calories 286, fat 10, fiber 2, carbs 16, protein 11

78. LUNCH OF COCONUT ZUCCHINI

Preparation Time: 23 minutes
Servings: 9

Ingredients:

- Veggie stock-1 cup
- Zucchinis-8 -cut in medium wedges
- Coconut cream-1 cup
- Soy sauce-1 tbsp
- Rosemary-1/4 tsp -dried

- Olive oil-2 tbsps
- Yellow onions-2 -chopped
- Salt and black pepper to taste
- Thyme-1/4 tsp -dried
- Basil-1/2 tsp -chopped

Directions:

1. Pick a pan that fits your air fryer and grease it with the oil.
2. Combine all other ingredients to the pan.
3. After tossing, place the pan in the fryer.
4. Cook at 360 o F for 16 minutes.
5. Divide the mix between plates, serve, and enjoy.

Nutrition Values:

calories 181, fat 4, fiber 4, carbs 10, protein 5

79. SIMPLE KALE AND MUSHROOM CHICKEN MIX

Preparation Time: 27 minutes
Servings: 7

Ingredients:

- A bunch of kale -torn
- Chicken stock-2 tbsps
- Salt and black pepper to taste
- Tomato sauce-1/4 cup
- Shiitake mushrooms-1-1/2 cups -roughly sliced
- Chicken breast-1 cup -skinless, boneless, cooked and shredded

Directions:

1. Pick a pan that fits your air fryer and mix all ingredients.
2. Toss and then put the pan in the fryer.
3. Cook at 350 o F for 20 minutes.
4. Divide between plates and serve.

Nutrition Values:

calories 210, fat 7, fiber 2, carbs 14, protein 5

80. CHICKEN CASSEROLE WITH BEANS

Preparation Time: 33 minutes
Servings: 7

Ingredients:

- Chicken breast-3 cups -skinless, boneless, cooked and shredded
- Cilantro-1/2 cup -chopped
- Canned black beans-24 ounces -drained and rinsed
- Mozzarella cheese-3 cups -shredded
- Kale leaves-6 -chopped
- Salsa-2 cups
- Green onions-1/2 cup -chopped
- A drizzle of olive oil
- Cumin-2 tsp -ground
- Chili powder-2 tsp
- Garlic powder-1 tbsp

Directions:

1. Take a baking dish that fits your air fryer and grease it with the oil.
2. Add all other ingredients except the cheese to the baking dish.
3. Then sprinkle the cheese all over and place the dish in the air fryer.
4. Cook at 350 o F for 20 minutes.
5. Divide between plates, serve, and enjoy!

Nutrition Values:

calories 285, fat 12, fiber 6, carbs 22, protein 15

81. JAPANESE STYLE CHICKEN

Preparation Time: 18 Minutes
Servings: 2

Ingredients:

- 2 chicken thighs; skinless and boneless
- 1/8 cup sake
- 1/2 tsp. sesame oil
- 1/8 cup water
- 2 ginger slices; chopped
- 3 garlic cloves; minced
- 1/4 cup soy sauce
- 1/4 cup mirin
- 2 tbsp. sugar
- 1 tbsp. cornstarch mixed with 2 tbsp. water
- Sesame seeds for serving

Directions:

1. In a bowl; mix chicken thighs with ginger, garlic, soy sauce, mirin, sake, oil, water,

sugar and cornstarch; toss well, transfer to preheated air fryer and cook at 360 °F, for 8 minutes. Divide among plates; sprinkle sesame seeds on top and serve with a side salad for lunch.

Nutrition Values: Calories: 300; Fat: 7; Fiber: 9; Carbs: 17; Protein: 10

82. CHICKEN PIE RECIPE

Preparation Time: 29 Minutes
Servings: 4

Ingredients:

- 2 chicken thighs; boneless, skinless and cubed
- 1 carrot; chopped
- 1 tsp. Worcestershire sauce
- 1 tbsp. flour
- 1 tbsp. milk
- 2 puff pastry sheets
- 1 tbsp. butter; melted
- 1 yellow onion; chopped
- 2 potatoes; chopped
- 2 mushrooms; chopped
- 1 tsp. soy sauce
- Salt and black pepper to the taste
- 1 tsp. Italian seasoning
- 1/2 tsp. garlic powder

Directions:

2. Heat up a pan over medium high heat, add potatoes, carrots and onion; stir and cook for 2 minutes.
3. Add chicken and mushrooms, salt, soy sauce, pepper, Italian seasoning, garlic powder, Worcestershire sauce, flour and milk; stir really well and take off heat.
4. Place 1 puff pastry sheet on the bottom of your air fryer's pan and trim edge excess.
5. Add chicken mix, top with the other puff pastry sheet; trim excess as well and brush pie with butter.
6. Place in your air fryer and cook at 360 °F, for 6 minutes. Leave pie to cool down; slice and serve for breakfast.

Nutrition Values: Calories: 300; Fat: 5; Fiber: 7; Carbs: 14; Protein: 7

83. CHICKEN FAJITAS

Preparation Time: 20 Minutes
Servings: 4

Ingredients:

- 1 lb. chicken breasts; cut into strips
- 1 tsp. garlic powder
- 1/4 tsp. cumin; ground
- 1/2 tsp. chili powder
- 1 green bell pepper; sliced
- 1 yellow onion; chopped.
- 1 tbsp. lime juice
- 1/4 tsp. coriander; ground
- 1 red bell pepper; sliced
- Salt and black pepper to the taste
- Cooking spray
- 4 tortillas; warmed up
- Salsa for serving
- 1 cup lettuce leaves; torn for serving
- Sour cream for serving

Directions:

1. In a bowl; mix chicken with garlic powder, cumin, chili, salt, pepper, coriander, lime juice, red bell pepper, green bell pepper and onion; toss, leave aside for 10 minutes, transfer to your air fryer and drizzle some cooking spray all over.
2. Toss and cook at 400 °F, for 10 minutes. Arrange tortillas on a working surface, divide chicken mix, also add salsa, sour cream and lettuce; wrap and serve for lunch.

Nutrition Values: Calories: 317; Fat: 6; Fiber: 8; Carbs: 14; Protein: 4

84. LENTILS FRITTERS

Preparation Time: 20 Minutes
Servings: 2

Ingredients:

- 1 cup yellow lentils; soaked in water for 1 hour and drained
- 1 hot chili pepper; chopped.
- 1-inch ginger piece; grated
- 1/2 tsp. turmeric powder
- 1 tsp. garam masala

- 1 tsp. baking powder
- 2 tsp. olive oil
- 1/3 cup water
- 1/2 cup cilantro; chopped
- 1 ½ cup spinach; chopped
- 4 garlic cloves; minced
- 3/4 cup red onion; chopped
- Salt and black pepper to the taste
- Mint chutney for serving

Directions:

1. In your blender; mix lentils with chili pepper, ginger, turmeric, garam masala, baking powder, salt, pepper, olive oil, water, cilantro, spinach, onion and garlic, blend well and shape medium balls out of this mix.
2. Place them all in your preheated air fryer at 400 °F and cook for 10 minutes. Serve your veggie fritters with a side salad for lunch.

Nutrition Values: Calories: 142; Fat: 2; Fiber: 8; Carbs: 12; Protein: 4

85. CORN CASSEROLE RECIPE

Preparation Time: 25 Minutes
Servings: 4

Ingredients:

- 2 cups corn
- 1/2 cup light cream
- 1/2 cup Swiss cheese; grated
- 2 tbsp. butter
- 3 tbsp. flour
- 1 egg
- 1/4 cup milk
- Salt and black pepper to the taste
- Cooking spray

Directions:

1. In a bowl; mix corn with flour, egg, milk, light cream, cheese, salt, pepper and butter and stir well.
2. Grease your air fryer's pan with cooking spray, pour cream mix; spread and cook at 320 °F, for 15 minutes. Serve warm for lunch.

Nutrition Values: Calories: 281; Fat: 7; Fiber:

8; Carbs: 9; Protein: 6

86. FISH AND KETTLE CHIPS

Preparation Time: 22 Minutes
Servings: 2

Ingredients:

- 2 medium cod fillets; skinless and boneless
- 1/4 cup buttermilk
- 3 cups kettle chips; cooked
- Salt and black pepper to the taste

Directions:

1. In a bowl mix fish with salt, pepper and buttermilk; toss and leave aside for 5 minutes.
2. Put chips in your food processor, crush them and spread them on a plate.
3. Add fish and press well on all sides.
4. Transfer fish to your air fryer's basket and cook at 400 °F, for 12 minutes. Serve hot for lunch.

Nutrition Values: Calories: 271; Fat: 7; Fiber: 9; Carbs: 14; Protein: 4

87. STEAK AND CABBAGE

Preparation Time: 20 Minutes
Servings: 4

Ingredients:

- 1/2 lb. sirloin steak; cut into strips
- 2 green onions; chopped.
- 2 garlic cloves; minced
- 2 tsp. cornstarch
- 1 tbsp. peanut oil
- 2 cups green cabbage; chopped
- 1 yellow bell pepper; chopped
- Salt and black pepper to the taste

Directions:

1. In a bowl; mix cabbage with salt, pepper and peanut oil; toss, transfer to air fryer's basket, cook at 370 °F, for 4 minutes and transfer to a bowl.
2. Add steak strips to your air fryer; also add green onions, bell pepper, garlic, salt and pepper, toss and cook for 5 minutes. Add over cabbage; toss, divide among plates

and serve for lunch.

Nutrition Values: Calories: 282; Fat: 6; Fiber: 8; Carbs: 14; Protein: 6

88. CHICKEN WINGS

Preparation Time: 55 Minutes
Servings: 4

Ingredients:

- 3 lbs. chicken wings
- 3/4 cup potato starch
- 1 tsp. lemon juice
- 1/2 cup butter
- 1 tbsp. old bay seasoning
- Lemon wedges for serving

Directions:

1. In a bowl; mix starch with old bay seasoning and chicken wings and toss well.
2. Place chicken wings in your air fryer's basket and cook them at 360 °F, for 35 minutes shaking the fryer from time to time.
3. Increase temperature to 400 degrees F; cook chicken wings for 10 minutes more and divide them on plates.
4. Heat up a pan over medium heat; add butter and melt it.
5. Add lemon juice; stir well, take off heat and drizzle over chicken wings. Serve them for lunch with lemon wedges on the side.

Nutrition Values: Calories: 271; Fat: 6; Fiber: 8; Carbs: 18; Protein: 18

89. SHRIMP CROQUETTES

Preparation Time: 18 Minutes
Servings: 4

Ingredients:

- 2/3 lb. shrimp; cooked; peeled; deveined and chopped.
- 1 ½ cups bread crumbs
- 1 egg; whisked
- 2 tbsp. olive oil
- 2 tbsp. lemon juice
- 3 green onions; chopped.

- 1/2 tsp. basil; dried
- Salt and black pepper to the taste

Directions:

1. In a bowl; mix half of the bread crumbs with egg and lemon juice and stir well.
2. Add green onions, basil, salt, pepper and shrimp and stir really well.
3. In a separate bowl; mix the rest of the bread crumbs with the oil and toss well.
4. Shape round balls out of shrimp mix, dredge them in bread crumbs; place them in preheated air fryer and cook the for 8 minutes at 400 degrees F. Serve them with a dip for lunch.

Nutrition Values: Calories: 142; Fat: 4; Fiber: 6; Carbs: 9; Protein: 4

90. SHRIMP PANCAKE

Preparation Time: 20 Minutes
Servings: 2

Ingredients:

- 1 cup small shrimp; peeled and deveined
- 1 tbsp. butter
- 3 eggs; whisked
- 1/2 cup flour
- 1/2 cup milk
- 1 cup salsa

Directions:

1. Preheat your air fryer at 400 degrees F; add fryer's pan, add 1 tbsp. butter and melt it.
2. In a bowl; mix eggs with flour and milk, whisk well and pour into air fryer's pan, spread, cook at 350 degrees for 12 minutes and transfer to a plate. In a bowl; mix shrimp with salsa; stir and serve your pancake with this on the side.

Nutrition Values: Calories: 200; Fat: 6; Fiber: 8; Carbs: 12; Protein: 4

91. PORK AND POTATOES RECIPE

Preparation Time: 35 Minutes
Servings: 2

Ingredients:

- 2 lbs. pork loin
- 2 red potatoes; cut into medium wedges
- 1/2 tsp. garlic powder
- 1/2 tsp. red pepper flakes
- 1 tsp. parsley; dried
- A drizzle of balsamic vinegar
- Salt and black pepper to the taste

Directions:

1. In your air fryer's pan; mix pork with potatoes, salt, pepper, garlic powder, pepper flakes, parsley and vinegar; toss and cook at 390 °F, for 25 minutes. Slice pork, divide it and potatoes on plates and serve for lunch.

Nutrition Values: Calories: 400; Fat: 15; Fiber: 7; Carbs: 27; Protein: 20

92. LUNCH PIZZAS

Preparation Time: 17 Minutes
Servings: 4

Ingredients:

- 3/4 cup pizza sauce
- 2 green onions; chopped
- 2 cup mozzarella; grated
- 4 pitas
- 1 tbsp. olive oil
- 4 oz. jarred mushrooms; sliced
- 1/2 tsp. basil; dried
- 1 cup grape tomatoes; sliced

Directions:

1. Spread pizza sauce on each pita bread; sprinkle green onions and basil, divide mushrooms and top with cheese.
2. Arrange pita pizzas in your air fryer and cook them at 400 °F, for 7 minutes. Top each pizza with tomato slices; divide among plates and serve.

Nutrition Values: Calories: 200; Fat: 4; Fiber: 6; Carbs: 7; Protein: 3

93. ASPARAGUS AND SALMON

Preparation Time: 33 Minutes
Servings: 4

Ingredients:

- 1 lb. asparagus; trimmed
- 1 tbsp. olive oil
- A pinch of sweet paprika
- A pinch of garlic powder
- A pinch of cayenne pepper
- 1 red bell pepper; cut into halves
- 4 oz. smoked salmon
- Salt and black pepper to the taste

Directions:

1. Put asparagus spears and bell pepper on a lined baking sheet that fits your air fryer; add salt, pepper, garlic powder, paprika, olive oil, cayenne pepper, toss to coat, introduce in the fryer; cook at 390 °F, for 8 minutes, flip and cook for 8 minutes more. Add salmon, cook for 5 minutes more; divide everything on plates and serve.

Nutrition Values: Calories: 90; Fat: 1; Fiber: 1; Carbs: 1.2; Protein: 4

94. DILL AND SCALLOPS

Preparation Time: 15 Minutes
Servings: 4

Ingredients:

- 1 lb. sea scallops; debearded
- 1 tsp. dill; chopped.
- 2 tsp. olive oil
- 1 tbsp. lemon juice
- Salt and black pepper to the taste

Directions:

1. In your air fryer, mix scallops with dill, oil, salt, pepper and lemon juice; cover and cook at 360 °F, for 5 minutes. Discard unopened ones, divide scallops and dill sauce on plates and serve for lunch.

Nutrition Values: Calories: 152; Fat: 4; Fiber: 7; Carbs: 19; Protein: 4

95. BEEF CUBES

Preparation Time: 22 Minutes
Servings: 4

Ingredients:

- 1 lb. sirloin; cubed

- 16 oz. jarred pasta sauce
- 1 ½ cups bread crumbs
- 1/2 tsp. marjoram; dried
- 2 tbsp. olive oil
- White rice; already cooked for serving

Directions:

1. In a bowl; mix beef cubes with pasta sauce and toss well.
2. In another bowl; mix bread crumbs with marjoram and oil and stir well.
3. Dip beef cubes in this mix, place them in your air fryer and cook at 360 °F, for 12 minutes. Divide among plates and serve with white rice on the side.

Nutrition Values: Calories: 271; Fat: 6; Fiber: 9; Carbs: 18; Protein: 12

96. ZUCCHINI AND TUNA TORTILLAS

Preparation Time: 20 Minutes
Servings: 4

Ingredients:

- 1 cup zucchini; shredded
- 1/3 cup mayonnaise
- 2 tbsp. mustard
- 4 corn tortillas
- 4 tbsp. butter; soft
- 6 oz. canned tuna; drained
- 1 cup cheddar cheese; grated

Directions:

1. Spread butter on tortillas; place them in your air fryer's basket and cook them at 400 °F, for 3 minutes.
2. Meanwhile; in a bowl, mix tuna with zucchini, mayo and mustard and stir.
3. Divide this mix on each tortilla, top with cheese, roll tortillas; place them in your air fryer's basket again and cook them at 400 °F, for 4 minutes more. Serve for lunch.

Nutrition Values: Calories: 162; Fat: 4; Fiber: 8; Carbs: 9; Protein: 4

97. SUMMER SQUASH FRITTERS

Preparation Time: 17 Minutes
Servings: 4

Ingredients:

- 3 oz. cream cheese
- 1 egg; whisked
- 1/2 tsp. oregano; dried
- 1/3 cup carrot; grated
- 2/3 cup bread crumbs
- A pinch of salt and black pepper
- 1 yellow summer squash; grated
- 2 tbsp. olive oil

Directions:

1. In a bowl; mix cream cheese with salt, pepper, oregano, egg, breadcrumbs, carrot and squash and stir well.
2. Shape medium patties out of this mix and brush them with the oil.
3. Place squash patties in your air fryer and cook them at 400 °F, for 7 minutes. Serve them for lunch.

Nutrition Values: Calories: 200; Fat: 4; Fiber: 7; Carbs: 8; Protein: 6

98. ASIAN CHICKEN

Preparation Time: 40 Minutes
Servings: 4

Ingredients:

- 2 chicken breasts; skinless, boneless and sliced
- 1 tsp. olive oil
- 1 yellow onion; sliced
- 1 tbsp. Worcestershire sauce
- 14 oz. pizza dough
- 1 ½ cups cheddar cheese; grated
- 1/2 cup jarred cheese sauce
- Salt and black pepper to the taste

Directions:

1. Preheat your air fryer at 400 degrees F; add half of the oil and onions and fry them for 8 minutes, stirring once.
2. Add chicken pieces, Worcestershire sauce, salt and pepper; toss, air fry for 8 minutes more, stirring once and transfer everything to a bowl.
3. Roll pizza dough on a working surface and shape a rectangle.
4. Spread half of the cheese all over, add

chicken and onion mix and top with cheese sauce.

5. Roll your dough and shape into a U.
6. Place your roll in your air fryer's basket, brush with the rest of the oil and cook at 370 degrees for 12 minutes, flipping the roll halfway. Slice your roll when it's warm and serve for lunch.

Nutrition Values: Calories: 300; Fat: 8; Fiber: 17; Carbs: 20; Protein: 6

99. PARMESAN GNOCCHI

Preparation Time: 27 Minutes
Servings: 4

Ingredients:

- 1/4 cup parmesan; grated
- 1 yellow onion; chopped
- 16 oz. gnocchi
- 1 tbsp. olive oil
- 3 garlic cloves; minced
- 8 oz. spinach pesto

Directions:

1. Grease your air fryer's pan with olive oil, add gnocchi, onion and garlic, toss; put pan in your air fryer and cook at 400 °F, for 10 minutes.
2. Add pesto, toss and cook for 7 minutes more at 350 degrees F. Divide among plates and serve for lunch.

Nutrition Values: Calories: 200; Fat: 4; Fiber: 4; Carbs: 12; Protein: 4

100. PROSCIUTTO SANDWICH

Preparation Time: 15 Minutes
Servings: 1

Ingredients:

- 2 bread slices
- 2 prosciutto slices
- 2 basil leaves
- 1 tsp. olive oil
- 2 mozzarella slices
- 2 tomato slices
- A pinch of salt and black pepper

Directions:

1. Arrange mozzarella and prosciutto on a bread slice.
2. Season with salt and pepper; place in your air fryer and cook at 400 °F, for 5 minutes. Drizzle oil over prosciutto, add tomato and basil; cover with the other bread slice, cut sandwich in half and serve.

Nutrition Values: Calories: 172; Fat: 3; Fiber: 7; Carbs: 9; Protein: 5

101. CHINESE STYLE PORK

Preparation Time: 22 Minutes
Servings: 4

Ingredients:

- 2 lbs. pork; cut into medium cubes
- 2 eggs
- 1 cup cornstarch
- 1 tsp. sesame oil
- A pinch of Chinese five spice
- 3 tbsp. canola oil
- Sweet tomato sauce for serving
- Salt and black pepper to the taste

Directions:

1. In a bowl; mix five spice with salt, pepper and cornstarch and stir.
2. In another bowl; mix eggs with sesame oil and whisk well.
3. Dredge pork cubes in cornstarch mix; then dip in eggs mix and place them in your air fryer which you've greased with the canola oil.
4. Cook at 340 °F, for 12 minutes; shaking the fryer once. Serve pork for lunch with the sweet tomato sauce on the side.

Nutrition Values: Calories: 320; Fat: 8; Fiber: 12; Carbs: 20; Protein: 5

102. HASH BROWN TOASTS

Preparation Time: 17 Minutes
Servings: 4

Ingredients:

- 4 hash brown patties; frozen
- 1 tbsp. olive oil
- 1 tbsp. balsamic vinegar
- 1 tbsp. basil; chopped.

- 1/4 cup cherry tomatoes; chopped.
- 3 tbsp. mozzarella; shredded
- 2 tbsp. parmesan; grated

Directions:

1. Put hash brown patties in your air fryer; drizzle the oil over them and cook them at 400 °F, for 7 minutes.
2. In a bowl; mix tomatoes with mozzarella, parmesan, vinegar and basil and stir well. Divide hash brown patties on plates; top each with tomatoes mix and serve for lunch.

Nutrition Values: Calories: 199; Fat: 3; Fiber: 8; Carbs: 12; Protein: 4

SIDES

103. CREAMY POTATOES

Preparation time: 5 minutes
Cooking time: 20 minutes
Servings: 4

Ingredients:

- 2 gold potatoes, cut into medium pieces
- 1 tablespoon olive oil
- Salt and black pepper to taste
- 3 tablespoons sour cream

Directions:

1. In a baking dish that fits your air fryer, mix all the ingredients and toss.
2. Place the dish in the air fryer and cook at 370 degrees F for 20 minutes.
3. Divide between plates and serve as a side dish.

Nutrition Values: calories 201, fat 8, fiber 9, carbs 18, protein 5

104. SWEET POTATO SIDE SALAD

Preparation time: 5 minutes
Cooking time: 20 minutes
Servings: 2

Ingredients:

- 2 sweet potatoes, peeled and cut into wedges
- Salt and black pepper to taste
- 2 tablespoons avocado oil
- ½ teaspoon curry powder
- ¼ teaspoon coriander, ground
- 4 tablespoons mayonnaise
- ½ teaspoon cumin, ground
- A pinch of ginger powder
- A pinch of cinnamon powder

Directions:

1. In your air fryer's basket, mix the sweet potato wedges with salt, pepper, coriander, curry powder, and the oil; toss well.
2. Cook at 370 degrees F for 20 minutes, flipping them once.

3. Transfer the potatoes to a bowl, then add the mayonnaise, cumin, ginger and the cinnamon.
4. Toss and serve as a side salad.

Nutrition Values: calories 190, fat 5, fiber 8, carbs 14, protein 5

105. MAYO BRUSSELS SPROUTS

Preparation time: 5 minutes
Cooking time: 15 minutes
Servings: 4

Ingredients:

- 1 pound Brussels sprouts, trimmed and halved
- Salt and black pepper to taste
- 6 teaspoons olive oil
- ½ cup mayonnaise
- 2 tablespoons garlic, minced

Directions:

1. In your air fryer, mix the sprouts, salt, pepper, and oil; toss well.
2. Cook the sprouts at 390 degrees F for 15 minutes.
3. Transfer them to a bowl; then add the mayo and the garlic and toss.
4. Divide between plates and serve as a side dish.

Nutrition Values: calories 202, fat 6, fiber 8, carbs 12, protein 8

106. GREEN BEANS AND SHALLOTS

Preparation time: 5 minutes
Cooking time: 25 minutes
Servings: 4

Ingredients:

- 1½ pounds green beans, trimmed
- Salt and black pepper to taste
- ½ pound shallots, chopped
- ¼ cup walnuts, chopped
- 2 tablespoons olive oil

Directions:

1. In your air fryer, mix all ingredients and toss.
2. Cook at 350 degrees F for 25 minutes.
3. Divide between plates and serve as a side dish.

Nutrition Values: calories 182, fat 3, fiber 6, carbs 11, protein 5

107. ITALIAN MUSHROOM MIX

Preparation time: 5 minutes
Cooking time: 15 minutes
Servings: 4

Ingredients:

- 1 pound button mushrooms, halved
- 2 tablespoons parmesan cheese, grated
- 1 teaspoon Italian seasoning
- A pinch of salt and black pepper
- 3 tablespoons butter, melted

Directions:

1. In a pan that fits your air fryer, mix all the ingredients and toss.
2. Place the pan in the air fryer and cook at 360 degrees F for 15 minutes.
3. Divide the mix between plates and serve.

Nutrition Values: calories 194, fat 4, fiber 4, carbs 14, protein 7

108. CRISPY FRIED PICKLE SPEARS

Preparation Time: 15 minutes
Servings 6

Nutrition Values: 58 Calories; 2g Fat; 6.8g Carbs; 3.2g Protein; 0.9g Sugars

Ingredients

- 1/3 cup milk
- 1 teaspoon garlic powder
- 2 medium-sized eggs
- 1 teaspoon fine sea salt
- 1/3 teaspoon chili powder
- 1/3 cup all-purpose flour
- 1/2 teaspoon shallot powder
- 2 jars sweet and sour pickle spears

Directions

1. Pat the pickle spears dry with a kitchen towel. Then, take two mixing bowls.
2. Whisk the egg and milk in a bowl. In another bowl, combine all dry ingredients.
3. Firstly, dip the pickle spears into the dry mix; then coat each pickle with the egg/milk mixture; dredge them in the flour mixture again for additional coating.
4. Air fry battered pickles for 15 minutes at 385 degrees. Enjoy!

109. SPICY WINTER SQUASH BITES

Preparation Time: 23 minutes
Servings 8

Nutrition Values: 113 Calories; 3g Fat; 22.6g Carbs; 1.6g Protein; 4.3g Sugars

Ingredients

- 2 teaspoons fresh mint leaves, chopped
- 1/3 cup brown sugar
- 1 ½ teaspoons red pepper chili flakes
- 2 tablespoons melted butter
- 3 pounds winter squash, peeled, seeded, and cubed

Directions

1. Toss all of the above ingredients in a large-sized mixing dish.
2. Roast the squash bites for 30 minutes at 325 degrees F in your Air Fryer, turning once or twice. Serve with a homemade dipping sauce.

110. BUTTER SQUASH FRITTERS

Preparation Time: 22 minutes
Servings 4

Nutrition Values: 152 Calories; 10.02g Fat; 9.4g Carbs; 5.8g Protein; 0.3g Sugars

Ingredients

- 1/3 cup all-purpose flour
- 1/3 teaspoon freshly ground black pepper, or more to taste
- 1/3 teaspoon dried sage
- 4 cloves garlic, minced
- 1 ½ tablespoons olive oil

- 1/3 butternut squash, peeled and grated
- 2 eggs, well whisked
- 1 teaspoon fine sea salt
- A pinch of ground allspice

Directions

1. Thoroughly combine all ingredients in a mixing bowl.
2. Preheat your air fryer to 345 degrees and set the timer for 17 minutes; cook until your fritters are browned; serve right away.

111. HERBED ROASTED POTATOES

Preparation Time: 24 minutes
Servings 4

Nutrition Values: 208 Calories; 7.1g Fat; 33.8g Carbs; 3.6g Protein; 2.5g Sugars

Ingredients

- 1 teaspoon crushed dried thyme
- 1 teaspoon ground black pepper
- 2 tablespoons olive oil
- 1/2 tablespoon crushed dried rosemary
- 3 potatoes, peeled, washed and cut into wedges
- 1/2 teaspoon seasoned salt

Directions

1. Lay the potatoes in the air fryer cooking basket; drizzle olive oil over your potatoes.
2. Then, cook for 17 minutes at 353 degrees F.
3. Toss with the seasonings and serve warm with your favorite salad on the side.

112. INDIAN-STYLE GARNET SWEET POTATOES

Preparation Time: 24 minutes
Servings 4

Nutrition Values: 103 Calories; 9.1g Fat; 4.9g Carbs; 1.9g Protein; 1.2g Sugars

Ingredients

- 1/3 teaspoon white pepper
- 1 tablespoon butter, melted
- 1/2 teaspoon turmeric powder
- 5 garnet sweet potatoes, peeled and diced
- 1 ½ tablespoons maple syrup
- 2 teaspoons tamarind paste
- 1 1/2 tablespoons fresh lime juice
- 1 1/2 teaspoon ground allspice

Directions

1. In a mixing bowl, toss all ingredients until sweet potatoes are well coated.
2. Air-fry them at 335 degrees F for 12 minutes.
3. Pause the air fryer and toss again. Increase the temperature to 390 degrees F and cook for an additional 10 minutes. Eat warm.

113. EASY FRIZZLED LEEKS

Preparation Time: 52 minutes
Servings 6

Nutrition Values: 291 Calories; 6g Fat; 53.3g Carbs; 5.7g Protein; 4.3g Sugars

Ingredients

- 1/2 teaspoon porcini powder
- 1 1/2 cup rice flour
- 1 tablespoon vegetable oil
- 3 medium-sized leeks, slice into julienne strips
- 2 large-sized dishes with ice water
- 2 teaspoons onion powder
- Fine sea salt and cayenne pepper, to taste

Directions

1. Allow the leeks to soak in ice water for about 25 minutes; drain well.
2. Place the rice flour, salt, cayenne pepper, onions powder, and porcini powder into a resealable bag. Add the celery and shake to coat well.
3. Drizzle vegetable oil over the seasoned leeks. Air fry at 390 degrees F for about 18 minutes; turn them halfway through the cooking time. Serve with homemade mayonnaise or any other sauce for dipping. Enjoy!

114. CREMINI MUSHROOMS IN

ZESTY TAHINI SAUCE

Preparation Time: 22 minutes
Servings 5

Nutrition Values: 372 Calories; 4g Fat; 80g Carbs; 11.2g Protein; 2.6g Sugars

Ingredients

- 1/2 tablespoon tahini
- 1/2 teaspoon turmeric powder
- 1/3 teaspoon cayenne pepper
- 2 tablespoons lemon juice, freshly squeezed
- 1 teaspoon kosher salt
- 1/3 teaspoon freshly cracked black pepper
- 1 1/2 tablespoons vermouth
- 1 ½ tablespoons olive oil
- 1 ½ pound Cremini mushrooms

Directions

1. Grab a mixing dish and toss the mushrooms with the olive oil, turmeric powder, salt, black pepper, and cayenne pepper.
2. Cook them in your air fryer for 9 minutes at 355 degrees F.
3. Pause your air fryer, give it a good stir and cook for 10 minutes longer.
4. Meanwhile, thoroughly combine lemon juice, vermouth, and tahini. Serve warm mushrooms with tahini sauce.

115. HASH BROWN CASSEROLE

Preparation Time: 23 minutes
Servings 6

Nutrition Values: 195 Calories; 11.1g Fat; 22g Carbs; 3.1g Protein; 3g Sugars

Ingredients

- 1/2 cup Cheddar cheese, shredded
- 1 tablespoon soft cheese, at room temperature
- 1/3 cup crushed bran cereal
- 1 ½ yellow or white medium-sized onion, chopped
- 5 ounces condensed cream of celery soup
- 1 tablespoons fresh cilantro, finely minced
- 1/3 cup sour cream

- 3 cloves garlic, peeled and finely minced
- 2 cups hash brown potatoes, shredded
- 1 1/2 tablespoons margarine or butter, melted
- Sea salt and freshly ground black pepper, to your liking
- Crushed red pepper flakes, to your liking

Directions

1. Grab a large-sized bowl and whisk the celery soup, sour cream, soft cheese, red pepper, salt, and black pepper. Stir in the hash browns, onion, garlic, cilantro, and Cheddar cheese. Mix until everything is thoroughly combined.
2. Scrape the mixture into a baking dish that is previously lightly greased.
3. In another mixing bowl, combine together the bran cereal and melted margarine -or butter. Spread the mixture evenly over the top of the hash brown mixture.
4. Bake for 17 minutes at 290 degrees F. Eat warm, garnished with some extra sour cream if desired.

116. PEPPER JACK CAULIFLOWER BITES

Preparation Time: 24 minutes
Servings 2

Nutrition Values: 271 Calories; 23g Fat; 8.9g Carbs; 9.8g Protein; 2.8g Sugars

Ingredients

- 1/3 teaspoon shallot powder
- 1 teaspoon ground black pepper
- 1 ½ large-sized heads of cauliflower, broken into florets
- 1/4 teaspoon cumin powder
- ½ teaspoon garlic salt
- 1/4 cup Pepper Jack cheese, grated
- 1 ½ tablespoons vegetable oil
- 1/3 teaspoon paprika

Directions

1. Boil cauliflower in a large pan of salted water approximately 5 minutes. After that, drain the cauliflower florets; now, transfer them to a baking dish.

2. Toss the cauliflower florets with the rest of the above ingredients.
3. Roast at 395 degrees F for 16 minutes, turn them halfway through the process. Enjoy!

117. CHEESY BROCCOLI CROQUETTES

Preparation Time: 50 minutes
Servings 6

Nutrition Values:246 Calories; 14g Fat; 15.2g Carbs; 14.5g Protein; 1.6g Sugars

Ingredients

- 1 1/2 cups Monterey Jack cheese
- 1 teaspoon dried dill weed
- 1/3 teaspoon ground black pepper
- 3 eggs, whisked
- 1 teaspoon cayenne pepper
- 1/2 teaspoon kosher salt
- 1 cup Panko crumbs
- 2 ½ cups broccoli florets
- 1/3 cup Parmesan cheese

Directions

1. Blitz the broccoli florets in a food processor until finely crumbed. Then, combine the broccoli with the rest of the above ingredients.
2. Roll the mixture into small balls; place the balls in the fridge for approximately half an hour.
3. Preheat your air fryer to 335 degrees F and set the timer to 14 minutes; cook until broccoli croquettes are browned and serve warm.

118. CAULIFLOWER CAKES OLE

Preparation Time: 48 minutes
Servings 6

Nutrition Values:190 Calories; 14.1g Fat; 4.7g Carbs; 11.5g Protein; 1.3g Sugars

Ingredients

- 2 teaspoons chili powder
- 1 1/2 teaspoon kosher salt
- 1 teaspoon dried marjoram, crushed
- 2 1/2 cups cauliflower, broken into florets

- 1 1/3 cups tortilla chip crumbs
- 1/2 teaspoon crushed red pepper flakes
- 3 eggs, whisked
- 1 ½ cups Queso cotija cheese, crumbled

Directions

1. Blitz the cauliflower florets in your food processor until they're crumbled -it is the size of rice. Then, combine the cauliflower "rice" with the other items.
2. Now, roll the cauliflower mixture into small balls; refrigerate for 30 minutes.
3. Preheat your air fryer to 345 degrees and set the timer for 14 minutes; cook until the balls are browned and serve right away.

119. CELERY AND CARROT CROQUETTES

Preparation Time: 25 minutes
Servings 4

Nutrition Values:142 Calories; 6g Fat; 15.8g Carbs; 7.2g Protein; 3g Sugars

Ingredients

- 2 small eggs, lightly beaten
- 1/3 teaspoon freshly cracked black pepper
- 1/3 cup Colby cheese, grated
- 1/2 tablespoon fresh dill, finely chopped
- 1/2 tablespoon garlic paste
- 1/3 cup onion, finely chopped
- 1/3 cup all-purpose flour
- 3 medium-sized carrots, trimmed and grated
- 2 teaspoons fine sea salt
- 3 medium-sized celery stalks, trimmed and grated
- 1/3 teaspoon baking powder

Directions

1. Place the carrots and celery on a paper towel and squeeze them to remove the excess liquid.
2. Combine the vegetables with the other ingredients in the order listed above. Shape the balls using 1 tablespoon of the vegetable mixture.
3. Then, gently flatten each ball with your

palm or a wide spatula. Spritz the croquettes with a nonstick cooking oil.
4. Bake the vegetable cakes in a single layer for 17 minutes at 318 degrees F. Serve warm with sour cream.

120. SMOKED VEGGIE OMELET

Preparation Time: 14 minutes
Servings 2

Nutrition Values: 226 Calories; 11.5g Fat; 14.2g Carbs; 16.3g Protein; 5.2g Sugars

Ingredients

- 1/3 cup cherry tomatoes, chopped
- 1 bell pepper, seeded and chopped
- 1/3 teaspoon freshly ground black pepper
- 1/2 purple onion, peeled and sliced
- 1 teaspoon smoked cayenne pepper
- 5 medium-sized eggs, well-beaten
- 1/3 cup smoked tofu, crumbled
- 1 teaspoon seasoned salt
- 1 1/2 tablespoons fresh chives, chopped

Directions

1. Brush a baking dish with a spray coating.
2. Throw all ingredients, minus fresh chives, into the baking dish; give it a good stir.
3. Cook about 15 minutes at 325 degrees F. Garnish with fresh chopped chives. Bon appétit!

121. SWEET POTATO AND CARROT CROQUETTES

Preparation Time: 22 minutes
Servings 4

Nutrition Values: 206 Calories; 5g Fat; 32g Carbs; 8.3g Protein; 5.7g Sugars

Ingredients

- 1/3 cup Swiss cheese, grated
- 1/3 teaspoon fine sea salt
- 1/3 teaspoon baking powder
- 1/3 cup scallions, finely chopped
- 1/2 tablespoon fresh basil, finely chopped
- 3 carrots, trimmed and grated
- 1/2 teaspoon freshly cracked black pepper
- 3 sweet potatoes, grated

- 1/3 cup all-purpose flour
- 2 small eggs, lightly beaten

Directions

1. Place grated sweet potatoes and carrots on a paper towel and pat them dry.
2. Combine the potatoes and carrots with the other ingredients in the order listed above. Then, create the balls using 1½ tablespoons of the vegetable mixture.
3. Then, gently flatten each ball. Spritz the croquettes with a nonstick cooking oil.
4. Bake your croquettes for 13 minutes at 305 degrees F; work with batches. Serve warm with tomato ketchup and mayonnaise.

122. MANCHEGO AND POTATO PATTIES

Preparation Time: 15 minutes
Servings 8

Nutrition Values: 191 Calories; 8.7g Fat; 22g Carbs; 7g Protein; 1.4g Sugars

Ingredients

- 1 cup Manchego cheese, shredded
- 1 teaspoon paprika
- 1 teaspoon freshly ground black pepper
- 1/2 tablespoon fine sea salt
- 2 cups scallions, finely chopped
- 2 pounds Russet potatoes, peeled and grated
- 2 tablespoons canola oil
- 2 teaspoons dried basil

Directions

1. Thoroughly combine all of the above ingredients. Then, shape the balls using your hands. Now, flatten the balls to make the patties.
2. Next, cook your patties at 360 degrees F approximately 10 minutes. Bon appétit!

123. MINT-BUTTER STUFFED MUSHROOMS

Preparation Time: 19 minutes
Servings 3

Nutrition Values: 290 Calories; 14.7g Fat; 13.4g

Carbs; 28g Protein; 3.3g Sugars

Ingredients

- 3 garlic cloves, minced
- 1 teaspoon ground black pepper, or more to taste
- 1/3 cup seasoned breadcrumbs
- 1½ tablespoons fresh mint, chopped
- 1 teaspoon salt, or more to taste
- 1½ tablespoons melted butter
- 14 medium-sized mushrooms, cleaned, stalks removed

Directions

1. Mix all of the above ingredients, minus the mushrooms, in a mixing bowl to prepare the filling.
2. Then, stuff the mushrooms with the prepared filling.
3. Air-fry stuffed mushrooms at 375 degrees F for about 12 minutes. Taste for doneness and serve at room temperature as a vegetarian appetizer.

124. RICOTTA AND LEAFY GREEN OMELET

Preparation Time: 17 minutes
Servings 2

Nutrition Values:409 Calories; 29.5g Fat; 6.9g Carbs; 27.9g Protein; 3g Sugars

Ingredients

- 1/3 cup Ricotta cheese
- 5 eggs, beaten
- 1/2 red bell pepper, seeded and sliced
- 1 cup mixed greens, roughly chopped
- 1/2 green bell pepper, seeded and sliced
- 1/2 teaspoon dried basil
- 1/2 chipotle pepper, finely minced
- 1/2 teaspoon dried oregano

Directions

1. Lightly coat the inside of a baking dish with a pan spray.
2. Then, throw all ingredients into the baking dish; give it a good stir.
3. Bake at 325 degrees F for 15 minutes.

125. BASIC PEPPER FRENCH FRIES

Preparation Time: 33 minutes
Servings 4

Nutrition Values:262 Calories; 9.1g Fat; 42g Carbs; 4.5g Protein; 3g Sugars

Ingredients

- 1 teaspoon fine sea salt
- 1/2 teaspoon freshly ground black pepper
- 2 ½ tablespoons canola oil
- 6 Russet potatoes, cut them into fries
- 1/2 teaspoon crushed red pepper flakes

Directions

1. Start by preheating your air fryer to 340 degrees F.
2. Place the fries in your air fryer and toss them with the oil. Add the seasonings and toss again.
3. Cook for 30 minutes, shaking your fries several times. Taste for doneness and eat warm.

126. OYSTER MUSHROOM AND LEMONGRASS OMELET

Preparation Time: 42 minutes
Servings 2

Nutrition Values:362 Calories; 29g Fat; 7.2g Carbs; 19g Protein; 2.8g Sugars

Ingredients

- 3 king oyster mushrooms, thinly sliced
- 1 lemongrass, chopped
- 1/2 teaspoon dried marjoram
- 5 eggs
- 1/3 cup Swiss cheese, grated
- 2 tablespoons sour cream
- 1 1/2 teaspoon dried rosemary
- 2 teaspoons red pepper flakes, crushed
- 2 tablespoons butter, melted
- 1/2 red onion, peeled and sliced into thin rounds
- ½ teaspoon garlic powder
- 1 teaspoon dried dill weed
- Fine sea salt and ground black pepper, to

your liking

Directions

1. Melt the margarine in a skillet that is placed over a medium flame. Then, sweat the onion, mushrooms, and lemongrass until they have softened; reserve.
2. Then, preheat the air fryer to 325 degrees F. Then, crack the eggs into a mixing bowl and whisk them well. Then, fold in the sour cream and give it a good stir.
3. Now, stir in the salt, black pepper, red pepper, rosemary, garlic powder, marjoram, and dill.
4. Next step, grease the inside of an air fryer baking dish with a thin layer of a cooking spray. Pour the egg/seasoning mixture into the baking dish; throw in the reserved mixture. Top with the Swiss cheese.
5. Set the timer for 35 minutes; cook until a knife inserted in the center comes out clean and dry

127. SPINACH AND CHEESE STUFFED BAKED POTATOES

Preparation Time: 18 minutes
Servings 4

Nutrition Values:327 Calories; 7g Fat; 59g Carbs; 9.4g Protein; 2.2g Sugars

Ingredients

- 3 tablespoons extra-virgin olive oil
- 2/3 cup sour cream, at room temperature
- 1½ cup baby spinach leaves, torn into small pieces
- 3 pounds russet potatoes
- 2 garlic cloves, peeled and finely minced
- 1/4 teaspoon fine sea salt, or more to taste
- 1/4 teaspoon freshly cracked black pepper, or more to taste
- 1/3 cup Cheddar cheese, freshly grated

Directions

1. Firstly, stab the potatoes with a fork. Preheat the air fryer to 345 degrees F. Now, cook the potatoes for 14 minutes.
2. Meanwhile, make the filling by mixing the rest of the above items.

3. Afterward that, open the potatoes up and stuff them with the prepared filling. Bon appétit!

128. PANTANO ROMANESCO WITH GOAT CHEESE APPETIZER

Preparation Time: 20 minutes
Servings 4

Nutrition Values:237 Calories; 20.4g Fat; 0.9g Carbs; 13g Protein; 0.9g Sugars

Ingredients

- 6 ounces goat cheese, sliced
- 2 shallots, thinly sliced
- 2 Pantano Romanesco tomatoes, cut into 1/2-inch slices
- 1 ½ tablespoons extra-virgin olive oil
- 3/4 teaspoon sea salt
- Fresh parsley, for garnish
- Fresh basil, chopped

Directions

1. Preheat your air fryer to 380 degrees F.
2. Now, pat each tomato slice dry using a paper towel. Sprinkle each slice with salt and chopped basil. Top with a slice of goat cheese.
3. Top with the shallot slices; drizzle with olive oil. Add the prepared tomato and feta "bites" to the air fryer food basket.
4. Cook in the air fryer for about 14 minutes. Lastly, adjust seasonings to taste and serve garnished with fresh parsley leaves. Enjoy!

129. SWISS CHARD AND CHEESE OMELET

Preparation Time: 25 minutes
Servings 2

Nutrition Values:388 Calories; 27g Fat; 6g Carbs; 29g Protein; 2.6g Sugars

Ingredients

- 1 teaspoon garlic paste
- 1 ½ tablespoons olive oil
- 1/2 cup crème fraîche
- 1/3 teaspoon ground black pepper, to your liking

- 1/3 cup Swiss cheese, crumbled
- 1 teaspoon cayenne pepper
- 1/3 cup Swiss chard, torn into pieces
- 5 eggs
- 1/4 cup yellow onions, chopped
- 1 teaspoon fine sea salt

Directions

1. Crack your eggs into a mixing dish; then, add the crème fraîche, salt, ground black pepper, and cayenne pepper.
2. Next, coat the inside of a baking dish with olive oil and tilt it to spread evenly. Scrape the egg/cream mixture into the baking dish. Add the other ingredients; mix to combine well.
3. Bake for 18 minutes at 292 degrees F. Serve immediately.

130. MOM'S JACKET POTATOES

Preparation Time: 23 minutes
Servings 4

Nutrition Values:270 Calories; 10.9g Fat; 35.2g Carbs; 8.8g Protein; 2.8g Sugars

Ingredients

- 1/3 cup Cottage cheese, softened
- 1/3 cup Parmigiano-Reggiano cheese, grated
- 1 teaspoon black pepper
- 1 ½ heaping tablespoons roughly chopped cilantro leaves
- 1/3 cup green onions, finely chopped
- 5 average-sized potatoes
- 2 ½ tablespoons softened butter
- 1 teaspoon salt

Directions

1. Firstly, stab your potatoes with a fork. Cook them in the air fryer basket for 20 minutes at 345 degrees F.
2. While the potatoes are cooking, make the filling by mixing the rest of the above ingredients.
3. Afterward, open the potatoes up and stuff them with the prepared filling. Bon appétit!

131. SKINNY ASPARAGUS AND

MUSHROOM CASSEROLE

Preparation Time: 27 minutes
Servings 2

Nutrition Values:207 Calories; 19.7g Fat; 30.2g Carbs; 20.6g Protein; 3.7g Sugars

Ingredients

- 1/3 cup milk
- 1/3 cup Colby cheese, grated
- 5 slices of Italian bread, cut into cubes
- 1 1/2 cups white mushrooms, sliced
- 2 asparagus spears, chopped
- 1 teaspoon table salt, or to taste
- 2 well-beaten eggs
- 1/3 teaspoon smoked cayenne pepper
- 1 teaspoon ground black pepper, or to taste
- 1/3 teaspoon dried rosemary, crushed

Directions

1. Throw the bread cubes into the baking dish.
2. In a mixing dish, thoroughly combine the eggs and milk. Stir in 1/2 of cheese; add the seasonings. Pour 3/4 of egg/cheese mixture over the bread cubes in the baking dish; press gently using a wide spatula.
3. Now, top with the mushrooms and chopped asparagus. Pour the remaining egg/cheese mixture over the top; make sure to spread it evenly.

Top with the remaining Colby cheese and bake for 20 minutes at 325 degrees F.

132. WINTER SAUSAGE WITH ROOT VEGETABLES

Preparation Time: 30 minutes
Servings 4

Nutrition Values:289 Calories; 13.6g Fat; 32.5g Carbs; 13.3g Protein; 6.7g Sugars

Ingredients

- 1/2 pound Italian sausage
- 3 sprigs rosemary
- 1 medium-sized parsnip, sliced
- 1/3 pound fingerling potatoes

- 3 sprigs thyme
- 1/3 pound carrots, trimmed and cut into matchsticks
- 1/2 celery stalk, sliced
- 2 garlic cloves, smashed
- 2 tablespoons extra-virgin olive oil
- 3 small-sized leeks, cut into halves lengthwise
- A pinch of grated nutmeg
- Salt and black pepper, to taste

Directions

1. Arrange fingerling potatoes, carrots, celery, parsnip, and leeks on the bottom of the air fryer baking dish. Tuck the garlic cloves around the vegetables.
2. Sprinkle with the seasonings and top with the sausage.
3. Roast approximately 33 minutes at 375 degrees F, stirring occasionally. Bon appétit!

133. CHINESE COD FILLETS

Preparation time: 10 minutes
Cooking time: 15 minutes
Servings: 4

Ingredients:

- 4 cod fillets, boneless
- Salt and black pepper to taste
- 1 cup water
- 4 tablespoons light soy sauce
- 1 tablespoon sugar
- 3 tablespoons olive oil + a drizzle
- 4 ginger slices
- 3 spring onions, chopped
- 2 tablespoons coriander, chopped

Directions:

1. Season the fish with salt and pepper, then drizzle some oil over it and rub well.
2. Put the fish in your air fryer and cook at 360 degrees F for 12 minutes.
3. Put the water in a pot and heat up over medium heat; add the soy sauce and sugar, stir, bring to a simmer, and remove from the heat.
4. Heat up a pan with the olive oil over medium heat; add the ginger and green onions, stir, cook for 2-3 minutes, and remove from the heat.
5. Divide the fish between plates and top with ginger, coriander, and green onions.
6. Drizzle the soy sauce mixture all over, serve, and enjoy!

Nutrition Values: calories 270, fat 12, fiber 8, carbs 16, protein 14

134. COD FILLETS WITH LEEKS

Preparation time: 10 minutes
Cooking time: 15 minutes
Servings: 2

Ingredients:

- 2 black cod fillets, boneless
- 1 tablespoon olive oil
- Salt and black pepper to taste
- 2 leeks, sliced
- ½ cup pecans, chopped

Directions:

1. In a bowl, mix the cod with the oil, salt, pepper, and the leeks; toss / coat well.
2. Transfer the cod to your air fryer and cook at 360 degrees F for 15 minutes.
3. Divide the fish and leeks between plates, sprinkle the pecans on top, and serve immediately.

Nutrition Values: calories 280, fat 4, fiber 2, carbs 12, protein 15

135. ROSEMARY SHRIMP KABOBS

Preparation time: 5 minutes
Cooking time: 7 minutes
Servings: 2

Ingredients:

- 8 shrimps, peeled and deveined
- 4 garlic cloves, minced
- Salt and black pepper to taste
- 8 red bell pepper slices
- 1 tablespoon rosemary, chopped
- 1 tablespoon olive oil

Directions:

1. Place all ingredients in a bowl and toss them well.
2. Thread 2 shrimp and 2 bell pepper slices on a skewer, and then repeat with 2 more shrimp and bell pepper slices.
3. Thred another 2 shrimp and 2 bell pepper slices on the other skewer and then repeat with the last 2 shrimp and 2 bell pepper slices.
4. Put the kabobs in your air fryer's basket., cook at 360 degrees F for 7 minutes and serve immediately with a side salad.

Nutrition Values: calories 200, fat 4, fiber 12, carbs 15, protein 6

136. SIMPLE BALSAMIC COD FILLETS

Preparation time: 5 minutes
Cooking time: 12 minutes
Servings: 2

Ingredients:

- 2 cod fillets, boneless
- 2 tablespoons lemon juice
- Salt and black pepper to taste
- ½ teaspoon garlic powder
- ⅓ cup water
- ⅓ cup balsamic vinegar
- 3 shallots, chopped
- 2 tablespoons olive oil

Directions:

1. In a bowl, toss the cod with the salt, pepper, lemon juice, garlic powder, water, vinegar, and oil; coat well.
2. Transfer the fish to your fryer's basket and cook at 360 degrees F for 12 minutes, flipping them halfway.
3. Divide the fish between plates, sprinkle the shallots on top, and serve.

Nutrition Values: calories 271, fat 12, fiber 10, carbs 16, protein 20

137. CHILI SALMON FILLETS

Preparation time: 5 minutes
Cooking time: 8 minutes
Servings: 2

Ingredients:

- 2 salmon fillets, boneless
- Salt and black pepper to taste
- 3 red chili peppers, chopped
- 2 tablespoons lemon juice
- 2 tablespoon olive oil
- 2 tablespoon garlic, minced

Directions:

1. In a bowl, combine the ingredients, toss, and coat fish well.
2. Transfer everything to your air fryer and cook at 365 degrees F for 8 minutes, flipping the fish halfway.
3. Divide between plates and serve right away.

Nutrition Values: calories 280, fat 4, fiber 8, carbs 15, protein 20

138. SHRIMP AND VEGGIE MIX

Preparation time: 10 minutes
Cooking time: 20 minutes
Servings: 4

Ingredients:

- ½ cup red onion, chopped
- 1 cup red bell pepper, chopped
- 1 cup celery, chopped
- 1 pound shrimp, peeled and deveined
- 1 teaspoon Worcestershire sauce
- Salt and black pepper to taste
- 1 tablespoon butter, melted
- 1 teaspoon sweet paprika

Directions:

1. Add all the ingredients to a bowl and mix well.
2. Transfer everything to your air fryer and cook 320 degrees F for 20 minutes, shaking halfway.
3. Divide between plates and serve.

Nutrition Values: calories 220, fat 14, fiber 9, carbs 17, protein 20

139. WHITE FISH AND PEAS

Preparation time: 10 minutes
Cooking time: 12 minutes
Servings: 4

Ingredients:

- 4 white fish fillets, boneless
- 2 tablespoons cilantro, chopped
- 2 cups peas, cooked and drained
- 4 tablespoons veggie stock
- ½ teaspoon basil, dried
- ½ teaspoon sweet paprika
- 2 garlic cloves, minced
- Salt and pepper to taste

Directions:

1. In a bowl, mix the fish with all ingredients except the peas; toss to coat the fish well.
2. Transfer everything to your air fryer and

cook at 360 degrees F for 12 minutes.

3. Add the peas, toss, and divide everything between plates.
4. Serve and enjoy.

Nutrition Values: calories 241, fat 8, fiber 12, carbs 15, protein 18

140. COD AND LIME SAUCE

Preparation time: 5 minutes
Cooking time: 12 minutes
Servings: 4

Ingredients:

- 4 cod fillets, boneless
- Salt and black pepper to taste
- 3 teaspoons lime zest
- 2 teaspoons lime juice
- 3 tablespoons chives, chopped
- 6 tablespoons butter, melted
- 2 tablespoons olive oil

Directions:

1. Season the fish with the salt and pepper, rub it with the oil, and then put it in your air fryer.
2. Cook at 360 degrees F for 10 minutes, flipping once.
3. Heat up a pan with the butter over medium heat, and then add the chives, salt, pepper, lime juice, and zest, whisk; cook for 1-2 minutes.
4. Divide the fish between plates, drizzle the lime sauce all over, and serve immediately.

Nutrition Values: calories 280, fat 12, fiber 9, carbs 17, protein 15

141. FLAVORED SALMON FILLETS

Preparation time: 5 minutes
Cooking time: 12 minutes
Servings: 4

Ingredients:

- 4 salmon fillets, boneless
- 1 tablespoon olive oil
- Salt and black pepper to taste
- 1 teaspoon cumin, ground
- 1 teaspoon sweet paprika
- ½ teaspoon chili powder

- 1 teaspoon garlic powder
- Juice of 1 lime

Directions:

1. In a bowl, mix the salmon with the other ingredients, rub / coat well, and transfer to your air fryer.
2. Cook at 350 degrees F for 6 minutes on each side.
3. Divide the fish between plates and serve right away with a side salad.

Nutrition Values: calories 280, fat 14, fiber 4, carbs 18, protein 20

142. TASTY AIR FRIED COD

Preparation time: 10 minutes
Cooking time: 12 minutes
Servings: 4

Ingredients:

- 2 cod fish, 7 ounces each
- A drizzle of sesame oil
- Salt and black pepper to the taste
- 1 cup water
- 1 teaspoon dark soy sauce
- 4 tablespoons light soy sauce
- 1 tablespoon sugar
- 3 tablespoons olive oil
- 4 ginger slices
- 3 spring onions, chopped
- 2 tablespoons coriander, chopped

Directions:

1. Season fish with salt, pepper, drizzle sesame oil, rub well and leave aside for 10 minutes.
2. Add fish to your air fryer and cook at 356 degrees F for 12 minutes.
3. Meanwhile, heat up a pot with the water over medium heat, add dark and light soy sauce and sugar, stir, bring to a simmer and take off heat.
4. Heat up a pan with the olive oil over medium heat, add ginger and green onions, stir, cook for a few minutes and take off heat.
5. Divide fish on plates, top with ginger and green onions, drizzle soy sauce mix, sprinkle coriander and serve right away.

6. Enjoy!

Nutrition Values: calories 300, fat 17, fiber 8, carbs 20, protein 22

143. DELICIOUS CATFISH

Preparation time: 10 minutes
Cooking time: 20 minutes
Servings: 4

Ingredients:

- 4 cat fish fillets
- Salt and black pepper to the taste
- A pinch of sweet paprika
- 1 tablespoon parsley, chopped
- 1 tablespoon lemon juice
- 1 tablespoon olive oil

Directions:

1. Season catfish fillets with salt, pepper, paprika, drizzle oil, rub well, place in your air fryer's basket and cook at 400 degrees F for 20 minutes, flipping the fish after 10 minutes.
2. Divide fish on plates, drizzle lemon juice all over, sprinkle parsley and serve.
3. Enjoy!

Nutrition Values: calories 253, fat 6, fiber 12, carbs 26, protein 22

144. COD FILLETS WITH FENNEL AND GRAPES SALAD

Preparation time: 10 minutes
Cooking time: 15 minutes
Servings: 2

Ingredients:

- 2 black cod fillets, boneless
- 1 tablespoon olive oil
- Salt and black pepper to the taste
- 1 fennel bulb, thinly sliced
- 1 cup grapes, halved
- ½ cup pecans

Directions:

1. Drizzle half of the oil over fish fillets, season with salt and pepper, rub well, place fillets in your air fryer's basket, cook for 10 minutes at 400 degrees F and

transfer to a plate.
2. In a bowl, mix pecans with grapes, fennel, the rest of the oil, salt and pepper, toss to coat, add to a pan that fits your air fryer and cook at 400 degrees F for 5 minutes.
3. Divide cod on plates, add fennel and grapes mix on the side and serve.
4. Enjoy!

Nutrition Values: calories 300, fat 4, fiber 2, carbs 32, protein 22

145. TABASCO SHRIMP

Preparation time: 10 minutes
Cooking time: 10 minutes
Servings: 4

Ingredients:

- 1 pound shrimp, peeled and deveined
- 1 teaspoon red pepper flakes
- 2 tablespoon olive oil
- 1 teaspoon Tabasco sauce
- 2 tablespoons water
- 1 teaspoon oregano, dried
- Salt and black pepper to the taste
- ½ teaspoon parsley, dried
- ½ teaspoon smoked paprika

Directions:

1. In a bowl, mix oil with water, Tabasco sauce, pepper flakes, oregano, parsley, salt, pepper, paprika and shrimp and toss well to coat.
2. Transfer shrimp to your preheated air fryer at 370 degrees F and cook for 10 minutes shaking the fryer once.
3. Divide shrimp on plates and serve with a side salad.
4. Enjoy!

Nutrition Values: calories 200, fat 5, fiber 6, carbs 13, protein 8

146. BUTTERED SHRIMP SKEWERS

Preparation time: 10 minutes
Cooking time: 6 minutes
Servings: 2

Ingredients:

- 8 shrimps, peeled and deveined
- 4 garlic cloves, minced
- Salt and black pepper to the taste
- 8 green bell pepper slices
- 1 tablespoon rosemary, chopped
- 1 tablespoon butter, melted

Directions:

1. In a bowl, mix shrimp with garlic, butter, salt, pepper, rosemary and bell pepper slices, toss to coat and leave aside for 10 minutes.
2. Arrange 2 shrimp and 2 bell pepper slices on a skewer and repeat with the rest of the shrimp and bell pepper pieces.
3. Place them all in your air fryer's basket and cook at 360 degrees F for 6 minutes.
4. Divide among plates and serve right away.
5. Enjoy!

Nutrition Values: calories 140, fat 1, fiber 12, carbs 15, protein 7

147. ASIAN SALMON

Preparation time: 1 hour
Cooking time: 15 minutes
Servings: 2

Ingredients:

- 2 medium salmon fillets
- 6 tablespoons light soy sauce
- 3 teaspoons mirin
- 1 teaspoon water
- 6 tablespoons honey

Directions:

1. In a bowl, mix soy sauce with honey, water and mirin, whisk well, add salmon, rub well and leave aside in the fridge for 1 hour.
2. Transfer salmon to your air fryer and cook at 360 degrees F for 15 minutes, flipping them after 7 minutes.
3. Meanwhile, put the soy marinade in a pan, heat up over medium heat, whisk well, cook for 2 minutes and take off heat.
4. Divide salmon on plates, drizzle marinade all over and serve.
5. Enjoy!

Nutrition Values: calories 300, fat 12, fiber 8,

carbs 13, protein 24

148. COD STEAKS WITH PLUM SAUCE

Preparation time: 10 minutes
Cooking time: 20 minutes
Servings: 2

Ingredients:

- 2 big cod steaks
- Salt and black pepper to the taste
- ½ teaspoon garlic powder
- ½ teaspoon ginger powder
- ¼ teaspoon turmeric powder
- 1 tablespoon plum sauce
- Cooking spray

Directions:

1. Season cod steaks with salt and pepper, spray them with cooking oil, add garlic powder, ginger powder and turmeric powder and rub well.
2. Place cod steaks in your air fryer and cook at 360 degrees F for 15 minutes, flipping them after 7 minutes.
3. Heat up a pan over medium heat, add plum sauce, stir and cook for 2 minutes.
4. Divide cod steaks on plates, drizzle plum sauce all over and serve.
5. Enjoy!

Nutrition Values: calories 250, fat 7, fiber 1, carbs 14, protein 12

149. FLAVORED AIR FRIED SALMON

Preparation time: 1 hour
Cooking time: 8 minutes
Servings: 2

Ingredients:

- 2 salmon fillets
- 2 tablespoons lemon juice
- Salt and black pepper to the taste
- ½ teaspoon garlic powder
- 1/3 cup water
- 1/3 cup soy sauce
- 3 scallions, chopped

- 1/3 cup brown sugar
- 2 tablespoons olive oil

Directions:

1. In a bowl, mix sugar with water, soy sauce, garlic powder, salt, pepper, oil and lemon juice, whisk well, add salmon fillets, toss to coat and leave aside in the fridge for 1 hour.
2. Transfer salmon fillets to the fryer's basket and cook at 360 degrees F for 8 minutes flipping them halfway.
3. Divide salmon on plates, sprinkle scallions on top and serve right away.
4. Enjoy!

Nutrition Values: calories 300, fat 12, fiber 10, carbs 23, protein 20

150. SALMON WITH CAPERS AND MASH

Preparation time: 10 minutes
Cooking time: 20 minutes
Servings: 4

Ingredients:

- 4 salmon fillets, skinless and boneless
- 1 tablespoon capers, drained
- Salt and black pepper to the taste
- Juice from 1 lemon
- 2 teaspoons olive oil
- For the potato mash:
- 2 tablespoons olive oil
- 1 tablespoon dill, dried
- 1 pound potatoes, chopped
- ½ cup milk

Directions:

1. Put potatoes in a pot, add water to cover, add some salt, bring to a boil over medium high heat, cook for 15 minutes, drain, transfer to a bowl, mash with a potato masher, add 2 tablespoons oil, dill, salt, pepper and milk, whisk well and leave aside for now.
2. Season salmon with salt and pepper, drizzle 2 teaspoons oil over them, rub, transfer to your air fryer's basket, add capers on top, cook at 360 degrees F and

cook for 8 minutes.
3. Divide salmon and capers on plates, add mashed potatoes on the side, drizzle lemon juice all over and serve.
4. Enjoy!

Nutrition Values: calories 300, fat 17, fiber 8, carbs 12, protein 18

151. LEMONY SABA FISH

Preparation time: 10 minutes
Cooking time: 8 minutes
Servings: 1

Ingredients:

- 4 Saba fish fillet, boneless
- Salt and black pepper to the taste
- 3 red chili pepper, chopped
- 2 tablespoons lemon juice
- 2 tablespoon olive oil
- 2 tablespoon garlic, minced

Directions:

1. Season fish fillets with salt and pepper and put in a bowl.
2. Add lemon juice, oil, chili and garlic toss to coat, transfer fish to your air fryer and cook at 360 degrees F for 8 minutes, flipping halfway.
3. Divide among plates and serve with some fries.
4. Enjoy!

Nutrition Values: calories 300, fat 4, fiber 8, carbs 15, protein 15

152. ASIAN HALIBUT

Preparation time: 30 minutes
Cooking time: 10 minutes
Servings: 3

Ingredients:

- 1 pound halibut steaks
- 2/3 cup soy sauce
- ¼ cup sugar
- 2 tablespoons lime juice
- ½ cup mirin
- ¼ teaspoon red pepper flakes, crushed
- ¼ cup orange juice
- ¼ teaspoon ginger, grated

- 1 garlic clove, minced

Directions:

1. Put soy sauce in a pan, heat up over medium heat, add mirin, sugar, lime and orange juice, pepper flakes, ginger and garlic, stir well, bring to a boil and take off heat.
2. Transfer half of the marinade to a bowl, add halibut, toss to coat and leave aside in the fridge for 30 minutes.
3. Transfer halibut to your air fryer and cook at 390 degrees F for 10 minutes, flipping once.
4. Divide halibut steaks on plates, drizzle the rest of the marinade all over and serve hot.
5. Enjoy!

Nutrition Values: calories 286, fat 5, fiber 12, carbs 14, protein 23

153. COD AND VINAIGRETTE

Preparation time: 10 minutes
Cooking time: 15 minutes
Servings: 4

Ingredients:

- 4 cod fillets, skinless and boneless
- 12 cherry tomatoes, halved
- 8 black olives, pitted and roughly chopped
- 2 tablespoons lemon juice
- Salt and black pepper to the taste
- 2 tablespoons olive oil
- Cooking spray
- 1 bunch basil, chopped

Directions:

1. Season cod with salt and pepper to the taste, place in your air fryer's basket and cook at 360 degrees F for 10 minutes, flipping after 5 minutes.
2. Meanwhile, heat up a pan with the oil over medium heat, add tomatoes, olives and lemon juice, stir, bring to a simmer, add basil, salt and pepper, stir well and take off heat.
3. Divide fish on plates and serve with the vinaigrette drizzled on top.
4. Enjoy!

Nutrition Values: calories 300, fat 5, fiber 8, carbs 12, protein 8

154. SHRIMP AND CRAB MIX

Preparation time: 10 minutes
Cooking time: 25 minutes
Servings: 4

Ingredients:

- ½ cup yellow onion, chopped
- 1 cup green bell pepper, chopped
- 1 cup celery, chopped
- 1 pound shrimp, peeled and deveined
- 1 cup crabmeat, flaked
- 1 cup mayonnaise
- 1 teaspoon Worcestershire sauce
- Salt and black pepper to the taste
- 2 tablespoons breadcrumbs
- 1 tablespoon butter, melted
- 1 teaspoon sweet paprika

Directions:

1. In a bowl, mix shrimp with crab meat, bell pepper, onion, mayo, celery, salt, pepper and Worcestershire sauce, toss well and transfer to a pan that fits your air fryer.
2. Sprinkle bread crumbs and paprika, add melted butter, place in your air fryer and cook at 320 degrees F for 25 minutes, shaking halfway.
3. Divide among plates and serve right away.
4. Enjoy!

Nutrition Values: calories 200, fat 13, fiber 9, carbs 17, protein 19

155. SEAFOOD CASSEROLE

Preparation time: 10 minutes
Cooking time: 40 minutes
Servings: 6

Ingredients:

- 6 tablespoons butter
- 2 ounces mushrooms, chopped
- 1 small green bell pepper, chopped
- 1 celery stalk, chopped
- 2 garlic cloves, minced
- 1 small yellow onion, chopped
- Salt and black pepper to the taste

- 4 tablespoons flour
- ½ cup white wine
- 1 and ½ cups milk
- ½ cup heavy cream
- 4 sea scallops, sliced
- 4 ounces haddock, skinless, boneless and cut into small pieces
- 4 ounces lobster meat, already cooked and cut into small pieces
- ½ teaspoon mustard powder
- 1 tablespoon lemon juice
- 1/3 cup bread crumbs
- Salt and black pepper to the taste
- 3 tablespoons cheddar cheese, grated
- A handful parsley, chopped
- 1 teaspoon sweet paprika

Directions:

1. Heat up a pan with 4 tablespoons butter over medium high heat, add bell pepper, mushrooms, celery, garlic, onion and wine, stir and cook for 10 minutes
2. Add flour, cream and milk, stir well and cook for 6 minutes.
3. Add lemon juice, salt, pepper, mustard powder, scallops, lobster meat and haddock, stir well, take off heat and transfer to a pan that fits your air fryer.
4. In a bowl, mix the rest of the butter with bread crumbs, paprika and cheese and sprinkle over seafood mix.
5. Transfer pan to your air fryer and cook at 360 degrees F for 16 minutes.
6. Divide among plates and serve with parsley sprinkled on top.
7. Enjoy!

Nutrition Values: calories 270, fat 32, fiber 14, carbs 15, protein 23

156. TROUT FILLET AND ORANGE SAUCE

Preparation time: 10 minutes
Cooking time: 10 minutes
Servings: 4

Ingredients:

- 4 trout fillets, skinless and boneless
- 4 spring onions, chopped
- 1 tablespoon olive oil
- 1 tablespoon ginger, minced
- Salt and black pepper to the taste
- Juice and zest from 1 orange

Directions:

1. Season trout fillets with salt, pepper, rub them with the olive oil, place in a pan that fits your air fryer, add ginger, green onions, orange zest and juice, toss well, place in your air fryer and cook at 360 degrees F for 10 minutes.
2. Divide fish and sauce on plates and serve right away.
3. Enjoy!

Nutrition Values: calories 239, fat 10, fiber 7, carbs 18, protein 23

157. COD FILLETS AND PEAS

Preparation time: 10 minutes
Cooking time: 10 minutes
Servings: 4

Ingredients:

- 4 cod fillets, boneless
- 2 tablespoons parsley, chopped
- 2 cups peas
- 4 tablespoons wine
- ½ teaspoon oregano, dried
- ½ teaspoon sweet paprika
- 2 garlic cloves, minced
- Salt and pepper to the taste

Directions:

1. In your food processor mix garlic with parsley, salt, pepper, oregano, paprika and wine and blend well.
2. Rub fish with half of this mix, place in your air fryer and cook at 360 degrees F for 10 minutes.
3. Meanwhile, put peas in a pot, add water to cover, add salt, bring to a boil over medium high heat, cook for 10 minutes, drain and divide among plates.
4. Also divide fish on plates, spread the rest of the herb dressing all over and serve.
5. Enjoy!

Nutrition Values: calories 261, fat 8, fiber 12,

carbs 20, protein 22

158. CRISPYLICIOUS CRAB CAKES

Servings: 2
Cooking Time: 10 minutes

Ingredients:

- 2 large eggs
- 1 teaspoon Dijon mustard
- 1 teaspoon Worcestershire sauce
- 1 ½ teaspoon old bay seasoning
- Salt and pepper to taste
- ¼ cup chopped green onion
- 1-pound lump crab meat
- ½ cup panko

Directions:

1. Preheat the air fryer at 3900F.
2. Place the grill pan accessory in the air fryer.
3. In a mixing bowl, combine all Ingredients: until everything is well-incorporated.
4. Use your hands to form small patties of crab cakes.
5. Place on the grill pan and cook for 10 minutes.
6. Flip the crab cakes halfway through the cooking time for even browning.

Nutrition Values:

Calories: 129; Carbs: 4.3g; Protein: 16.2g; Fat: 5.1g

159. COCONUT SHRIMPS WITH PINA COLADA DIP

Servings: 4
Cooking Time: 6 minutes

Ingredients:

- 1 ½ pounds jumbo shrimps, peeled and deveined
- ½ cup cornstarch
- 2/3 cup coconut milk
- 2 tablespoons honey
- 1 cup shredded coconut flakes
- ¾ cups panko bread crumbs
- 1/3 cup light coconut milk
- 1/3 cup non-fat Greek yogurt

- ¼ cup pineapple chunks, drained
- Salt and pepper to taste
- Toasted coconut meat for garnish

Directions:

1. Preheat the air fryer at 3900F.
2. Place the shrimps and cornstarch in a Ziploc bag and give a good shake.
3. In a bowl, stir in coconut milk and honey. Set aside.
4. In another bowl, mix the coconut flakes and bread crumbs. Set aside.
5. Dip the shrimps in the milk mixture then dredge in the bread crumbs.
6. Place in the double layer rack and cook for 6 minutes.
7. Meanwhile, combine the rest of the Ingredients: to create the dipping sauce.

Nutrition Values:

Calories: 493; Carbs: 21.4g; Protein: 38.9g; Fat: 27.9g

160. ALASKAN COD FISH WITH APPLE SLAW

Servings: 3
Cooking Time: 15 minutes

Ingredients:

- 1 ½ pounds frozen Alaskan cod
- 1 tablespoon vegetable oil
- 1 box whole wheat panko bread crumbs
- 1 granny smith apple, julienned
- 2 cups Napa cabbage, shredded
- ½ red onion, diced
- ¼ cup mayonnaise
- 1 teaspoon paprika
- Salt and pepper to taste

Directions:

1. Preheat the air fryer at 3900F.
2. Place the grill pan accessory in the air fryer.
3. Brush the fish with oil and dredge in the breadcrumbs.
4. Place the fish on the grill pan and cook for 15 minutes. Make sure to flip the fish halfway through the cooking time.
5. Meanwhile, prepare the slaw by mixing the

remaining Ingredients: in a bowl.
6. Serve the fish with the slaw.

Nutrition Values:

Calories: 316; Carbs: 13.5g; Protein: 37.8g; Fat: 12.2g

161. BEER BATTERED AIR FRIED FISH

Servings: 2
Cooking Time: 15 minutes

Ingredients:

- 2 cod fillets
- 2 eggs, beaten
- 1 ¼ cup lager beer
- ½ cup all-purpose flour
- ¾ teaspoon baking powder
- Salt and pepper to taste

Directions:

1. Preheat the air fryer at 3900F.
2. Pat the fish fillets dry then set aside.
3. In a bowl, combine the rest of the Ingredients: to create a batter.
4. Dip the fillets on the batter and place on the double layer rack.
5. Cook for 15 minutes.

Nutrition Values:

Calories: 229; Carbs: 33.2g; Protein: 31.1g; Fat: 10.2g

162. BLACKENED SHRIMPS IN AIR FRYER

Servings: 4
Cooking Time: 6 minutes

Ingredients:

- 20 jumbo shrimps, peeled and deveined
- 2 tablespoons coconut oil
- 2 teaspoons cilantro
- 2 teaspoons smoked paprika
- 2 teaspoons onion powder
- 1 teaspoon cumin
- 1 teaspoon salt
- 1 teaspoon thyme
- 1 teaspoon oregano
- ¼ teaspoon cayenne pepper
- ¼ teaspoon red chili flakes

Directions:

1. Preheat the air fryer at 3900F.
2. Season the shrimps with all the Ingredients.
3. Place the seasoned shrimps in the double layer rack.
4. Cook for 6 minutes.

Nutrition Values:

Calories: 220; Carbs: 2.5g; Protein: 34.2g; Fat: 8.1g

163. HERB AND GARLIC FISH FINGERS

Servings: 1
Cooking Time: 10 minutes

Ingredients:

- ½ pound fish, cut into fingers
- ½ teaspoon salt
- 2 tablespoons lemon juice
- ½ teaspoon turmeric powder
- ½ teaspoon red chili flakes
- 2 teaspoons garlic powder
- ½ teaspoon crushed black pepper
- 1 teaspoon ginger garlic paste
- 2 teaspoons corn flour
- 2 eggs, beaten
- ¼ teaspoon baking soda
- 1 cup bread crumbs
- Oil for brushing

Directions:

1. Preheat the air fryer at 3900F.
2. Season the fish fingers with salt, lemon juice, turmeric powder, chili flakes, garlic powder, black pepper, and garlic paste. Add the corn flour, eggs, and baking soda.
3. Dredge the seasoned fish in breadcrumbs and brush with cooking oil.
4. Place on the double layer rack.
5. Cook for 10 minutes.

Nutrition Values:

Calories: 773; Carbs: 32.7g; Protein: 64.9g; Fat: 42.5gUBSCRIBE TO WHISKAFFAIR

164. CRISPY COD NUGGETS WITH TARTAR SAUCE

Servings: 3
Cooking Time: 10 minutes

Ingredients:

- 1 ½ pounds cod fillet
- Salt and pepper to taste
- ½ cup flour
- 1 egg, beaten
- 1 cup cracker crumbs
- 1 tablespoon vegetable oil
- ½ cup non-fat mayonnaise
- 1 teaspoon honey
- Zest from half of a lemon
- Juice from half a lemon
- ½ teaspoon Worcestershire sauce
- 1 tablespoon sweet pickle relish
- Salt and pepper to taste

Directions:

1. Preheat the air fryer at 3900F.
2. Season the cods with salt and pepper.
3. Dredge the fish on flour and dip in the beaten egg before dredging on the cracker crumbs. Brush with oil.
4. Place the fish on the double layer rack and cook for 10 minutes.
5. Meanwhile, prepare the sauce by mixing all ingredients in a bowl.
6. Serve the fish with the sauce.

Nutrition Values:

Calories: 470; Carbs: 25.4g; Protein: 42.9g; Fat: 21.8g

165. GARLIC AND BLACK PEPPER SHRIMP GRILL

Servings: 2
Cooking Time: 6 minutes

Ingredients:

- 1 red chili, seeds removed
- 3 cloves of garlic, grated
- 1 tablespoon ground pepper
- 1 tablespoon fresh lime juice
- 1-pound large shrimps, peeled and deveined
- Salt to taste

Directions:

1. Preheat the air fryer at 3900F.
2. Place the grill pan accessory in the air fryer.
3. Grill the shrimps for 6 minutes.

Nutrition Values:

Calories:179 ; Carbs: 6.3g; Protein: 31.6g; Fat: 2.3g

166. GRILLED SALMON WITH CUCUMBERS

Servings: 4
Cooking Time: 10 minutes

Ingredients:

- 4 6-ounces salmon fillets
- 1 teaspoon lemon zest
- Juice from 1 lemon, freshly squeezed
- 1 tablespoon fresh dill
- Salt and pepper to taste
- ½ cup mayonnaise
- ½ cup sour cream
- 2 cucumbers peeled and sliced

Directions:

1. Preheat the air fryer at 3900F.
2. Place the grill pan accessory in the air fryer.
3. Season the salmon fillets with lemon zest, lemon juice, dill, salt and pepper.
4. 10Grill the salmon for 10 minutes making sure to flip halfway through the cooking time.
5. 11Meanwhile, prepare the cucumber salad by mixing in a bowl the mayonnaise, sour cream and cucumber slices. Season with salt and pepper.
6. 12Serve the salmon with the cucumber salad.

Nutrition Values:

Calories: 409; Carbs: 5.9g; Protein: 38.4g; Fat: 25.1g

167. SHRIMPS, ZUCCHINI, AND TOMATOES ON THE GRILL

Servings: 2
Cooking Time: 15 minutes

Ingredients:

- 10 jumbo shrimps, peeled and deveined
- Salt and pepper to taste
- 1 clove of garlic, minced
- 1 medium zucchini, sliced
- 1-pint cherry tomatoes
- ¼ cup feta cheese

Directions:

1. Preheat the air fryer at 3900F.
2. Place the grill pan accessory in the air fryer.
3. In a mixing bowl, season the shrimps with salt and pepper. Stir in the garlic, zucchini, and tomatoes.
4. Place on the grill pan and cook for 15 minutes.
5. 10Once cooked, transfer to a bowl and sprinkle with feta cheese.

Nutrition Values:

Calories: 257; Carbs:4.2 g; Protein: 48.9g; Fat: 5.3g

168. GRILLED HALIBUT WITH TOMATOES AND HEARTS OF PALM

Servings: 4
Cooking Time: 15 minutes

Ingredients:

- 4 halibut fillets
- Juice from 1 lemon
- Salt and pepper to taste
- 2 tablespoons oil
- ½ cup hearts of palm, rinse and drained
- 1 cup cherry tomatoes

Directions:

1. Preheat the air fryer at 3900F.
2. Place the grill pan accessory in the air fryer.
3. Season the halibut fillets with lemon juice, salt and pepper. Brush with oil.
4. 10Place the fish on the grill pan.
5. 11Arrange the hearts of palms and cherry tomatoes on the side and sprinkle with

more salt and pepper.

6. 12Cook for 15 minutes.

Nutrition Values:

Calories: 208; Carbs: 7g; Protein: 21 g; Fat: 11g

169. CHAT MASALA GRILLED SNAPPER

Servings: 5
Cooking Time: 25 minutes

Ingredients:

- 2 ½ pounds whole fish
- Salt to taste
- 1/3 cup chat masala
- 3 tablespoons fresh lime juice
- 5 tablespoons olive oil

Directions:

1. Preheat the air fryer at 3900F.
2. Place the grill pan accessory in the air fryer.
3. Season the fish with salt, chat masala and lime juice.
4. 10Brush with oil
5. 11Place the fish on a foil basket and place inside the grill.
6. 12Cook for 25 minutes.

Nutrition Values:

Calories:308 ; Carbs: 0.7g; Protein: 35.2g; Fat: 17.4g

170. ONE-PAN SHRIMP AND CHORIZO MIX GRILL

Servings: 4
Cooking Time: 15 minutes

Ingredients:

- 1 ½ pounds large shrimps, peeled and deveined
- Salt and pepper to taste
- 6 links fresh chorizo sausage
- 2 bunches asparagus spears, trimmed
- Lime wedges

Directions:

1. Preheat the air fryer at 3900F.
2. Place the grill pan accessory in the air fryer.

3. 10Season the shrimps with salt and pepper to taste. Set aside.
4. 11Place the chorizo on the grill pan and the sausage.
5. 12Place the asparagus on top.
6. 13Grill for 15 minutes.
7. 14Serve with lime wedges.

Nutrition Values:

Calories:124 ; Carbs: 9.4g; Protein: 8.2g; Fat: 7.1g

171. GRILLED TASTY SCALLOPS

Servings: 2
Cooking Time: 10 minutes

Ingredients:

- 1-pound sea scallops, cleaned and patted dry
- Salt and pepper to taste
- 3 dried chilies
- 2 tablespoon dried thyme
- 1 tablespoon dried oregano
- 1 tablespoon ground coriander
- 1 tablespoon ground fennel
- 2 teaspoons chipotle pepper

Directions:

1. Preheat the air fryer at 3900F.
2. Place the grill pan accessory in the air fryer.
3. Mix all Ingredients: in a bowl.
4. Dump the scallops on the grill pan and cook for 10 minutes.

Nutrition Values:

Calories:291 ; Carbs: 20.7g; Protein: 48.6g; Fat: 2.5g

172. CLAM WITH LEMONS ON THE GRILL

Servings: 6
Cooking Time: 6 minutes

Ingredients:

- 4 pounds littleneck clams
- Salt and pepper to taste
- 1 clove of garlic, minced
- ½ cup parsley, chopped
- 1 teaspoon crushed red pepper flakes

- 5 tablespoons olive oil
- 1 loaf crusty bread, halved
- ½ cup parmesan cheese, grated

Directions:

1. Preheat the air fryer at 3900F.
2. Place the grill pan accessory in the air fryer.
3. 10Place the clams on the grill pan and cook for 6 minutes.
4. 11Once the clams have opened, take them out and extract the meat.
5. 12Transfer the meat into a bowl and season with salt and pepper.
6. 13Stir in the garlic, parsley, red pepper flakes, and olive oil.
7. 14Serve on top of bread and sprinkle with parmesan cheese.

Nutrition Values:

Calories: 341; Carbs: 26g; Protein:48.3g; Fat: 17.2g

173. SALMON STEAK GRILLED WITH CILANTRO GARLIC SAUCE

Servings: 2
Cooking Time: 15 minutes

Ingredients:

- 2 salmon steaks
- Salt and pepper to taste
- 2 tablespoons vegetable oil
- 2 cloves of garlic, minced
- 1 cup cilantro leaves
- ½ cup Greek yogurt
- 1 teaspoon honey

Directions:

1. Preheat the air fryer at 3900F.
2. Place the grill pan accessory in the air fryer.
3. Season the salmon steaks with salt and pepper. Brush with oil.
4. Grill for 15 minutes and make sure to flip halfway through the cooking time.
5. In a food processor, mix the garlic, cilantro leaves, yogurt and honey. Season with salt and pepper to taste. Pulse until smooth.
6. Serve the salmon steaks with the cilantro

sauce.

Nutrition Values:

Calories: 485; Carbs: 6.3g; Protein: 47.6g; Fat: 29.9g

174. TASTY GRILLED RED MULLET

Servings: 8
Cooking Time: 15 minutes

Ingredients:

- 8 whole red mullets, gutted and scales removed
- Salt and pepper to taste
- Juice from 1 lemon
- 1 tablespoon olive oil

Directions:

1. Preheat the air fryer at 3900F.
2. Place the grill pan accessory in the air fryer.
3. Season the red mullet with salt, pepper, and lemon juice.
4. Brush with olive oil.
5. Grill for 15 minutes.

Nutrition Values:

Calories: 152; Carbs: 0.9g; Protein: 23.1g; Fat: 6.2g

175. CHARGRILLED HALIBUT NIÇOISE WITH VEGETABLES

Servings: 6
Cooking Time: 15 minutes

Ingredients:

- 1 ½ pounds halibut fillets
- Salt and pepper to taste
- 2 tablespoons olive oil
- 2 pounds mixed vegetables
- 4 cups torn lettuce leaves
- 1 cup cherry tomatoes, halved
- 4 large hard-boiled eggs, peeled and sliced

Directions:

1. Preheat the air fryer at 3900F.
2. Place the grill pan accessory in the air fryer.
3. Rub the halibut with salt and pepper.

Brush the fish with oil.
4. Place on the grill.
5. Surround the fish fillet with the mixed vegetables and cook for 15 minutes.
6. Assemble the salad by serving the fish fillet with grilled mixed vegetables, lettuce, cherry tomatoes, and hard-boiled eggs.

Nutrition Values:

Calories: 312; Carbs:16.8 g; Protein: 19.8g; Fat: 18.3g

176. SPICED SALMON KEBABS

Servings: 3
Cooking Time: 15 minutes

Ingredients:

- 2 tablespoons chopped fresh oregano
- 2 teaspoons sesame seeds
- 1 teaspoon ground cumin
- Salt and pepper to taste
- 1 ½ pounds salmon fillets
- 2 tablespoons olive oil
- 2 lemons, sliced into rounds

Directions:

1. Preheat the air fryer at 3900F.
2. Place the grill pan accessory in the air fryer.
3. Create the dry rub by combining the oregano, sesame seeds, cumin, salt and pepper.
4. Rub the salmon fillets with the dry rub and brush with oil.
5. Grill the salmon for 15 minutes.
6. Serve with lemon slices once cooked.

Nutrition Values:

Calories per serving 447 ; Carbs: 4.1g; Protein:47.6 g; Fat:26.6 g

177. ROASTED TUNA ON LINGUINE

Servings: 2
Cooking Time: 20 minutes

Ingredients:

- 1-pound fresh tuna fillets
- Salt and pepper to taste
- 1 tablespoon olive oil

- 12 ounces linguine, cooked according to package Directions:
- 2 cups parsley leaves, chopped
- 1 tablespoon capers, chopped
- Juice from 1 lemon

Directions:

1. Preheat the air fryer at 3900F.
2. Place the grill pan accessory in the air fryer.
3. Season the tuna with salt and pepper. Brush with oil.
4. Grill for 20 minutes.
5. Once the tuna is cooked, shred using forks and place on top of cooked linguine. Add parsley and capers. Season with salt and pepper and add lemon juice.

Nutrition Values:

Calories: 520; Carbs: 60.6g; Protein: 47.7g; Fat: 9.6g

178. CHILI LIME CLAMS WITH TOMATOES

Servings: 3
Cooking Time: 15 minutes

Ingredients:

- 25 littleneck clams
- 1 tablespoon fresh lime juice
- Salt and pepper to taste
- 6 tablespoons unsalted butter
- 4 cloves of garlic, minced
- ½ cup tomatoes, chopped
- ½ cup basil leaves

Directions:

1. Preheat the air fryer at 3900F.
2. Place the grill pan accessory in the air fryer.
3. On a large foil, place all ingredients. Fold over the foil and close by crimping the edges.
4. Place on the grill pan and cook for 15 minutes.
5. Serve with bread.

Nutrition Values:

Calories: 163; Carbs: 4.1g; Protein: 1.7g; Fat: 15.5g

179. AIR FRYER GARLICKY-GRILLED TURBOT

Servings: 2
Cooking Time: 20 minutes

Ingredients:

- 2 whole turbot, scaled and head removed
- Salt and pepper to taste
- 1 clove of garlic, minced
- ½ cup chopped celery leaves
- 2 tablespoons olive oil

Directions:

1. Preheat the air fryer at 3900F.
2. Place the grill pan accessory in the air fryer.
3. Season the turbot with salt, pepper, garlic, and celery leaves.
4. Brush with oil.
5. Place on the grill pan and cook for 20 minutes until the fish becomes flaky.

Nutrition Values:

Calories: 269; Carbs: 3.3g; Protein: 66.2g; Fat: 25.6g

180. BROILED SPICED-LEMON SQUID

Servings: 4
Cooking Time: 15 minutes

Ingredients:

- 2 pounds squid, gutted and cleaned
- Salt and pepper to taste
- 1 tablespoon fresh lemon juice
- 5 cloves of garlic
- ½ cup tomatoes, chopped
- ½ cup green onions, chopped
- 2 tablespoons olive oil

Directions:

1. Preheat the air fryer at 3900F.
2. Place the grill pan accessory in the air fryer.
3. Season the squid with salt, pepper, and lemon juice.
4. Stuff the cavity with garlic, tomatoes, and onions.

5. Brush the squid with olive oil.
6. Place on the grill pan and cook for 15 minutes.
7. Halfway through the cooking time, flip the squid.

Nutrition Values:

Calories: 277; Carbs: 10.7g; Protein: 36g; Fat: 10g

181. TUNA GRILL WITH GINGER SAUCE

Servings: 3
Cooking Time: 20 minutes

Ingredients:

- 1 ½ pounds tuna, thick slices
- 2 tablespoons rice vinegar
- 2 tablespoons grated fresh ginger
- 2 tablespoons peanut oil
- 2 tablespoons soy sauce
- 2 tablespoons honey
- 1 serrano chili, seeded and minced

Directions:

1. Place all ingredients in a Ziploc bag.
2. Allow to marinate in the fridge for at least 2 hours.
3. Preheat the air fryer at 3900F.
4. Place the grill pan accessory in the air fryer.
5. Grill the fish for 15 to 20 minutes.
6. Flip the fish halfway through the cooking time.
7. Meanwhile, pour the marinade in a saucepan and allow to simmer for 10 minutes until the sauce thickens.
8. Brush the tuna with the sauce before serving.

Nutrition Values:

Calories: 357; Carbs:14.8 g; Protein: 44.9g; Fat: 13.1g

182. CHAR-GRILLED SPICY HALIBUT

Servings: 6
Cooking Time: 20 minutes

Ingredients:

- 3 pounds halibut fillet, skin removed
- Salt and pepper to taste
- 4 tablespoons dry white wine
- 4 tablespoons olive oil
- 2 cloves of garlic, minced
- 1 tablespoon chili powder

Directions:

1. Place all ingredients in a Ziploc bag.
2. Allow to marinate in the fridge for at least 2 hours.
3. Preheat the air fryer at 3900F.
4. Place the grill pan accessory in the air fryer.
5. Grill the fish for 20 minutes making sure to flip every 5 minutes.

Nutrition Values:

Calories: 385; Carbs: 1.7g; Protein: 33g; Fat: 40.6g

183. ROASTED SWORDFISH WITH CHARRED LEEKS

Servings: 4
Cooking Time: 20 minutes

Ingredients:

- 4 swordfish steaks
- Salt and pepper to taste
- 3 tablespoons lime juice
- 2 tablespoons olive oil
- 4 medium leeks, cut into an inch long

Directions:

1. Preheat the air fryer at 3900F.
2. Place the grill pan accessory in the air fryer.
3. Season the swordfish with salt, pepper and lime juice.
4. Brush the fish with olive oil
5. Place fish fillets on grill pan and top with leeks.
6. Grill for 20 minutes.

Nutrition Values:

Calories: 611; Carbs: 14.6g; Protein: 48g; Fat: 40g

POULTRY

184. CHINESE STUFFED CHICKEN RECIPE

Preparation Time: 45 Minutes
Servings: 8

Ingredients:

- 1 whole chicken
- 10 wolfberries
- 2 red chilies; chopped
- 4 ginger slices
- 1 yam; cubed
- 1 tsp. soy sauce
- 3 tsp. sesame oil
- Salt and white pepper to the taste

Directions:

1. Season chicken with salt, pepper, rub with soy sauce and sesame oil and stuff with wolfberries, yam cubes, chilies and ginger.
2. Place in your air fryer, cook at 400 °F, for 20 minutes and then at 360 °F, for 15 minutes. Carve chicken, divide among plates and serve.

Nutrition Values: Calories: 320; Fat: 12; Fiber: 17; Carbs: 22; Protein: 12

185. CHICKEN AND ASPARAGUS RECIPE

Preparation Time: 30 Minutes
Servings: 4

Ingredients:

- 8 chicken wings; halved
- 8 asparagus spears
- 1 tbsp. rosemary; chopped
- 1 tsp. cumin; ground
- Salt and black pepper to the taste

Directions:

1. Pat dry chicken wings, season with salt, pepper, cumin and rosemary, put them in your air fryer's basket and cook at 360 °F, for 20 minutes.
2. Meanwhile; heat up a pan over medium heat, add asparagus, add water to cover, steam for a few minutes; transfer to a bowl filled with ice water, drain and arrange on plates. Add chicken wings on the side and serve.

Nutrition Values: Calories: 270; Fat: 8; Fiber: 12; Carbs: 24; Protein: 22

186. ITALIAN CHICKEN RECIPE

Preparation Time: 26 Minutes
Servings: 4

Ingredients:

- 5 chicken thighs
- 1 tbsp. olive oil
- 1/4 cup parmesan; grated
- 1/2 cup sun dried tomatoes
- 2 garlic cloves; minced
- 1 tbsp. thyme; chopped.
- 1/2 cup heavy cream
- 3/4 cup chicken stock
- 1 tsp. red pepper flakes; crushed
- 2 tbsp. basil; chopped
- Salt and black pepper to the taste

Directions:

1. Season chicken with salt and pepper, rub with half of the oil, place in your preheated air fryer at 350 °F and cook for 4 minutes.
2. Meanwhile; heat up a pan with the rest of the oil over medium high heat, add thyme garlic, pepper flakes, sun dried tomatoes, heavy cream, stock, parmesan, salt and pepper; stir, bring to a simmer, take off heat and transfer to a dish that fits your air fryer.
3. Add chicken thighs on top, introduce in your air fryer and cook at 320 °F, for 12 minutes. Divide among plates and serve with basil sprinkled on top.

Nutrition Values: Calories: 272; Fat: 9; Fiber: 12; Carbs: 37; Protein: 23

187. CHINESE CHICKEN WINGS

RECIPE

Preparation Time: 2 hours 15 Minutes
Servings: 6

Ingredients:

- 16 chicken wings
- 2 tbsp. honey
- 2 tbsp. soy sauce
- Salt and black pepper to the taste
- 1/4 tsp. white pepper
- 3 tbsp. lime juice

Directions:

1. In a bowl, mix honey with soy sauce, salt, black and white pepper and lime juice, whisk well, add chicken pieces, toss to coat and keep in the fridge for 2 hours.
2. Transfer chicken to your air fryer, cook at 370 °F, for 6 minutes on each side, increase heat to 400 °F and cook for 3 minutes more. Serve hot.

Nutrition Values: Calories: 372; Fat: 9; Fiber: 10; Carbs: 37; Protein: 24

188. CREAMY CHICKEN, PEAS AND RICE

Preparation Time: 40 Minutes
Servings: 4

Ingredients:

- 1 lb. chicken breasts; skinless, boneless and cut into quarters
- 1 cup white rice; already cooked
- 1 cup chicken stock
- 1/4 cup parsley; chopped.
- 2 cups peas; frozen
- 1 ½ cups parmesan; grated
- 1 tbsp. olive oil
- 3 garlic cloves; minced
- 1 yellow onion; chopped
- 1/2 cup white wine
- 1/4 cup heavy cream
- Salt and black pepper to the taste

Directions:

1. Season chicken breasts with salt and pepper, drizzle half of the oil over them,

rub well, put in your air fryer's basket and cook them at 360 °F, for 6 minutes.
2. Heat up a pan with the rest of the oil over medium high heat, add garlic, onion, wine, stock, salt, pepper and heavy cream; stir, bring to a simmer and cook for 9 minutes.
3. Transfer chicken breasts to a heat proof dish that fits your air fryer, add peas, rice and cream mix over them, toss, sprinkle parmesan and parsley all over, place in your air fryer and cook at 420 °F, for 10 minutes. Divide among plates and serve hot.

Nutrition Values: Calories: 313; Fat: 12; Fiber: 14; Carbs: 27; Protein: 44

198. CHICKEN AND GREEN ONIONS SAUCE RECIPE

Preparation Time: 26 Minutes
Servings: 4

Ingredients:

- 10 green onions; roughly chopped.
- 1-inch piece ginger root; chopped
- 4 garlic cloves; minced
- 2 tbsp. fish sauce
- 3 tbsp. soy sauce
- 1 tsp. Chinese five spice
- 10 chicken drumsticks
- 1 cup coconut milk
- 1 tsp. butter; melted
- 1/4 cup cilantro; chopped.
- 1 tbsp. lime juice
- Salt and black pepper to the taste

Directions:

1. In your food processor, mix green onions with ginger, garlic, soy sauce, fish sauce, five spice, salt, pepper, butter and coconut milk and pulse well.
2. In a bowl, mix chicken with green onions mix; toss well, transfer everything to a pan that fits your air fryer and cook at 370 °F, for 16 minutes; shaking the fryer once. Divide among plates, sprinkle cilantro on top, drizzle lime juice and serve with a side salad.

Nutrition Values: Calories: 321; Fat: 12; Fiber:

12; Carbs: 22; Protein: 20

190. CHICKEN CACCIATORE RECIPE

Preparation Time: 30 Minutes
Servings: 4

Ingredients:

- 8 chicken drumsticks; bone-in
- 1/2 cup black olives; pitted and sliced
- 1 bay leaf
- 1 tsp. garlic powder
- 1 yellow onion; chopped
- 28 oz. canned tomatoes and juice; crushed
- 1 tsp. oregano; dried
- Salt and black pepper to the taste

Directions:

1. In a heat proof dish that fits your air fryer, mix chicken with salt, pepper, garlic powder, bay leaf, onion, tomatoes and juice, oregano and olives; toss, introduce in your preheated air fryer and cook at 365 °F, for 20 minutes. Divide among plates and serve.

Nutrition Values: Calories: 300; Fat: 12; Fiber: 8; Carbs: 20; Protein: 24

191. HERBED CHICKEN RECIPE

Preparation Time: 70 Minutes
Servings: 4

Ingredients:

- 1 whole chicken
- 1 tsp. garlic powder
- 1 tsp. onion powder
- 1/2 tsp. thyme; dried
- 1 tsp. rosemary; dried
- 1 tbsp. lemon juice
- 2 tbsp. olive oil
- Salt and black pepper to the taste

Directions:

1. Season chicken with salt and pepper, rub with thyme, rosemary, garlic powder and onion powder, rub with lemon juice and olive oil and leave aside for 30 minutes.
2. Put chicken in your air fryer and cook at

360 °F, for 20 minutes on each side. Leave chicken aside to cool down, carve and serve.

Nutrition Values: Calories: 390; Fat: 10; Fiber: 5; Carbs: 22; Protein: 20

192. AIR FRIED CHICKEN WITH HONEY AND LEMON

Preparation Time: 100 min
Servings: 6

Nutrition Values: Calories: 342; Carbs: 68g; Fat: 28g; Protein: 33g

Ingredients

The Stuffing:

- 1 whole chicken, 3 lb
- 2 red and peeled onions
- 2 tbsp olive oil
- 2 apricots
- 1 zucchini
- 1 apple
- 2 cloves finely chopped garlic
- Fresh chopped thyme
- Salt and pepper

The Marinade:

- 5 oz honey
- juice from 1 lemon
- 2 tbsp olive oil
- Salt and pepper

Directions

1. For the stuffing, chop all ingredients into tiny pieces. Transfer to a large bowl and add the olive oil. Season with salt and black pepper. Fill the cavity of the chicken with the stuffing, without packing it tightly.
2. Place the chicken in the Air Fryer and cook for 35 minutes at 340 F. Warm the honey and the lemon juice in a large pan; season with salt and pepper. Reduce the temperature of the Air Fryer to 320 F.
3. Brush the chicken with some of the honey-lemon marinade and return it to the fryer. Cook for another 70 minutes; brush the chicken every 20-25 minutes with the marinade. Garnish with parsley, and serve with potatoes.

193. SPICY HONEY ORANGE CHICKEN

Preparation Time: 20 min
Servings: 4

Nutrition Values: Calories: 246; Carbs: 21g; Fat: 6g; Protein: 25g

Ingredients

- 1 ½ pounds chicken breast, washed and sliced
- Parsley to taste
- 1 cup coconut, shredded
- ¾ cup breadcrumbs
- 2 whole eggs, beaten
- ½ cup flour
- ½ tsp pepper
- Salt to taste
- ½ cup orange marmalade
- 1 tbsp red pepper flakes
- ¼ cup honey
- 3 tbsp dijon mustard

Directions

1. Preheat your Air Fryer to 400 F. In a mixing bowl, combine coconut, flour, salt, parsley and pepper. In another bowl, add the beaten eggs. Place breadcrumbs in a third bowl. Dredge chicken in egg mix, flour and finally in the breadcrumbs. Place the chicken in the Air Fryer cooking basket and bake for 15 minutes.
2. In a separate bowl, mix honey, orange marmalade, mustard and pepper flakes. Cover chicken with marmalade mixture and fry for 5 more minutes. Enjoy!

194. CRUNCHY CHICKEN FINGERS

Preparation Time: 8 min
Servings: 2

Nutrition Values: Calories: 253; Carbs: 31g; Fat: 18g; Protein: 28g

Ingredients

- 2 medium-sized chicken breasts, cut in stripes
- 3 tbsp parmesan cheese

- ¼ tbsp fresh chives, chopped
- ⅓ cup breadcrumbs
- 1 egg white
- 2 tbsp plum sauce, optional
- ½ tbsp fresh thyme, chopped
- ½ tbsp black pepper
- 1 tbsp water

Directions

1. Preheat the Air Fryer to 360 F. Mix the chives, parmesan, thyme, pepper and breadcrumbs. In another bowl, whisk the egg white and mix with the water. Dip the chicken strips into the egg mixture and the breadcrumb mixture. Place the strips in the air fryer basket and cook for 10 minutes. Serve with plum sauce.

195. MUSTARD AND MAPLE TURKEY BREAST

Preparation Time: 1 hr
Servings: 6

Nutrition Values: Calories: 529; Carbs: 77g; Fat: 20g; Protein: 13g

Ingredients

- 5 lb of whole turkey breast
- ¼ cup maple syrup
- 2 tbsp dijon mustard
- ½ tbsp smoked paprika
- 1 tbsp thyme
- 2 tbsp olive oil
- ½ tbsp sage
- ½ tbsp salt and black pepper
- 1 tbsp butter, melted

Directions

1. Preheat the Air fryer to 350 F and brush the turkey with the olive oil. Combine all herbs and seasoning, in a small bowl, and rub the turkey with the mixture. Air fry the turkey for 25 minutes. Flip the turkey on its side and continue to cook for 12 more minutes.
2. Now, turn on the opposite side, and again, cook for an additional 12 minutes. Whisk the butter, maple and mustard together in a small bowl. When done, brush the glaze

all over the turkey. Return to the air fryer and cook for 5 more minutes, until nice and crispy.

196. CHICKEN BREASTS WITH TARRAGON

Preparation Time: 15 min
Servings: 3

Nutrition Values: Calories: 493; Carbs: 36.5g; Fat: 11g; Protein: 57.5g

Ingredients

- 1 boneless and skinless chicken breast
- ½ tbsp butter
- ¼ tbsp kosher salt
- ¼ cup dried tarragon
- ¼ tbsp black and fresh ground pepper

Directions

1. Preheat the Air Fryer to 380 F and place each chicken breast on a 12x12 inches foil wrap. Top the chicken with tarragon and butter; season with salt and pepper to taste. Wrap the foil around the chicken breast in a loose way to create a flow of air. Cook the in the Air Fryer for 15 minutes. Carefully unwrap the chicken and serve.

197. CAJUN CHICKEN TENDERS

Preparation Time: 25 min
Servings: 4

Nutrition Values: Calories: 253; Carbs: 16g; Fat: 11g; Protein: 23.5g

Ingredients

- 3 lb chicken breast cut into slices
- 3 eggs
- 2 ¼ cup flour, divided
- 1 tbsp olive oil
- ½ tbsp plus
- ½ tbsp garlic powder, divided
- 1 tbsp salt
- 3 tbsp cajun seasoning, divided
- ¼ cup milk

Directions

1. Season the chicken with salt, pepper, ½

tbsp garlic powder and 2 tbsp Cajun seasoning.

2. Combine 2 cups flour, the rest of the Cajun seasoning and the rest of the garlic powder, in a bowl. In another bowl, whisk the eggs, milk, olive oil, and quarter cup flour. Preheat the Air fryer to 370 F.

3. Line a baking sheet with parchment paper. Dip the chicken into the egg mixture first, and then into the flour mixture. Arrange on the sheet. If there isn't enough room, work in two batches. Cook for 12 to 15 minutes.

198. CHICKEN WITH CASHEW NUTS

Preparation Time: 30 min
Servings: 4

Nutrition Values: Calories: 425; Carbs: 25g; Fat: 35g; Protein: 53g

Ingredients

- 1 lb chicken cubes
- 2 tbsp soy sauce
- 1 tbsp corn flour
- 2 ½ onion cubes
- 1 carrot, chopped
- ⅓ cup cashew nuts, fried
- 1 capsicum, cut
- 2 tbsp garlic, crushed
- Salt and white pepper

Directions

1. Marinate the chicken cubes with ½ tbsp of white pepper, ½ tsp salt, 2 tbsp soya sauce, and add 1 tbsp corn flour.

2. Set aside for 25 minutes. Preheat the Air Fryer to 380 F and transfer the marinated chicken. Add the garlic, the onion, the capsicum, and the carrot; fry for 5-6 minutes. Roll it in the cashew nuts before serving.

199. CRUNCHY COCONUT CHICKEN

Preparation Time: 22 min
Servings: 4

Nutrition Values: Calories: 651; Carbs: 21.6g; Fat: 47g; Protein: 66g

Ingredients

- 3 ½ cups coconut flakes
- 4 chicken breasts cut into strips
- ½ cup cornstarch
- ¼ tsp pepper
- ¼ tsp salt
- 3 eggs, beaten

Directions

1. Preheat the Air fryer to 350 F. Mix salt, pepper, and cornstarch in a small bowl. Line a baking sheet with parchment paper. Dip the chicken first in the cornstarch, then into the eggs, and finally, coat with coconut flakes. Arrange on the sheet and cook for 8 minutes. Flip the chicken over, and cook for 8 more minutes, until crispy.

200. AIR FRIED SOUTHERN DRUMSTICKS

Preparation Time: 50 min
Servings: 4

Nutrition Values: Calories: 197; Carbs: 5.2g; Fat: 6g; Protein: 29.2g

Ingredients

- 8 chicken drumsticks
- 2 tbsp oregano
- 2 tbsp thyme
- 2 oz oats
- ¼ cup milk
- ¼ steamed cauliflower florets
- 1 egg
- 1 tbsp ground cayenne
- Salt and pepper, to taste

Directions

1. Preheat the Air fryer to 350 F and season the drumsticks with salt and pepper; rub them with the milk. Place all the other ingredients, except the egg, in a food processor. Process until smooth. Dip each drumstick in the egg first, and then in the oat mixture. Arrange half of them on a baking mat inside the air fryer. Cook for

20 minutes. Repeat with the other batch.

201. FRIED CHICKEN LEGS

Preparation Time: 50 min
Servings: 5

Nutrition Values: Calories: 288; Carbs: 15g; Fat: 11g; Protein: 35g

Ingredients

- 5 quarters chicken legs
- 2 lemons, halved
- 5 tbsp garlic powder
- 5 tbsp dried basil
- 5 tbsp oregano, dried
- ⅓ cup olive oil
- Salt and black pepper

Directions

1. Set the Air Fryer to 350 F. Place the chicken in a large deep bowl. Brush the chicken legs with a tbsp of olive oil.
2. Sprinkle with the lemon juice and arrange in the Air Fryer. In another bowl, combine basil, oregano, garlic powder, salt and pepper. Sprinkle the seasoning mixture on the chicken. Cook in the preheated Air Fryer for 50 minutes, shaking every 10-15 minutes.

202. TURKEY CORDON BLEU

Preparation Time: 35 min
Servings: 4

Nutrition Values: Calories: 316; Carbs: 17g; Fat: 9 g; Protein: 37 g

Ingredients

- 2 turkey breasts
- 1 ham slice
- 1 slice cheddar cheese
- 2 oz breadcrumbs
- 1 tbsp cream cheese
- 1 tbsp garlic powder
- 1 tbsp thyme
- 1 tbsp tarragon
- 1 egg, beaten
- Salt and pepper, to taste

Directions

1. Preheat the air fryer to 350 F. Cut the turkey in the middle, that way so you can add ingredients in the center. Season with salt, pepper, thyme and tarragon. Combine the cream cheese and garlic powder, in a small bowl.
2. Spread the mixture on the inside of the breasts. Place half cheddar slice and half ham slice in the center of each breast. Dip the cordon bleu in egg first, then sprinkle with breadcrumbs. Cook on a baking mat for 30 minutes.

203. TOM YUM WINGS

Preparation Time: 4 hrs 20 min
Servings: 2

Nutrition Values: Calories: 287; Carbs: 20g; Fat: 7g; Protein: 26g

Ingredients

- 8 chicken wings
- 1 tbsp water
- 2 tbsp potato starch
- 2 tbsp cornstarch
- 2 tbsp tom yum paste
- ½ tbsp baking powder

Directions

1. Combine the tom yum paste and water, in a small bowl. Place the wings in a large bowl, add the tom yum mixture and coat well. Cover the bowl and refrigerate for 4 hours. Preheat the air fryer to 370 degrees.
2. Combine the baking powder, cornstarch and potato starch. Dip each wing in the starch mixture. Place on a lined baking dish in the air fryer and cook for 7 minutes. Flip over and cook for 5 to 7 minutes more.

204. CORDON BLEU CHICKEN

Preparation Time: 40 min
Servings: 4

Nutrition Values: Calories: 317; Carbs: 48g; Fat: 22g; Protein: 35g

Ingredients

- 4 skinless and boneless chicken breasts
- 4 slices ham
- 4 slices Swiss cheese
- 3 tbsp all-purpose flour
- 4 tbsp butter
- 1 tbsp paprika
- 1 tbsp chicken bouillon granules
- ½ cup dry white wine
- 1 cup heavy whipping cream
- 1 tbsp cornstarch

Directions

1. Preheat the Air Fryer to 380 F. Pound the chicken breasts and put a slice of ham on each of the chicken breasts. Fold the edges of the chicken over the filling and secure the edges with toothpicks. In a medium bowl, combine the paprika and the flour, and coat the chicken pieces. Fry the chicken for 20 minutes.
2. In a large skillet, heat the butter and add the bouillon and wine; reduce the heat to low. Remove the chicken from the Air Fryer and place it in the skillet. Let simmer for around 20-25 minutes.

205. CHICKEN WITH PRUNES

Preparation Time: 55 min
Servings: 6

Nutrition Values: Calories: 288; Carbs: 44g; Fat: 18g; Protein: 39g

Ingredients

- 1 whole chicken, 3 lb
- ½ cup pitted prunes
- 3 minced cloves of garlic
- 2 tbsp capers
- 2 bay leaves
- 2 tbsp red wine vinegar
- 2 tbsp olive oil
- 1 tbsp dried oregano
- ¼ cup packed brown sugar
- 1 tbsp chopped and fresh parsley
- Salt and black pepper

Directions

1. In a big and deep bowl, mix the prunes, the olives, capers, garlic, olive oil, bay leaves, oregano, vinegar, salt and pepper. Spread the mixture on the bottom of a

baking tray, and place the chicken.

2. Preheat the Air Fryer to 360 F. Sprinkle a little bit of brown sugar on top of the chicken; cook for 55 minutes.

206. ROSEMARY LEMON CHICKEN

Preparation Time: 60 min
Servings: 2

Nutrition Values: Calories: 275; Carbs: 19g; Fat: 7.6g; Protein: 36g

Ingredients

- 2 chicken breasts
- 1 tbsp minced ginger
- 2 rosemary sprigs
- ½ lemon, cut into wedges
- 1 tbsp soy sauce
- ½ tbsp olive oil
- 1 tbsp oyster sauce
- 3 tbsp brown sugar

Directions

1. Add the ginger, soy sauce, and olive oil, in a bowl; add the chicken and coat well. Cover the bowl and refrigerate for 30 minutes. Preheat the air fryer to 370 F. Transfer the marinated chicken to a baking dish; cook for 6 minutes.
2. Meanwhile, mix the oyster sauce, rosemary and brown sugar, in a small bowl. Pour the sauce over the chicken. Arrange the lemon wedges in the dish. Return to the air fryer and cook for 13 more minutes.

207. SIMPLE PANKO TURKEY

Preparation Time: 25 min
Servings: 6

Nutrition Values: Calories: 286; Carbs: 6.6g; Fat: 18g; Protein: 24g

Ingredients

- 6 turkey breasts, boneless and skinless
- 2 cups panko1 tbsp salt
- ½ tsp cayenne pepper
- ½ tbsp black pepper
- 1 stick butter, melted

Directions

1. In a bowl, combine the panko, half of the black pepper, cayenne pepper, and half of the salt. In another small bowl, combine the melted butter with salt and pepper. Don't add salt if you use salted butter.
2. Brush the butter mixture over the turkey breast. Coat the turkey with the panko mixture. Arrange them on a lined baking dish. Air fry for 15 minutes at 390 degrees F. If the turkey breasts are thinner, cook only for 8 minutes.

208. GREEK-STYLE CHICKEN

Preparation Time: 45 min
Servings: 6

Nutrition Values: Calories: 283; Carbs: 34g; Fat: 12g; Protein: 27g

Ingredients

- 1 whole chicken, around 3 lb, cut in pieces
- 3 chopped cloves of garlic
- ½ cup olive oil
- ½ cup white wine
- 1 tbsp fresh rosemary
- 1 tbsp chopped fresh oregano
- 1 tbsp fresh thyme
- Juice from 1 lemon
- Salt and black pepper, to taste

Directions

1. In a large bowl, combine cloves of garlic, rosemary, thyme, olive oil, lemon juice, oregano, salt and pepper. Mix all ingredients very well and spread the mixture into a baking dish. Add the chicken and stir.
2. Preheat the Air Fryer to 380 F, and transfer in the chicken mixture. Sprinkle with wine and cook for 45 minutes.

209. CHICKEN QUARTERS WITH BROCCOLI AND RICE

Preparation Time: 60 min
Servings: 3

Nutrition Values: Calories: 256; Carbs: 29g; Fat: 15g; Protein: 23g

Ingredients

- 3 chicken leg quarters
- 1 package instant long grain rice
- 1 cup chopped broccoli
- 2 cups water
- 1 can condensed cream chicken soup
- 1 tbsp minced garlic

Directions

1. Preheat the Air Fryer to 390 F, and place the chicken quarters in the Air Fryer. Season with salt, pepper and one tbsp of oil; cook for 30 minutes. Meanwhile, in a large deep bowl, mix the rice, water, minced garlic, soup and broccoli. Combine the mixture very well.
2. Remove the chicken from the Air fryer and place it on a platter to drain. Spread the rice mixture on the bottom of the dish and place the chicken on top of the rice. Cook again for 30 minutes.

210. ASIAN-STYLE CHICKEN

Preparation Time: 35 min
Servings: 4

Nutrition Values: Calories: 313; Carbs: 64g; Fat: 14g; Protein: 31g

Ingredients

- 1 lb chicken, cut in stripes
- 2 tomatoes, cubed
- 3 green peppers, cut in stripes
- 1 tbsp cumin powder
- 1 large onion
- 2 tbsp oil
- 1 tbsp mustard
- A pinch of ginger
- A pinch of fresh and chopped coriander
- Salt and black pepper

Directions

1. Heat the oil in a deep pan. Add the mustard, the onion, the ginger, the cumin and the green chili peppers. Sauté the mixture for 2-3 minutes. Then, add the tomatoes, the coriander and salt and keep stirring.
2. Preheat the Air Fryer to 380 F. Coat the chicken with oil, salt and pepper and cook it for 25 minutes. Remove from the Air Fryer and pour the sauce over and around.

211. CRUMBED SAGE CHICKEN SCALLOPINI

Preparation Time: 12 min
Servings: 4

Nutrition Values: Calories: 218; Carbs: 8.9g; Fat: 5.9g; Protein: 30.4g

Ingredients

- 4 chicken breasts, skinless and boneless
- 3 oz breadcrumbs
- 2 tbsp grated Parmesan cheese
- 2 oz flour
- 2 eggs, beaten
- 1 tbsp fresh, chopped sage
- Cooking spray

Directions

1. Preheat the air fryer to 370 F. Place some plastic wrap underneath and on top of the chicken breasts. Using a rolling pin, beat the meat until it becomes really thin. In a bowl, combine the Parmesan, sage and breadcrumbs.
2. Dip the chicken in the egg first, and then in the sage mixture. Spray with cooking oil and arrange the meat in the air fryer. Cook for 7 minutes.

212. BUTTERMILK CHICKEN THIGHS

Preparation Time: 4 hrs 40 min
Servings: 6

Nutrition Values: Calories: 322; Carbs: 36g; Fat: 4g; Protein: 33g

Ingredients

- 1 ½ lb chicken thighs
- 1 tbsp cayenne pepper
- 3 tbsp salt divided
- 2 cups flour
- 2 tbsp black pepper
- 1 tbsp paprika
- 1 tbsp baking powder

- 2 cups buttermilk

Directions

1. Rinse and pat dry the chicken thighs. Place the chicken thighs in a bowl. Add cayenne pepper, 2 tbsp of salt, black pepper and buttermilk, and stir to coat well. Refrigerate for 4 hours. Preheat the air fryer to 350 F.
2. In another bowl, mix the flour, paprika, 1 tbsp of salt, and baking powder. Dredge half of the chicken thighs, one at a time, in the flour, and then place on a lined dish. Cook for 10 minutes, flip over and cook for 8 more minutes. Repeat with the other batch.

213. BUTTERMILK FRIED CHICKEN TENDERS

Preparation Time: 1 hour 15 minutes
Servings 4

Nutrition Values:386 Calories; 11.7g Fat; 32.5g Carbs; 35.2g Protein; 2.5g Sugars

Ingredients

- 3/4 cup of buttermilk
- 1 pound chicken tenders
- 1 ½ cups all-purpose flour
- Salt, to your liking
- 1/2 teaspoon pink peppercorns, freshly cracked
- 1 teaspoon shallot powder
- 1/2 teaspoon cumin powder
- 1 ½ teaspoon smoked cayenne pepper
- 1 tablespoon sesame oil

Directions

1. Place the buttermilk and chicken tenders in the mixing dish; gently stir to coat and let it soak for 1 hour.
2. Then, mix the flour with all seasonings. Coat the soaked chicken tenders with the flour mixture; now, dip them into the buttermilk. Finally, dredge them in the flour.
3. Brush the prepared chicken tenders with sesame oil and lower them onto the bottom of a cooking basket.
4. Air-fry for 15 minutes at 365 degrees F;

make sure to shake them once or twice. Bon appétit!

214. PENNE WITH CHICKEN SAUSAGE MEATBALLS

Preparation Time: 20 minutes
Servings 4

Nutrition Values:384 Calories; 5.3g Fat; 60.2g Carbs; 22.5g Protein; 0.6g Sugars

Ingredients

- 1 cup chicken meat, ground
- 1 sweet red pepper, minced
- 1/4 cup green onions, chopped
- 1 green garlic, minced
- 4 tablespoons seasoned breadcrumbs
- 1/2 teaspoon cumin powder
- 1 tablespoon fresh coriander, minced
- 1/2 teaspoon sea salt
- 1/4 teaspoon mixed peppercorns, ground
- 1 package penne pasta, cooked

Directions

1. Place the chicken, red pepper, green onions, and garlic into a mixing bowl; mix to combine well.
2. Now, add seasoned breadcrumbs, followed by all seasonings; mix again until everything is well incorporated.
3. Next, shape into small balls -e.g. the size of a golf ball; cook them in the preheated Air Fryer at 350 degrees F for 15 minutes; shaking once or twice to ensure evenness of cooking. Serve over cooked penne pasta.

215. CAJUN CHICKEN WINGS WITH CABBAGE-POTATO CAKES

Preparation Time: 40 minutes
Servings 4

Nutrition Values:306 Calories; 12.8g Fat; 14.5g Carbs; 32.2g Protein; 1.3g Sugars

Ingredients

- 4 large-sized chicken wings
- 1 teaspoon Cajun seasoning
- 1 teaspoon maple syrup

- 3/4 teaspoon sea salt flakes
- 1/4 teaspoon red pepper flakes, crushed
- 1 teaspoon onion powder
- 1 teaspoon porcini powder
- 1/2 teaspoon celery seeds
- 1 small-seized head of cabbage, shredded
- 1 cup mashed potatoes
- 1 small-sized brown onion, coarsely grated
- 1 teaspoon garlic puree
- 1 medium-sized whole egg, well whisked
- 1/2 teaspoon table salt
- 1/2 teaspoon ground black pepper
- 1 ½ tablespoons all-purpose flour
- 3/4 teaspoon baking powder
- 1 heaping tablespoon cilantro
- 1 tablespoon sesame oil

Directions

1. Start by preheating your Air Fryer to 390 degrees F. Dry the chicken wings. Now, prepare the rub by mixing Cajun seasoning, maple syrup, sea salt flakes, red pepper, onion powder, porcini powder, and celery seeds.
2. Cook for 25 to 30 minutes or until the wings are no longer pink in the middle.
3. Then, mix the shredded cabbage, potato, onion, garlic puree, egg, table salt, black pepper, flour, baking powder and cilantro in a mixing bowl.
4. Divide the cabbage mixture into 4 portions and create four cabbage/potato cakes. Sprinkle each cake with the sesame oil.
5. Bake cabbage/potato cakes for 10 minutes, flipping them once and working in batches. Finally, serve with the chicken wings and enjoy!

216. MAJESTIC MAPLE-GLAZED CHICKEN

Preparation Time: 20 minutes + marinating time
Servings 4

Nutrition Values:189 Calories; 3.1g Fat; 9.1g Carbs; 29.5g Protein; 7.6g Sugars

Ingredients

- 2 ½ tablespoons maple syrup
- 1 tablespoon tamari soy sauce
- 1 tablespoon oyster sauce
- 1 teaspoon fresh lemon juice
- 1 teaspoon minced fresh ginger
- 1 teaspoon garlic puree
- Seasoned salt and freshly ground pepper, to your liking
- 2 chicken breasts, boneless and skinless

Directions

1. To prepare the marinade, in a mixing dish, combine maple syrup, tamari sauce, oyster sauce, lemon juice, fresh ginger and garlic puree.
2. Now, season the chicken breasts with salt and pepper. Put the chicken breast into the bowl with the marinade and make sure to coat them well; cover with foil and place in the refrigerator for 3 hours or overnight.
3. Discard the marinade. Air-fry marinated chicken breast for 15 minutes at 365 degrees F; turn them once or twice.
4. Meanwhile, add the remaining marinade to a pan that is preheated over a moderate flame; let it simmer until reduced by half; it will take 3 to 5 minutes. Serve the chicken with the sauce. Bon appétit!

217. SAUCY PROVENÇAL CHICKEN WITH BACON

Preparation Time: 25 minutes
Servings 4

Nutrition Values:296 Calories; 13.7g Fat; 6.9g Carbs; 34.7g Protein; 2.9g Sugars

Ingredients

- 4 medium-sized skin-on chicken drumsticks
- 1 ½ teaspoons herbs de Provence
- Salt and pepper, to your liking
- 1 tablespoon rice vinegar
- 2 tablespoons olive oil
- 2 garlic cloves, crushed
- 12 ounces crushed canned tomatoes
- 1 small-size leek, thinly sliced

- 2 slices smoked bacon, chopped

Directions

1. Sprinkle the chicken drumsticks with herbs de Provence, salt and pepper; then, drizzle them with rice vinegar and olive oil. Cook in the baking pan at 360 degrees F for 8 to 10 minutes.
2. Pause the Air Fryer; stir in the remaining ingredients and continue to cook for 15 minutes longer; make sure to check them periodically. Serve over rice garnished with lemon wedges. Bon appétit!

218. MELT-IN-YOUR-MOUTH MARJORAM CHICKEN

Preparation Time: 1 hour
Servings 2

Nutrition Values:328 Calories; 16.1g Fat; 0.0g Carbs; 43.6g Protein; 0.0 g Sugars

Ingredients

- 2 small-sized chicken breasts, skinless and boneless
- 2 tablespoons butter
- 1 teaspoon sea salt
- 1/2 teaspoon red pepper flakes, crushed
- 2 teaspoons marjoram
- 1/4 teaspoon lemon pepper

Directions

1. Add all of the above ingredients to a mixing dish; let it marinate for 30 minutes to 1 hour.
2. Then, set your Air Fryer to cook at 390 degrees. Cook for 20 minutes, turning halfway through cooking time.
3. Check for doneness using an instant-read thermometer. Serve over jasmine rice. Bon appétit!

219. CHICKEN WITH CREMINI MUSHROOM SAUCE

Preparation Time: 25 minutes
Servings 6

Nutrition Values:403 Calories; 17.2g Fat; 31g Carbs; 34.3g Protein; 1g Sugars

Ingredients

- 1/2 pound Cremini mushrooms, thinly sliced
- 1/2 cup chicken stock
- 1/3 cup rice wine
- 1/3 teaspoon Chinese 5 spice powder
- 3 medium-sized chicken breasts, sliced
- 1/2 teaspoon ground ginger
- 1 ½ tablespoons flour
- 1 teaspoon smoked paprika
- 1 ½ tablespoons peanut oil
- 1/3 teaspoon dried dill weed
- 3 cloves garlic, minced
- 1 teaspoon kosher salt
- 1 teaspoon red pepper flakes, crushed

Directions

1. Rub the chicken with all the seasonings.
2. Lower the seasoned chicken onto the baking dish. Air-fry for 18 minutes at 365 degrees F.
3. Then, pause the machine; add the Cremini mushrooms, followed by the other ingredients. Air-fry an additional 8 to 10 minutes. Eat warm. Bon appétit!

220. CHICKEN AND ASIAGO CRESCENT SQUARES

Preparation Time: 10 minutes
Servings 6

Nutrition Values:311 Calories; 21.6g Fat; 3.7g Carbs; 25.9g Protein; 0.2g Sugars

Ingredients

- 1 pound chicken breasts, shredded
- 6 large-sized eggs, well beaten
- 6 slices Asiago cheese
- 1/2 can crescent roll, refrigerated
- 1 ½ teaspoon hot paprika
- ½ tablespoon fresh parsley, minced
- 1 teaspoon kosher salt
- ½ teaspoon ground black pepper, or more to taste

Directions

1. Begin by unrolling the crescent rolls and split the dough into 4 rectangles. Now, fold up the edges of each rectangle.

2. Lower 1 rectangle onto the bottom of the air fryer cooking basket; now, crack 1 egg into it. Sprinkle with the seasonings.
3. Add 1/3 of the shredded chicken meat; top with 1 slice of Asiago cheese. Repeat with the other crescent rolls.
4. Air-fry for 8 minutes at 325 degrees F, or until all sides are golden brown. Bon appétit!

221. THE BEST ORANGE AND SHOYU WINGS

Preparation Time: 50 minutes
Servings 4

Nutrition Values:78 Calories; 2.6g Fat; 1.4g Carbs; 12.9g Protein; 0.8g Sugars

Ingredients

- ½ teaspoon smoked paprika
- 2 teaspoons garlic powder
- 1/3 teaspoon ground black pepper, preferably freshly ground
- ½ pound chicken wings
- 1 ½ tablespoons plain flour
- 1 teaspoon salt
- For the Glaze:
- 1/3 cup orange juice
- 1/2 teaspoon Shoyu sauce
- 2 cloves garlic, minced
- 1/2 tablespoon brown sugar
- 1/3 cup hoisin sauce
- 1 ½ teaspoons olive oil
- 1/2 teaspoon fresh ginger root, finely grated

Directions

1. Toss the chicken wings with the flour, garlic powder, paprika, salt, and ground black pepper in a baking dish.
2. Air-fry the chicken wings at 365 degrees F for 24 minutes.
3. In the meantime, prepare the glaze; heat the oil in a saucepan and sauté the garlic until just tender.
4. Throw in the remaining ingredients; simmer for about 30 minutes or until the sauce has thickened. Pour the glaze over the prepared chicken wings; toss to coat.

Bon appétit!

222. BAKED ZA'ATAR EGGS WITH CHICKEN

Preparation Time: 15 minutes
Servings 2

Nutrition Values:440 Calories; 28.5g Fat; 8.7g Carbs; 36.9g Protein; 5.2g Sugars

Ingredients

- 1/3 cup milk
- 1 1/2 Roma tomato, chopped
- 1/3 cup Provolone cheese, grated
- 1 teaspoon freshly cracked pink peppercorns
- 3 eggs
- 1 teaspoon Za'atar
- ½ chicken breast, cooked
- 1 teaspoon fine sea salt
- 1 teaspoon freshly cracked pink peppercorns

Directions

1. Preheat your air fryer to cook at 365 degrees F. In a medium-sized mixing dish, whisk the eggs together with the milk, Za'atar, sea salt, and cracked pink peppercorns.
2. Spritz the ramekins with cooking oil; divide the prepared egg mixture among the greased ramekins.
3. Shred the chicken with two forks or a stand mixer. Add the shredded chicken to the ramekins, followed by the tomato and the cheese.
4. To finish, air-fry for 18 minutes or until it is done. Bon appétit!

223. CHICKEN IN YOGURT-MUSTARD SAUCE

Preparation Time: 1 hours 10 minutes
Servings 6

Nutrition Values:283 Calories; 15.8g Fat; 2.8g Carbs; 31g Protein; 0.7g Sugars

Ingredients

- 3 chicken breasts, skinless, boneless and cubed

- 1/3 cup Greek-style yogurt
- 3 cloves garlic, minced
- 1 teaspoon paprika
- 1/3 cup reduced-fat thickened cooking cream
- 1 teaspoon turmeric powder
- 2 ½ tablespoons yellow mustard
- 1 tablespoon melted butter
- 1/3 teaspoon freshly cracked mixed peppercorns
- 1 teaspoon fine sea salt

Directions

1. Toss the cubes of the chicken breasts with the turmeric, paprika, sea salt, and cracked pepper.
2. Add the rest of the above ingredients and let it stand for about 1 hour.
3. Discard the sauce and air-fry the chicken cubes for 10 minutes at 365 degrees F. Serve with the reserved yogurt/mustard sauce and enjoy!

224. BRIOCHE WITH CHICKEN AND CACIOCAVALLO

Preparation Time: 10 minutes
Servings 6

Nutrition Values:430 Calories; 19g Fat; 22.4g Carbs; 42.9g Protein; 3g Sugars

Ingredients

- 6 brioche rolls
- 3 tablespoons sesame oil
- 2 teaspoons dried thyme
- 1/3 cup Caciocavallo, grated
- 1 cup leftover chicken, shredded
- 3 eggs
- 1 teaspoon kosher salt
- 1 teaspoon freshly cracked black pepper, or more to taste
- 1/3 teaspoon gremolata

Directions

1. Firstly, slice off the top of each brioche; then, scoop out the insides.
2. Brush each brioche with sesame oil. Add the remaining ingredients in the order listed above.

3. Place the prepared brioche onto the bottom of the cooking basket. Bake for 7 minutes at 345 degrees F. Bon appétit!

225. CHEESE AND CHIVE STUFFED CHICKEN ROLLS

Preparation Time: 20 minutes
Servings 6

Nutrition Values:311 Calories; 18.3g Fat; 1.3g Carbs; 33.4g Protein; 0.3 g Sugars

Ingredients

- 2 eggs, well-whisked
- Tortilla chips, crushed
- 1 1/2 tablespoons extra-virgin olive oil
- 1 ½ tablespoons fresh chives, chopped
- 3 chicken breasts, halved lengthwise
- 1 ½ cup soft cheese
- 2 teaspoons sweet paprika
- 1/2 teaspoon whole grain mustard
- 1/2 teaspoon cumin powder
- 1/3 teaspoon fine sea salt
- 1/3 cup fresh cilantro, chopped
- 1/3 teaspoon freshly ground black pepper, or more to taste

Directions

1. Flatten out each piece of the chicken breast using a rolling pin. Then, grab three mixing dishes.
2. In the first one, combine the soft cheese with the cilantro, fresh chives, cumin, and mustard.
3. In another mixing dish, whisk the eggs together with the sweet paprika. In the third dish, combine the salt, black pepper, and crushed tortilla chips.
4. Spread the cheese mixture over each piece of chicken. Repeat with the remaining pieces of the chicken breasts; now, roll them up.
5. Coat each chicken roll with the whisked egg; dredge each chicken roll into the tortilla chips mixture. Lower the rolls onto the air fryer cooking basket. Drizzle extra-virgin olive oil over all rolls.
6. Air fry at 345 degrees F for 28 minutes, working in batches. Serve warm, garnished

with sour cream if desired.

226. CHICKEN DRUMSTICKS WITH KETCHUP-LEMON SAUCE

Preparation Time: 20 minutes + marinating time
Servings 6

Nutrition Values:274 Calories; 12g Fat; 17.3g Carbs; 23.3g Protein; 16.2g Sugars

Ingredients

- 3 tablespoons lemon juice
- 1 cup tomato ketchup
- 1 ½ tablespoons fresh rosemary, chopped
- 6 skin-on chicken drumsticks, boneless
- 1/2 teaspoon ground black pepper
- 2 teaspoons lemon zest, grated
- 1/3 cup honey
- 3 cloves garlic, minced

Directions

1. Dump the chicken drumsticks into a mixing dish. Now, add the other items and give it a good stir; let it marinate overnight in your refrigerator.
2. Discard the marinade; roast the chicken legs in your air fryer at 375 degrees F for 22 minutes, turning once.
3. Now, add the marinade and cook an additional 6 minutes or until everything is warmed through.

227. CREAMED CAJUN CHICKEN

Preparation Time: 10 minutes
Servings 6

Nutrition Values:400 Calories; 10.2g Fat; 48.2g Carbs; 27.3g Protein; 3.5g Sugars

Ingredients

- 3 green onions, thinly sliced
- ½ tablespoon Cajun seasoning
- 1 ½ cup buttermilk
- 2 large-sized chicken breasts, cut into strips
- 1/2 teaspoon garlic powder
- 1 teaspoon salt
- 1 cup cornmeal mix
- 1 teaspoon shallot powder

- 1 ½ cup flour
- 1 teaspoon ground black pepper, or to taste

Directions

1. Prepare three mixing bowls. Combine 1/2 cup of the plain flour together with the cornmeal and Cajun seasoning in your bowl. In another bowl, place the buttermilk.
2. Pour the remaining 1 cup of flour into the third bowl.
3. Sprinkle the chicken strips with all the seasonings. Then, dip each chicken strip in the 1 cup of flour, then in the buttermilk; finally, dredge them in the cornmeal mixture.
4. Cook the chicken strips in the air fryer baking pan for 16 minutes at 365 degrees F. Serve garnished with green onions. Bon appétit!

228. CHIVE, FETA AND CHICKEN FRITTATA

Preparation Time: 10 minutes
Servings 4

Nutrition Values:176 Calories; 7.7g Fat; 2.4g Carbs; 22.8g Protein; 1.5g Sugars

Ingredients

- 1/3 cup Feta cheese, crumbled
- 1 teaspoon dried rosemary
- ½ teaspoon brown sugar
- 2 tablespoons fish sauce
- 1 ½ cup cooked chicken breasts, boneless and shredded
- 1/2 teaspoon coriander sprig, finely chopped
- 3 medium-sized whisked eggs
- 1/3 teaspoon ground white pepper
- 1 cup fresh chives, chopped
- 1/2 teaspoon garlic paste
- Fine sea salt, to taste
- Nonstick cooking spray

Directions

1. Grab a baking dish that fit in your air fryer.

2. Lightly coat the inside of the baking dish with a nonstick cooking spray of choice. Stir in all ingredients, minus Feta cheese. Stir to combine well.

3. Set your machine to cook at 335 degrees for 8 minutes; check for doneness. Scatter crumbled Feta over the top and eat immediately!

229. GRILLED CHICKEN TIKKA MASALA

Preparation Time: 35 minutes + marinating time
Servings 4

Nutrition Values:319 Calories; 20.1g Fat; 1.9g Carbs; 30.5g Protein; 0.1g Sugars

Ingredients

- 1 teaspoon Tikka Masala
- 1 teaspoon fine sea salt
- 2 heaping teaspoons whole grain mustard
- 2 teaspoons coriander, ground
- 2 tablespoon olive oil
- 2 large-sized chicken breasts, skinless and halved lengthwise
- 2 teaspoons onion powder
- 1 ½ tablespoons cider vinegar
- Basmati rice, steamed
- 1/3 teaspoon red pepper flakes, crushed

Directions

1. Preheat the air fryer to 335 degrees for 4 minutes.
2. Toss your chicken together with the other ingredients, minus basmati rice. Let it stand at least 3 hours.
3. Cook for 25 minutes in your air fryer; check for doneness because the time depending on the size of the piece of chicken.
4. Serve immediately over warm basmati rice. Enjoy!

230. AWARD WINNING BREADED CHICKEN

Preparation Time: 10 minutes + marinating time
Servings 4

Nutrition Values:262 Calories; 14.9g Fat; 2.7g Carbs; 27.5g Protein; 0.3g Sugars

Ingredients

For the Marinade:

- 1 1/2 teaspoons olive oil
- 1 teaspoon red pepper flakes, crushed
- 1/3 teaspoon chicken bouillon granules
- 1/3 teaspoon shallot powder
- 1 1/2 tablespoons tamari soy sauce
- 1/3 teaspoon cumin powder
- 1 ½ tablespoons mayo
- 1 teaspoon kosher salt

For the chicken:

- 2 beaten eggs
- Breadcrumbs
- 1 ½ chicken breasts, boneless and skinless
- 1 ½ tablespoons plain flour

Directions

1. Butterfly the chicken breasts, and then, marinate them for at least 55 minutes.
2. Coat the chicken with plain flour; then, coat with the beaten eggs; finally, roll them in the breadcrumbs.
3. Lightly grease the cooking basket. Air-fry the breaded chicken at 345 degrees F for 12 minutes, flipping them halfway.

231. CHEESE AND GARLIC STUFFED CHICKEN BREASTS

Preparation Time: 20 minutes
Servings 2

Nutrition Values:424 Calories; 24.5g Fat; 7.5g Carbs; 43.4g Protein; 5.3g Sugars

Ingredients

- 1/2 cup Cottage cheese
- 2 eggs, beaten
- 2 medium-sized chicken breasts, halved
- 2 tablespoons fresh coriander, chopped
- 1teaspoon fine sea salt
- Seasoned breadcrumbs
- 1/3teaspoon freshly ground black pepper, to savor
- 3 cloves garlic, finely minced

Directions

1. Firstly, flatten out the chicken breast using

a meat tenderizer.

2. In a medium-sized mixing dish, combine the Cottage cheese with the garlic, coriander, salt, and black pepper.

3. Spread 1/3 of the mixture over the first chicken breast. Repeat with the remaining ingredients. Roll the chicken around the filling; make sure to secure with toothpicks.

4. Now, whisk the egg in a shallow bowl. In another shallow bowl, combine the salt, ground black pepper, and seasoned breadcrumbs.

5. Coat the chicken breasts with the whisked egg; now, roll them in the breadcrumbs.

6. Cook in the air fryer cooking basket at 365 degrees F for 22 minutes. Serve immediately.

232. DINNER AVOCADO CHICKEN SLIDERS

Preparation Time: 10 minutes
Servings 4

Nutrition Values:321 Calories; 18.7g Fat; 15.8g Carbs; 23.5g Protein; 1.2g Sugars

Ingredients

- ½ pounds ground chicken meat
- 4 burger buns
- 1/2 cup Romaine lettuce, loosely packed
- ½ teaspoon dried parsley flakes
- 1/3 teaspoon mustard seeds
- 1 teaspoon onion powder
- 1 ripe fresh avocado, mashed
- 1 teaspoon garlic powder
- 1 ½ tablespoon extra-virgin olive oil
- 1 cloves garlic, minced
- Nonstick cooking spray
- Salt and cracked black pepper - peppercorns, to taste

Directions

1. Firstly, spritz an air fryer cooking basket with a nonstick cooking spray.

2. Mix ground chicken meat, mustard seeds, garlic powder, onion powder, parsley, salt, and black pepper until everything is thoroughly combined. Make sure not to

overwork the meat to avoid tough chicken burgers.

3. Shape the meat mixture into patties and roll them in breadcrumbs; transfer your burgers to the prepared cooking basket. Brush the patties with the cooking spray.

4. Air-fry at 355 F for 9 minutes, working in batches. Slice burger buns into halves. In the meantime, combine olive oil with mashed avocado and pressed garlic.

5. To finish, lay Romaine lettuce and avocado spread on bun bottoms; now, add burgers and bun tops. Bon appétit!

233. PEANUT BUTTER AND CHICKEN BITES

Preparation Time: 10 minutes
Servings 8

Nutrition Values:150 Calories; 9.7g Fat; 2.1g Carbs; 12.9g Protein; 1.6g Sugars

Ingredients

- 1 ½ tablespoons soy sauce
- 1/2 teaspoon smoked cayenne pepper
- 8 ounces soft cheese
- 1 1/2 tablespoons peanut butter
- 1/3 leftover chicken
- 1 teaspoon sea salt
- 32 wonton wrappers
- 1/3 teaspoon freshly cracked mixed peppercorns
- 1/2 tablespoon pear cider vinegar

Directions

1. Combine all of the above ingredients, minus the wonton wrappers, in a mixing dish.

2. Lay out the wrappers on a clean surface. Now, spread the wonton wrappers with the prepared chicken filling.

3. Fold the outside corners to the center over the filling; after that, roll up the wrappers tightly; you can moisten the edges with a little water.

4. Set the air fryer to cook at 360 degrees F. Air fry the rolls for 6 minutes, working in batches. Serve with marinara sauce. Bon appétit!

234. TANGY PAPRIKA CHICKEN

Preparation Time: 30 minutes
Servings 4

Nutrition Values:312 Calories; 17.6g Fat; 2.6g Carbs; 30.4g Protein; 1.2g Sugars

Ingredients

- 1 ½ tablespoons freshly squeezed lemon juice
- 2 small-sized chicken breasts, boneless
- 1/2 teaspoon ground cumin
- 1 teaspoon dry mustard powder
- 1 teaspoon paprika
- 2 teaspoons cup pear cider vinegar
- 1 tablespoon olive oil
- 2 garlic cloves, minced
- Kosher salt and freshly ground mixed peppercorns, to savor

Directions

1. Warm the olive oil in a nonstick pan over a moderate flame. Sauté the garlic for just 1 minutes.
2. Remove your pan from the heat; add cider vinegar, lemon juice, paprika, cumin, mustard powder, kosher salt, and black pepper. Pour this paprika sauce into a baking dish.
3. Pat the chicken breasts dry; transfer them to the prepared sauce. Bake in the preheated air fryer for about 28 minutes at 335 degrees F; check for doneness using a thermometer or a fork.
4. Allow to rest for 8 to 9 minutes before slicing and serving. Serve with dressing.

235. CHICKEN AND YOGURT

Preparation Time: 1 hour 15 minutes
Servings: 4

Ingredients:

- 17 oz. chicken meat; boneless and cubed
- 14 oz. yogurt
- 3½ oz. cherry tomatoes; halved
- 1 red bell pepper; deseeded and cubed
- 1 yellow bell pepper; deseeded and cubed
- 2 tbsp. coriander powder
- 2 tsp. olive oil

- 1 tsp. turmeric powder
- 3 mint leaves; torn
- 1 green bell pepper; deseeded and cubed
- 1 tbsp. ginger; grated
- 2 tbsp. red chili powder
- 2 tbsp. cumin powder
- Salt and black pepper to taste

Directions:

1. In a bowl, mix all of the ingredients, toss well and place in the fridge for 1 hour
2. Transfer the whole mix to a pan that fits your air fryer and cook at 400°F for 15 minutes, shaking the pan halfway. Divide everything between plates and serve

236. CHICKEN AND PEPPERCORNS

Preparation Time: 25 minutes
Servings: 4

Ingredients:

- 8 chicken thighs; boneless
- 1 tsp. black peppercorns
- 4 garlic cloves; minced
- 1/2 cup soy sauce
- 1/2 cup balsamic vinegar
- Salt and black pepper to taste

Directions:

1. In a pan that fits your air fryer; mix the chicken with all the other ingredients and toss
2. Place the pan in the fryer and cook at 380°F for 20 minutes. Divide everything between plates and serve.

237. DUCK AND SAUCE

Preparation Time: 30 minutes
Servings: 4

Ingredients:

- 2 duck breasts; skin scored
- 8 oz. white wine
- 1 tbsp. garlic; minced
- 2 tbsp. heavy cream
- 1 tbsp. sugar
- 2 tbsp. cranberries

- 1 tbsp. olive oil
- Salt and black pepper to taste

Directions:

1. Season the duck breasts with salt and pepper and put them in preheated air fryer
2. Cook at 350°F for 10 minutes on each side and divide between plates
3. Heat up a pan with the oil over medium heat and add the cranberries, sugar, wine, garlic and the cream; whisk well. Cook for 3-4 minutes, drizzle over the duck and serve.

238. BARBEQUE CHICKEN WINGS

Preparation Time: 40 minutes
Servings: 4

Ingredients:

- 1/2 cup BBQ sauce
- 2 lbs. chicken wings; cut into drumettes and flats

Directions:

1. Set the temperature of Air Fryer to 380°F. Grease an Air Fryer basket. Arrange chicken wings into the prepared Air Fryer basket in a single layer.
2. Air Fry for about 24 minutes, flipping once halfway through. Now, set the temperature of Air Fryer to 400°F.
3. Air Fry for about 6 minutes. Remove from Air Fryer and transfer the chicken wings into a bowl. Drizzle with the BBQ sauce and toss to coat well. Serve immediately.

239. TURKEY AND SPRING ONIONS

Preparation Time: 40 minutes
Servings: 2

Ingredients:

- 2 small turkey breasts; boneless and skinless
- 1 bunch spring onions; chopped.
- 2 red chilies; chopped.
- 1 tbsp. Chinese rice wine

- 1 tbsp. oyster sauce
- 1 cup chicken stock
- 1 tbsp. olive oil
- 1 tbsp. soy sauce

Directions:

1. Add the oil to a pan that fits your air fryer and place it over medium heat
2. Then add the chilies, spring onions, oyster sauce, soy sauce, stock and rice wine; whisk and simmer for 3-4 minutes
3. Add the turkey, toss and place the pan in the air fryer and cook at 380°F for 30 minutes. Divide everything between plates and serve.

240. CHICKEN AND SQUASH

Preparation Time: 35 minutes
Servings: 4

Ingredients:

- 14 oz. coconut milk
- 6 cups squash; cubed
- 8 chicken drumsticks
- 1/2 cup cilantro; chopped.
- 2 tbsp. olive oil
- 2 tbsp. green curry paste
- 1/4 tsp. coriander; ground
- 1/2 cup basil; chopped.
- 2 red chilies; minced
- 3 garlic cloves; minced
- A pinch of cumin; ground
- Salt and black pepper to taste

Directions:

1. Heat up a pan that fits your air fryer with the oil over medium heat.
2. Add the garlic, chilies, curry paste, cumin, coriander, salt and pepper; stir and cook for 3-4 minutes.
3. Add the chicken pieces and the coconut milk and stir
4. Place the pan in the fryer and cook at 380°F for 15 minutes
5. Add the squash, cilantro and basil; toss and cook for 5-6 minutes more. Divide into bowls and serve. Enjoy!

241. SOY SAUCE CHICKEN

Preparation Time: 50 minutes
Servings: 6

Ingredients:

- 1 whole chicken; cut into pieces
- 1 tsp. sesame oil
- 2 tsp. soy sauce
- 1 chili pepper; minced
- 1 tbsp. ginger; grated
- Salt and black pepper to taste

Directions:

1. In a bowl, mix the chicken with all the other ingredients and rub well
2. Transfer the chicken pieces to your air fryer's basket
3. Cook at 400°F for 30 minutes and then at 380°F for 10 minutes more. Divide everything between plates and serve

242. CHICKEN AND VEGGIES

Preparation Time: 35 minutes
Servings: 4

Ingredients:

- 4 chicken breasts; boneless and skinless
- 3 garlic cloves; minced
- 1 celery stalk; chopped.
- 1 red onion; chopped.
- 2 tbsp. olive oil
- 1 tsp. sage; dried
- 1 carrot; chopped.
- 1 cup chicken stock
- 1/2 tsp. rosemary; dried
- Salt and black pepper to taste

Directions:

1. In a pan that fits your air fryer, place all ingredients and toss well
2. Put the pan in the fryer and cook at 360°F for 25 minutes. Divide everything between plates, serve and enjoy!

243. ROSEMARY CHICKEN BREASTS

Preparation Time: 35 minutes
Servings: 4

Ingredients:

- 2 chicken breasts; skinless, boneless and halved
- 1 yellow onion; sliced
- 1 cup chicken stock
- 4 garlic cloves; chopped.
- 2 tbsp. cornstarch mixed with 2½ tbsp. water
- 2 tbsp. butter; melted
- 1 tbsp. soy sauce
- 1 tsp. rosemary; dried
- 1 tbsp. fresh rosemary; chopped.
- Salt and black pepper to taste

Directions:

1. Heat up the butter in a pan that fits your air fryer over medium heat.
2. Add the onions, garlic, dried and fresh rosemary, stock, soy sauce, salt and pepper; stir and simmer for 2-3 minutes
3. Add the cornstarch mixture, whisk, cook for 2 minutes more and take off the heat
4. Add the chicken, toss gently and place the pan in the fryer; cook at 370°F for 20 minutes. Divide between plates and serve hot.

244. SESAME CHICKEN

Preparation Time: 30 minutes
Servings: 4

Ingredients:

- 2 lbs. chicken breasts; skinless, boneless and cubed
- 1/2 cup soy sauce
- 1/2 cup honey
- 1 tbsp. olive oil
- 2 tsp. sesame oil
- 1/4 tsp. red pepper flakes
- 1/2 cup yellow onion; chopped.
- 2 garlic cloves; minced
- 1 tbsp. sesame seeds; toasted
- Salt and black pepper to taste

Directions:

1. Heat up the oil in a pan that fits your air fryer oil over medium heat.
2. Add the chicken, toss and brown for 3 minutes

3. Add the onions, garlic, salt and pepper; stir and cook for 2 minutes more.
4. Add the soy sauce, sesame oil, honey and pepper flakes; toss well
5. Place the pan in the fryer and cook at 380°F for 15 minutes
6. Top with the sesame seeds and toss. Divide between plates and serve.

245. TURKEY WITH FIG SAUCE

Preparation Time: 40 minutes
Servings: 4

Ingredients:

- 2 turkey breasts; halved
- 1 shallot; chopped.
- 1 cup chicken stock
- 1/2 cup red wine
- 1 tbsp. olive oil
- 3 tbsp. butter; melted
- 1 tbsp. white flour
- 1/2 tsp. garlic powder
- 1/4 tsp. sweet paprika
- 4 tbsp. figs; chopped.
- Salt and black pepper to taste

Directions:

1. Heat up a pan with the olive oil and 1½ tbsp. of the butter over medium-high heat.
2. Add the shallots, stir and cook for 2 minutes
3. Add the garlic powder, paprika, stock, salt, pepper, wine and the figs; stir and cook for 7-8 minutes.
4. Next add the flour, stir well and cook the sauce for 1-2 minutes more; take off heat
5. Season the turkey with salt and pepper and drizzle the remaining 1½ tbsp. of butter over them
6. Place the turkey in your air fryer's basket and cook at 380°F for 15 minutes, flipping them halfway. Divide between plates, drizzle the sauce all over and serve.

246. DUCK BREAST AND POTATOES

Preparation Time: 40 minutes
Servings: 2

Ingredients:

- 1 duck breast; halved and scored
- 1 oz. red wine
- 2 tbsp. butter; melted
- 2 gold potatoes; cubed
- Salt and black pepper to taste

Directions:

1. Season the duck pieces with salt and pepper, put them in a pan and heat up over medium-high heat.
2. Cook for 4 minutes on each side, transfer to your air fryer's basket and cook at 360°F for 8 minutes
3. Put the butter in a pan and heat it up over medium heat; then add the potatoes, salt, pepper and the wine and cook for 8 minutes
4. Add the duck pieces, toss and cook everything for 3-4 minutes more. Divide all between plates and serve.

247. CAJUN CHICKEN AND OKRA

Preparation Time: 40 minutes
Servings: 4

Ingredients:

- 1 lb. chicken thighs; halved
- 1/2 lb. okra
- 1 red bell pepper; chopped.
- 1 yellow onion; chopped.
- 1 cup chicken stock
- 1 tbsp. Cajun spice
- 4 garlic cloves; minced
- 1 tbsp. olive oil
- Salt and black pepper to taste

Directions:

1. Add the oil to a pan that fits your air fryer and heat up over medium heat.
2. Then add the chicken and brown for 2-3 minutes
3. Next, add all remaining ingredients, toss and cook for 3-4 minutes more
4. Place the pan into the air fryer and cook at 380°F for 22 minutes. Divide everything between plates and serve.

248. CHICKEN AND BEER

Preparation Time: 40 minutes
Servings: 4

Ingredients:

- 15 oz. beer
- 1 yellow onion; minced
- 1 chili pepper; chopped.
- 2 tbsp. olive oil
- 4 chicken drumsticks
- 1 tbsp. balsamic vinegar
- Salt and black pepper to taste

Directions:

1. Put the oil in a pan that fits your air fryer and heat up over medium heat.
2. Add the onion and the chili pepper, stir and cook for 2 minutes
3. Add the vinegar, beer, salt and pepper; stir and cook for 3 more minutes
4. Add the chicken, toss and put the pan in the fryer and cook at 370°F for 20 minutes. Divide everything between plates and serve.

249. TURKEY MEATBALLS

Preparation Time: 25 minutes
Servings: 8

Ingredients:

- 1 lb. turkey meat; ground
- 1/4 cup parsley; chopped.
- 1/4 cup milk
- 1/2 cup panko breadcrumbs
- 1 tsp. fish sauce
- 1 tsp. oregano; dried
- 1 egg; whisked
- 1/4 cup parmesan cheese; grated
- 1 yellow onion; minced
- 4 garlic cloves; minced
- 2 tsp. soy sauce
- Cooking spray
- Salt and black pepper to taste

Directions:

1. In a bowl, mix together all of the ingredients -except the cooking spray, stir well and then shape into medium-sized meatballs
2. Place the meatballs in your air fryer's basket, grease them with cooking spray and cook at 380°F for 15 minutes. Serve the meatballs with a side salad

250. CHICKEN AND BABY CARROTS

Preparation Time: 35 minutes
Servings: 4

Ingredients:

- 6 chicken thighs
- 1/2 lb. baby carrots; halved
- 15 oz. canned tomatoes; chopped.
- 1 cup chicken stock
- 1 yellow onion; chopped.
- 1 tsp. olive oil
- 1/2 tsp. thyme; dried
- 1/2 cup white wine
- 2 tbsp. tomato paste
- Salt and black pepper to taste

Directions:

1. Put the oil into a pan that fits your air fryer and heat up over medium heat.
2. Add the chicken thighs and brown them for 1-2 minutes on each side
3. Add all the remaining ingredients, toss and cook for 4-5 minutes more
4. Place the pan in the air fryer and cook at 380°F for 22 minutes. Divide the chicken and carrots mix between plates and serve.

251. BALSAMIC CHICKEN

Preparation Time: 30 minutes
Servings: 4

Ingredients:

- 4 chicken breasts; skinless and boneless
- 1 yellow onion; minced
- 1/4 cup cheddar cheese; grated
- 1/4 tsp. garlic powder
- 1/4 cup balsamic vinegar
- 12 oz. canned tomatoes; chopped.
- Salt and black pepper to taste

Directions:

1. In a baking dish that fits your air fryer, mix the chicken with the onions, vinegar, tomatoes, salt, pepper and garlic powder
2. Sprinkle the cheese on top and place the pan in the air fryer; cook at 400°F for 20 minutes. Divide between plates and serve.

252. CHICKEN CURRY

Preparation Time: 40 minutes
Servings: 4

Ingredients:

- 15 oz. chicken breast; skinless, boneless, cubed
- 6 potatoes; peeled and cubed
- 5 oz. heavy cream
- 1/2 bunch coriander; chopped
- 1 yellow onion; sliced
- 1 tbsp. olive oil
- 1 tsp. curry powder
- Salt and black pepper to taste

Directions:

1. Heat up the oil in a pan that fits your air fryer over medium heat.
2. Add the chicken, toss and brown for 2 minutes
3. Then add the onions, curry powder, salt and pepper; toss and cook for 3 minutes.
4. Next add the potatoes and the cream; toss well
5. Place the pan in the air fryer and cook at 370°F for 20 minutes
6. Add the coriander and stir. Divide the curry into bowls and serve.

253. ASIAN ATYLE CHICKEN

Preparation Time: 40 minutes
Servings: 4

Ingredients:

- 1 lb. spinach; chopped.
- 1½ lbs. chicken drumsticks
- 15 oz. canned tomatoes; crushed
- 1/4 cup lemon juice
- 1/2 cup chicken stock
- 1/2 cup heavy cream
- 1/2 cup cilantro; chopped.
- 4 garlic cloves; minced

- 1 yellow onion; chopped.
- 2 tbsp. butter; melted
- 1 tbsp. ginger; grated
- 1½ tsp. coriander; ground
- 1½ tsp. paprika
- 1 tsp. turmeric powder
- Salt and black pepper to taste

Directions:

1. Place the butter in a pan that fits your air fryer and heat over medium heat.
2. Add the onions and the garlic, stir and cook for 3 minutes
3. Add the ginger, paprika, coriander, turmeric, salt, pepper and the chicken; toss and cook for 4 minutes more.
4. Add the tomatoes and the stock and stir
5. Place the pan in the fryer and cook at 370°F for 15 minutes
6. Add the spinach, lemon juice, cilantro and the cream; stir and cook for 5-6 minutes more. Divide everything into bowls and serve.

254. LEMONGRASS CHICKEN

Preparation Time: 40 minutes
Servings: 4

Ingredients:

- 10 chicken drumsticks
- 1 cup coconut milk
- 1 bunch lemongrass; trimmed
- 1/4 cup parsley; chopped.
- 1 yellow onion; chopped.
- 2 tbsp. fish sauce
- 3 tbsp. soy sauce
- 1 tsp. butter; melted
- 1 tbsp. ginger; chopped.
- 4 garlic cloves; minced
- 1 tbsp. lemon juice
- Salt and black pepper to taste

Directions:

1. In a blender, combine the lemongrass, ginger, garlic, soy sauce, fish sauce and coconut milk; pulse well.
2. Put the butter in a pan that fits your air fryer and heat it up over medium heat; add

the onions, stir and cook for 2-3 minutes

3. Add the chicken, salt, pepper and the lemongrass mix; toss well
4. Place the pan in the fryer and cook at 380°F for 25 minutes
5. Add the lemon juice and the parsley and toss. Divide everything between plates and serve.

255. CHICKEN AND CHICKPEAS

Preparation Time: 35 minutes
Servings: 4

Ingredients:

- 2 lbs. chicken thighs; boneless
- 8 oz. canned chickpeas; drained
- 5 oz. bacon; cooked and crumbled
- 1 cup chicken stock
- 1 tsp. balsamic vinegar
- 2 tbsp. olive oil
- 1 cup yellow onion; chopped.
- 2 carrots; chopped.
- 1 tbsp. parsley; chopped.
- Salt and black pepper to taste

Directions:

1. Heat up a pan that fits your air fryer with the oil over medium heat.
2. Add the onions, carrots, salt and pepper; stir and sauté for 3-4 minutes.
3. Add the chicken, stock, vinegar and chickpeas; then toss
4. Place the pan in the fryer and cook at 380°F for 20 minutes
5. Add the bacon and the parsley and toss again. Divide everything between plates and serve.

MEAT

256. PORK WITH COUSCOUS RECIPE

Preparation Time: 45 Minutes
Servings: 6

Ingredients:

- 2 ½ lbs. pork loin; boneless and trimmed
- 2 ¼ tsp. sage; dried
- 3/4 cup chicken stock
- 1/2 tbsp. sweet paprika
- 1/2 tbsp. garlic powder
- 1/4 tsp. marjoram; dried
- 1/4 tsp. rosemary; dried
- 1 tsp. basil; dried
- 2 tbsp. olive oil
- 2 cups couscous; cooked
- 1 tsp. oregano; dried
- Salt and black pepper to the taste

Directions:

1. In a bowl; mix oil with stock, paprika, garlic powder, sage, rosemary, thyme, marjoram, oregano, salt and pepper to the taste, whisk well, add pork loin, toss well and leave aside for 1 hour.
2. Transfer everything to a pan that fits your air fryer and cook at 370 °F, for 35 minutes. Divide among plates and serve with couscous on the side.

Nutrition Values: Calories: 310; Fat: 4; Fiber: 6; Carbs: 37; Protein: 34

257. CREAMY PORK RECIPE

Preparation Time: 32 Minutes
Servings: 6

Ingredients:

- 2 lbs. pork meat; boneless and cubed
- 2 yellow onions; chopped.
- 2 tbsp. dill; chopped.
- 2 tbsp. sweet paprika
- 1 tbsp. olive oil
- 1 garlic clove; minced

- 3 cups chicken stock
- 2 tbsp. white flour
- 1 ½ cups sour cream
- Salt and black pepper to the taste

Directions:

1. In a pan that fits your air fryer, mix pork with salt, pepper and oil, toss, introduce in your air fryer and cook at 360 °F, for 7 minutes.
2. Add onion, garlic, stock, paprika, flour, sour cream and dill, toss and cook at 370 °F, for 15 minutes more. Divide everything on plates and serve right away.

Nutrition Values: Calories: 300; Fat: 4; Fiber: 10; Carbs: 26; Protein: 34

258. LAMB ROAST AND POTATOES RECIPE

Preparation Time: 55 Minutes
Servings: 6

Ingredients:

- 4 lbs. lamb roast
- 4 bay leaves
- 3 garlic cloves; minced
- 1 spring rosemary
- 6 potatoes; halved
- 1/2 cup lamb stock
- Salt and black pepper to the taste

Directions:

1. Put potatoes in a dish that fits your air fryer, add lamb, garlic, rosemary spring, salt, pepper, bay leaves and stock, toss, introduce in your air fryer and cook at 360 °F, for 45 minutes. Slice lamb, divide among plates and serve with potatoes and cooking juices.

Nutrition Values: Calories: 273; Fat: 4; Fiber: 12; Carbs: 25; Protein: 29

259. CHINESE STEAK AND BROCCOLI RECIPE

Preparation Time: 57 Minutes
Servings: 4

Ingredients:

- 3/4 lb. round steak; cut into strips
- 1 lb. broccoli florets
- 1 tsp. sugar
- 1/3 cup sherry
- 1/3 cup oyster sauce
- 1 tbsp. olive oil
- 1 garlic clove; minced
- 2 tsp. sesame oil
- 1 tsp. soy sauce

Directions:

1. In a bowl; mix sesame oil with oyster sauce, soy sauce, sherry and sugar; stir well, add beef, toss and leave aside for 30 minutes.
2. Transfer beef to a pan that fits your air fryer, also add broccoli, garlic and oil, toss everything and cook at 380 °F, for 12 minutes. Divide among plates and serve.

Nutrition Values: Calories: 330; Fat: 12; Fiber: 7; Carbs: 23; Protein: 23

260. BEEF FILLETS WITH GARLIC MAYO RECIPE

Preparation Time: 50 Minutes
Servings: 8

Ingredients:

- 3 lbs. beef fillet
- 1 cup mayonnaise
- 1/3 cup sour cream
- 2 tbsp. chives; chopped
- 2 tbsp. mustard
- 2 tbsp. mustard
- 1/4 cup tarragon; chopped
- 2 garlic cloves; minced
- Salt and black pepper to the taste

Directions:

1. Season beef with salt and pepper to the taste, place in your air fryer, cook at 370 °F, for 20 minutes; transfer to a plate and leave aside for a few minutes.
2. In a bowl; mix garlic with sour cream, chives, mayo, some salt and pepper, whisk and leave aside.
3. In another bowl, mix mustard with Dijon mustard and tarragon, whisk, add beef, toss, return to your air fryer and cook at 350 °F, for 20 minutes more. Divide beef on plates, spread garlic mayo on top and serve.

Nutrition Values: Calories: 400; Fat: 12; Fiber: 2; Carbs: 27; Protein: 19

261. SIMPLE BRAISED PORK RECIPE

Preparation Time: 1 hour 20 Minutes
Servings: 4

Ingredients:

- 2 lbs. pork loin roast; boneless and cubed
- 4 tbsp. butter; melted
- 2 cups chicken stock
- 1/2 lb. red grapes
- 1 bay leaf
- 1/2 yellow onion; chopped.
- 1/2 cup dry white wine
- 2 garlic cloves; minced
- 1 tsp. thyme; chopped
- 1 thyme spring
- 2 tbsp. white flour
- Salt and black pepper to the taste

Directions:

1. Season pork cubes with salt and pepper, rub with 2 tbsp. melted butter, put in your air fryer and cook at 370 °F, for 8 minutes.
2. Meanwhile; heat up a pan that fits your air fryer with 2 tbsp. butter over medium high heat, add garlic and onion; stir and cook for 2 minutes.
3. Add wine, stock, salt, pepper, thyme, flour and bay leaf; stir well, bring to a simmer and take off heat.
4. Add pork cubes and grapes, toss, introduce in your air fryer and cook at 360 °F, for 30 minutes more.
5. Divide everything on plates and serve.

Nutrition Values: Calories: 320; Fat: 4; Fiber: 5; Carbs: 29; Protein: 38

262. LAMB AND LEMON SAUCE RECIPE

Preparation Time: 40 Minutes
Servings: 4

Ingredients:

- 2 lamb shanks
- 2 garlic cloves; minced
- 4 tbsp. olive oil
- Juice from 1/2 lemon
- Zest from 1/2 lemon
- 1/2 tsp. oregano; dried
- Salt and black pepper to the taste

Directions:

1. Season lamb with salt, pepper, rub with garlic, put in your air fryer and cook at 350 °F, for 30 minutes.
2. Meanwhile; in a bowl, mix lemon juice with lemon zest, some salt and pepper, the olive oil and oregano and whisk very well. Shred lamb, discard bone, divide among plates, drizzle the lemon dressing all over and serve.

Nutrition Values: Calories: 260; Fat: 7; Fiber: 3; Carbs: 15; Protein: 12

263. PROVENCAL PORK RECIPE

Preparation Time: 25 Minutes
Servings: 2

Ingredients:

- 7 oz. pork tenderloin
- 1 red onion; sliced
- 1 yellow bell pepper; cut into strips
- 2 tsp. Provencal herbs
- 1/2 tbsp. mustard
- 1 tbsp. olive oil
- 1 green bell pepper; cut into strips
- Salt and black pepper to the taste

Directions:

1. In a baking dish that fits your air fryer, mix yellow bell pepper with green bell pepper, onion, salt, pepper, Provencal herbs and half of the oil and toss well.
2. Season pork with salt, pepper, mustard and the rest of the oil, toss well and add to

veggies. Introduce everything in your air fryer,
3. Cook at 370 °F, for 15 minutes; divide among plates and serve.

Nutrition Values: Calories: 300; Fat: 8; Fiber: 7; Carbs: 21; Protein: 23

264. LEMONY LAMB LEG RECIPE

Preparation Time: 1 hour 10 Minutes
Servings: 6

Ingredients:

- 4 lbs. lamb leg
- 2 tbsp. olive oil
- 2 springs rosemary; chopped.
- 2 tbsp. lemon juice
- 2 lbs. baby potatoes
- 1 cup beef stock
- 2 tbsp. parsley; chopped
- 2 tbsp. oregano; chopped
- 1 tbsp. lemon rind; grated
- 3 garlic cloves; minced
- Salt and black pepper to the taste

Directions:

1. Make small cuts all over lamb, insert rosemary springs and season with salt and pepper.
2. In a bowl; mix 1 tbsp. oil with oregano, parsley, garlic, lemon juice and rind; stir and rub lamb with this mix.
3. Heat up a pan that fits your air fryer with the rest of the oil over medium high heat, add potatoes; stir and cook for 3 minutes.
4. Add lamb and stock; stir, introduce in your air fryer and cook at 360 °F, for 1 hour. Divide everything on plates and serve.

Nutrition Values: Calories: 264; Fat: 4; Fiber: 12; Carbs: 27; Protein: 32

265. BEEF ROAST AND WINE SAUCE RECIPE

Preparation Time: 55 Minutes
Servings: 6

Ingredients:

- 3 lbs. beef roast

- 17 oz. beef stock
- 4 garlic cloves; minced
- 3 carrots; chopped
- 5 potatoes; chopped
- 3 oz. red wine
- 1/2 tsp. chicken salt
- Salt and black pepper to the taste
- 1/2 tsp. smoked paprika
- 1 yellow onion; chopped

Directions:

1. In a bowl; mix salt, pepper, chicken salt and paprika; stir, rub beef with this mix and put it in a big pan that fits your air fryer.
2. Add onion, garlic, stock, wine, potatoes and carrots, introduce in your air fryer and cook at 360 °F, for 45 minutes. Divide everything on plates and serve.

Nutrition Values: Calories: 304; Fat: 20; Fiber: 7; Carbs: 20; Protein: 32

266. FENNEL FLAVORED PORK ROAST RECIPE

Preparation Time: 1 hour 10 Minutes
Servings: 10

Ingredients:

- 5 ½ lbs. pork loin roast; trimmed
- 1 tbsp. fennel seeds
- 2 tsp. red pepper; crushed
- 1/4 cup olive oil
- 3 garlic cloves; minced
- 2 tbsp. rosemary; chopped.
- 1 tsp. fennel; ground
- Salt and black pepper to the taste

Directions:

1. In your food processor mix garlic with fennel seeds, fennel, rosemary, red pepper, some black pepper and the olive oil and blend until you obtain a paste.
2. Spread 2 tbsp. garlic paste on pork loin, rub well, season with salt and pepper, introduce in your preheated air fryer and cook at 350 °F, for 30 minutes.
3. Reduce heat to 300 °F and cook for 15 minutes more. Slice pork, divide among

plates and serve.

Nutrition Values: Calories: 300; Fat: 14; Fiber: 9; Carbs: 26; Protein: 22

267. BEEF BRISKET AND ONION SAUCE RECIPE

Preparation Time: 2 hours 10 Minutes
Servings: 6

Ingredients:

- 1 lb. yellow onion; chopped
- 4 lbs. beef brisket
- 8 earl grey tea bags
- 1/2 lb. celery; chopped.
- 1 lb. carrot; chopped
- Salt and black pepper to the taste
- 4 cups water

For the sauce:

- 16 oz. canned tomatoes; chopped
- 1 lb. sweet onion; chopped
- 1 cup brown sugar
- 8 earl grey tea bags
- 1/2 lb. celery; chopped
- 1 oz. garlic; minced
- 4 oz. vegetable oil
- 1 cup white vinegar

Directions:

1. Put the water in a heat proof dish that fits your air fryer, add 1 lb. onion, 1 lb. carrot, 1/2 lb. celery, salt and pepper; stir and bring to a simmer over medium high heat.
2. Add beef brisket and 8 tea bags; stir, transfer to your air fryer and cook at 300 °F, for 1 hour and 30 minutes.
3. Meanwhile; heat up a pan with the vegetable oil over medium high heat, add 1 lb. onion; stir and sauté for 10 minutes.
4. Add garlic, 1/2 lb. celery, tomatoes, sugar, vinegar, salt, pepper and 8 tea bags; stir, bring to a simmer, cook for 10 minutes and discard tea bags. Transfer beef brisket to a cutting board, slice, divide among plates, drizzle onion sauce all over and serve.

Nutrition Values: Calories: 400; Fat: 12; Fiber: 4; Carbs: 38; Protein: 34

268. LAMB SHANKS AND CARROTS RECIPE

Preparation Time: 55 Minutes
Servings: 4

Ingredients:

- 4 lamb shanks
- 2 tbsp. olive oil
- 1 yellow onion; finely chopped.
- 1 tsp. oregano; dried
- 1 tomato; roughly chopped.
- 2 tbsp. water
- 4 oz. red wine
- 6 carrots; roughly chopped.
- 2 garlic cloves; minced
- 2 tbsp. tomato paste
- Salt and black pepper to the taste

Directions:

1. Season lamb with salt and pepper, rub with oil, put in your air fryer and cook at 360 °F, for 10 minutes.
2. In a pan that fits your air fryer, mix onion with carrots, garlic, tomato paste, tomato, oregano, wine and water and toss.
3. Add lamb, toss, introduce in your air fryer and cook at 370 °F, for 35 minutes. Divide everything on plates and serve.

Nutrition Values: Calories: 432; Fat: 17; Fiber: 8; Carbs: 17; Protein: 43

269. MARINATED PORK CHOPS AND ONIONS RECIPE

Preparation Time: 24 hours 25 Minutes
Servings: 6

Ingredients:

- 2 pork chops
- 1/2 tsp. oregano; dried
- 1/2 tsp. thyme; dried
- 1/4 cup olive oil
- 2 yellow onions; sliced
- 2 garlic cloves; minced
- 2 tsp. mustard
- 1 tsp. sweet paprika
- A pinch of cayenne pepper

- Salt and black pepper to the taste

Directions:

1. In a bowl; mix oil with garlic, mustard, paprika, black pepper, oregano, thyme and cayenne and whisk well.
2. Combine onions with meat and mustard mix, toss to coat, cover and keep in the fridge for 1 day.
3. Transfer meat and onions mix to a pan that fits your air fryer and cook at 360 °F, for 25 minutes.
4. Divide everything on plates and serve.

Nutrition Values: Calories: 384; Fat: 4; Fiber: 4; Carbs: 17; Protein: 25

270. BEEF AND GREEN ONIONS MARINADE RECIPE

Preparation Time: 30 Minutes
Servings: 4

Ingredients:

- 1 cup green onion; chopped
- 1 cup soy sauce
- 1/2 cup water
- 1/4 cup sesame seeds
- 5 garlic cloves; minced
- 1 tsp. black pepper
- 1/4 cup brown sugar
- 1 lb. lean beef

Directions:

1. In a bowl; mix onion with soy sauce, water, sugar, garlic, sesame seeds and pepper, whisk, add meat, toss and leave aside for 10 minutes.
2. Drain beef, transfer to your preheated air fryer and cook at 390 °F, for 20 minutes. Slice, divide among plates and serve with a side salad.

Nutrition Values: Calories: 329; Fat: 8; Fiber: 12; Carbs: 26; Protein: 22

271. RIB EYE STEAK RECIPE

Preparation Time: 30 Minutes
Servings: 4

Ingredients:

- 2 lbs. rib eye steak
- Salt and black pepper to the taste
- 1 tbsp. olive oil

For the rub:

- 3 tbsp. sweet paprika
- 1 tbsp. brown sugar
- 1 tbsp. cumin; ground
- 2 tbsp. onion powder
- 2 tbsp. oregano; dried
- 2 tbsp. garlic powder
- 1 tbsp. rosemary; dried

Directions:

1. In a bowl; mix paprika with onion and garlic powder, sugar, oregano, rosemary, salt, pepper and cumin; stir and rub steak with this mix.
2. Season steak with salt and pepper, rub again with the oil, put in your air fryer and cook at 400 °F, for 20 minutes; flipping them halfway. Transfer steak to a cutting board, slice and serve with a side salad.

Nutrition Values: Calories: 320; Fat: 8; Fiber: 7; Carbs: 22; Protein: 21

272. BEEF STRIPS WITH SNOW PEAS AND MUSHROOMS RECIPE

Preparation Time: 32 Minutes
Servings: 2

Ingredients:

- 7 oz. snow peas
- 2 tbsp. soy sauce
- 2 beef steaks; cut into strips
- 8 oz. white mushrooms; halved
- 1 yellow onion; cut into rings
- 1 tsp. olive oil
- Salt and black pepper to the taste

Directions:

1. In a bowl; mix olive oil with soy sauce, whisk, add beef strips and toss.
2. In another bowl, mix snow peas, onion and mushrooms with salt, pepper and the oil, toss well, put in a pan that fits your air fryer and cook at 350 °F, for 16 minutes.
3. Add beef strips to the pan as well and cook at 400 °F, for 6 minutes more.

4. Divide everything on plates and serve.

Nutrition Values: Calories: 235; Fat: 8; Fiber: 2; Carbs: 22; Protein: 24

273. ORIENTAL FRIED LAMB RECIPE

Preparation Time: 52 Minutes
Servings: 8

Ingredients:

- 2 ½ lbs. lamb shoulder; chopped.
- 3 tbsp. honey
- 3 oz. almonds; peeled and chopped.
- 9 oz. plumps; pitted
- 8 oz. veggie stock
- 2 yellow onions; chopped
- 2 garlic cloves; minced
- 1 tsp. cumin powder
- 1 tsp. turmeric powder
- 1 tsp. ginger powder
- 1 tsp. cinnamon powder
- Salt and black pepper to the tastes
- 3 tbsp. olive oil

Directions:

1. In a bowl; mix cinnamon powder with ginger, cumin, turmeric, garlic, olive oil and lamb, toss to coat, place in your preheated air fryer and cook at 350 °F, for 8 minutes.
2. Transfer meat to a dish that fits your air fryer, add onions, stock, honey and plums; stir, introduce in your air fryer and cook at 350 °F, for 35 minutes. Divide everything on plates and serve with almond sprinkled on top.

Nutrition Values: Calories: 432; Fat: 23; Fiber: 6; Carbs: 30; Protein: 20

274. GREEK BEEF MEATBALLS SALAD RECIPE

Preparation Time: 20 Minutes
Servings: 6

Ingredients:

- 17 oz. beef; ground
- 1 yellow onion; grated

- 5 bread slices; cubed
- 2 garlic cloves; minced
- 1/4 cup mint; chopped.
- 2 ½ tsp. oregano; dried
- 1/4 cup milk
- 1 egg; whisked
- 1/4 cup parsley; chopped.
- Salt and black pepper to the taste
- 1 tbsp. olive oil
- 7 oz. cherry tomatoes; halved
- 1 cup baby spinach
- 1 ½ tbsp. lemon juice
- 7 oz. Greek yogurt
- Cooking spray

Directions:

1. Put torn bread In a bowl; add milk, soak for a few minutes; squeeze and transfer to another bowl.
2. Add beef, egg, salt, pepper, oregano, mint, parsley, garlic and onion; stir and shape medium meatballs out of this mix.
3. Spray them with cooking spray, place them in your air fryer and cook at 370 °F, for 10 minutes.
4. In a salad bowl, mix spinach with cucumber and tomato. Add meatballs, the oil, some salt, pepper, lemon juice and yogurt, toss and serve.

Nutrition Values: Calories: 200; Fat: 4; Fiber: 8; Carbs: 13; Protein: 27

275.BEEF AND CABBAGE MIX RECIPE

Preparation Time: 50 Minutes
Servings: 6

Ingredients:

- 2 ½ lbs. beef brisket
- 1 cup beef stock
- 3 garlic cloves; chopped
- 4 carrots; chopped
- 2 bay leaves
- 1 cabbage head; cut into medium wedges
- 3 turnips; cut into quarters
- Salt and black pepper to the taste

Directions:

1. Put beef brisket and stock in a large pan that fits your air fryer, season beef with salt and pepper, add garlic and bay leaves, carrots, cabbage, potatoes and turnips, toss, introduce in your air fryer and cook at 360 °F and cook for 40 minutes. Divide among plates and serve.

Nutrition Values: Calories: 353; Fat: 16; Fiber: 7; Carbs: 20; Protein: 24

276. PORK CHOPS AND GREEN BEANS RECIPE

Preparation Time: 25 Minutes
Servings: 4

Ingredients:

- 4 pork chops; bone in
- 2 tbsp. olive oil
- 16 oz. green beans
- 3 garlic cloves; minced
- 2 tbsp. parsley; chopped
- 1 tbsp. sage; chopped
- Salt and black pepper to the taste

Directions:

1. In a pan that fits your air fryer, mix pork chops with olive oil, sage, salt, pepper, green beans, garlic and parsley, toss, introduce in your air fryer and cook at 360 °F, for 15 minutes
2. Divide everything on plates and serve

Nutrition Values: Calories: 261; Fat: 7; Fiber: 9; Carbs: 14; Protein: 20

277. ASIAN PORK RECIPE

Preparation Time: 45 Minutes
Servings: 4

Ingredients:

- 1 tsp. ginger powder
- 2 tsp. chili paste
- 2 garlic cloves; minced
- 2 tbsp. olive oil
- 3 oz. peanuts; ground
- 3 tbsp. soy sauce
- 1 shallot; chopped

- 1 tsp. coriander; ground
- 14 oz. pork chops; cubed
- 7 oz. coconut milk
- Salt and black pepper to the taste

Directions:

1. In a bowl; mix ginger with 1 tsp. chili paste, half of the garlic, half of the soy sauce and half of the oil, whisk, add meat, toss and leave aside for 10 minutes.
2. Transfer meat to your air fryer's basket and cook at 400 °F, for 12 minutes; turning halfway.
3. Meanwhile; heat up a pan with the rest of the oil over medium high heat, add shallot, the rest of the garlic, coriander, coconut milk, the rest of the peanuts, the rest of the chili paste and the rest of the soy sauce; stir and cook for 5 minutes. Divide pork on plates, spread coconut mix on top and serve.

Nutrition Values: Calories: 423; Fat: 11; Fiber: 4; Carbs: 42; Protein: 18

278. SPICED PORK CHOPS

Preparation time: 5 minutes
Cooking time: 15 minutes
Servings: 4

Ingredients:

- 4 medium pork chops
- Salt and black pepper to taste
- 1 tablespoon olive oil
- 2 tablespoons sweet paprika
- 2 tablespoons onion powder
- 2 tablespoons garlic powder
- 2 tablespoons oregano, dried
- 1 tablespoon cumin, ground
- 1 tablespoon rosemary, dried

Directions:

1. In a bowl, mix all of the ingredients and rub the pork chops well.
2. Put the pork chops in your air fryer's basket and cook at 400 degrees F for 15 minutes, flipping them halfway.
3. Divide between plates, serve, and enjoy.

Nutrition Values: calories 281, fat 8, fiber 7,

carbs 17, protein 19

279. CHINESE PORK AND BROCCOLI MIX

Preparation time: 5 minutes
Cooking time: 15 minutes
Servings: 4

Ingredients:

- 1 pound pork stew meat, cut into strips
- 1 pound broccoli florets
- ⅓ cup oyster sauce
- 2 teaspoons olive oil
- 1 teaspoon soy sauce
- 1 garlic clove, minced

Directions:

1. In a bowl, mix the pork with all the other ingredients and toss well.
2. Put the mixture into your air fryer and cook at 390 degrees F for 15 minutes.
3. Divide into bowls and serve.

Nutrition Values: calories 281, fat 12, fiber 7, carbs 19, protein 20

280. FRENCH BEEF MIX

Preparation time: 5 minutes
Cooking time: 15 minutes
Servings: 2

Ingredients:

- 1 red onion, sliced
- 1 green bell pepper, cut in strips
- Salt and black pepper to taste
- 2 teaspoons Provencal herbs
- ½ tablespoon mustard
- 1 tablespoon olive oil
- 7 ounces beef fillets, cut into strips

Directions:

1. Place all the ingredients in a baking dish that fits your air fryer and mix well.
2. Put the pan in the fryer and cook at 400 degrees F for 15 minutes.
3. Divide the mixture between bowls and serve.

Nutrition Values: calories 291, fat 8, fiber 7, carbs 19, protein 20

281. BEEF AND MUSHROOM MIX

Preparation time: 5 minutes
Cooking time: 17 minutes
Servings: 2

Ingredients:

- 2 beef steaks, cut into strips
- Salt and black pepper to taste
- 8 ounces white mushrooms, sliced
- 1 yellow onion, chopped
- 2 tablespoons dark soy sauce
- 1 teaspoon olive oil

Directions:

1. In a baking dish that fits your air fryer, combine all ingredients; toss well.
2. Place the pan in the fryer and cook at 390 degrees F for 17 minutes.
3. Divide everything between plates and serve.

Nutrition Values: calories 285, fat 8, fiber 2, carbs 18, protein 20

282. OREGANO PORK CHOPS

Preparation time: 5 minutes
Cooking time: 15 minutes
Servings: 4

Ingredients:

- 2 tablespoons olive oil
- 4 pork chops
- Salt and black pepper to taste
- 4 garlic cloves, minced
- 2 tablespoon oregano, chopped

Directions:

1. Place all of the ingredients in a bowl and toss / mix well.
2. Transfer the chops to your air fryer's basket and cook at 400 degrees F for 15 minutes.
3. Serve with a side salad and enjoy!

Nutrition Values: calories 301, fat 7, fiber 5, carbs 19, protein 22

283. CRUSTED RACK OF LAMB

Preparation time: 10 minutes
Cooking time: 20 minutes

Servings: 4

Ingredients:

- 2 tablespoons macadamia nuts, toasted and crushed
- 1 tablespoon vegetable oil
- 2 garlic cloves, minced
- 28 ounces rack of lamb
- Salt and black pepper to taste
- 1 egg, whisked
- 1 tablespoon oregano, chopped

Directions:

1. In a bowl, mix the lamb with the salt, pepper, garlic, and the oil; rub the lamb well.
2. In another bowl, mix the macadamia nuts with the oregano, salt, and pepper; stir.
3. Put the egg in a third bowl.
4. Dredge the lamb in the egg, then in the macadamia nuts mix.
5. Place the lamb in your air fryer's basket and cook at 380 degrees F for 10 minutes on each side.
6. Divide between plates and serve with a side salad.

Nutrition Values: calories 280, fat 12, fiber 8, carbs 20, protein 19

284. COCONUT PORK MIX

Preparation time: 5 minutes
Cooking time: 15 minutes
Servings: 4

Ingredients:

- 1 teaspoon ginger, grated
- 2 teaspoons chili paste
- 2 garlic cloves, minced
- 14 ounces pork chops, cut into strips
- 1 shallot, chopped
- 7 ounces coconut milk
- 2 tablespoons olive oil
- 3 tablespoons soy sauce
- Salt and black pepper to taste

Directions:

1. In a baking dish that fits your air fryer, mix the pork with the ginger, chili paste, garlic, shallots, oil soy sauce, salt, and

pepper; toss well.

2. Place the pan in the fryer and cook at 400 degrees F for 12 minutes, shaking the fryer halfway.
3. Add the coconut milk, toss, and cook for 3-4 minutes more.
4. Divide everything into bowls and serve.

Nutrition Values: calories 283, fat 11, fiber 9, carbs 22, protein 14

285. CREAMY PORK AND SPROUTS

Preparation time: 10 minutes
Cooking time: 25 minutes
Servings: 4

Ingredients:

- 1 pound pork tenderloin, cubed
- 2 tablespoons olive oil
- 2 tablespoons rosemary, chopped
- Salt and black pepper to taste
- 1 garlic clove, minced
- 1½ pounds Brussels sprouts, trimmed
- ½ cup sour cream
- Salt and black pepper to taste

Directions:

1. In a pan that fits your air fryer, mix the pork with the oil, rosemary, salt, pepper, garlic, salt, and pepper; toss well.
2. Place the pan in the fryer and cook at 400 degrees F for 17 minutes.
3. Next add the sprouts and the sour cream and toss.
4. Place the pan in the fryer and cook for 8 more minutes.
5. Divide everything into bowls and serve.

Nutrition Values: calories 280, fat 13, fiber 9, carbs 22, protein 18

286. PORK AND CHIVES MIX

Preparation time: 10 minutes
Cooking time: 22 minutes
Servings: 6

Ingredients:

- 1 cup mayonnaise
- 2 garlic cloves, minced

- 1 pound pork tenderloin, cubed
- 2 tablespoons chives, chopped
- 2 tablespoons mustard
- ¼ cup tarragon, chopped
- Salt and black pepper to taste

Directions:

1. Place all ingredients except the mayo into a pan that fits your air fryer; mix well.
2. Put the pan in the fryer and cook at 400 degrees F for 15 minutes.
3. Add the mayo and toss.
4. Put the pan in the fryer for 7 more minutes.
5. Divide into bowls and serve.

Nutrition Values: calories 280, fat 12, fiber 2, carbs 17, protein 14

287. BEEF AND WINE SAUCE

Preparation time: 10 minutes
Cooking time: 40 minutes
Servings: 6

Ingredients:

- 2 tablespoons butter, melted
- 3 garlic cloves, minced
- Salt and black pepper to taste
- 1 tablespoon mustard
- 3 pounds beef roast
- 1¾ cups beef stock
- ¾ cup red wine

Directions:

1. In a bowl, mix the beef with the butter, mustard, garlic, salt, and pepper; rub the meat thoroughly.
2. Put the beef roast in your air fryer's basket and cook at 400 degrees F for 15 minutes.
3. Heat up a pan over medium-high heat and add the stock and the wine.
4. Then add the beef roast and place the pan in the fryer; cook at 380 degrees F for 25 minutes more.
5. Divide into bowls and serve.

Nutrition Values: calories 300, fat 11, fiber 4, carbs 18, protein 22

288. LAMB CHOPS AND DILL

Preparation time: 10 minutes
Cooking time: 20 minutes
Servings: 6

Ingredients:

- 1 pound lamb chops
- 2 yellow onions, chopped
- 1 tablespoon olive oil
- 1 garlic clove, minced
- 3 cups chicken stock
- 2 tablespoons sweet paprika
- Salt and black pepper to taste
- 1½ cups heavy cream
- 2 tablespoons dill, chopped

Directions:

1. Put the lamb chops in your air fryer and season with the salt, pepper, garlic, and paprika; rub the chops thoroughly.
2. Cook at 380 degrees F for 10 minutes.
3. Transfer the lamb to a baking dish that fits your air fryer. Then add the onions, stock, cream, and dill, and toss.
4. Place the pan in the fryer and cook everything for 7-8 minutes more.
5. Divide everything between plates and serve hot.

Nutrition Values: calories 310, fat 8, fiber 10, carbs 19, protein 25

289. MUSTARD PORK CHOPS

Preparation time: 10 minutes
Cooking time: 15 minutes
Servings: 6

Ingredients:

- 2 pork chops
- ¼ cup olive oil
- 2 garlic cloves, minced
- 1 tablespoon mustard
- 1 teaspoon sweet paprika
- Salt and black pepper to taste

Directions:

1. Place all of the ingredients in a bowl, and coat the pork chops well.
2. Transfer the pork chops to your air fryer's basket and cook at 400 degrees F for 15 minutes.

3. Divide the chops between plates and serve

Nutrition Values: calories 284, fat 14, fiber 4, carbs 17, protein 28

290. FLAVORED RIB EYE STEAK

Preparation time: 10 minutes
Cooking time: 20 minutes
Servings: 4

Ingredients:

- 2 pounds rib eye steak
- Salt and black pepper to the taste
- 1 tablespoons olive oil

For the rub:

- 3 tablespoons sweet paprika
- 2 tablespoons onion powder
- 2 tablespoons garlic powder
- 1 tablespoon brown sugar
- 2 tablespoons oregano, dried
- 1 tablespoon cumin, ground
- 1 tablespoon rosemary, dried

Directions:

1. In a bowl, mix paprika with onion and garlic powder, sugar, oregano, rosemary, salt, pepper and cumin, stir and rub steak with this mix.
2. Season steak with salt and pepper, rub again with the oil, put in your air fryer and cook at 400 degrees F for 20 minutes, flipping them halfway.
3. Transfer steak to a cutting board, slice and serve with a side salad.
4. Enjoy!

Nutrition Values: calories 320, fat 8, fiber 7, carbs 22, protein 21

291. CHINESE STEAK AND BROCCOLI

Preparation time: 45 minutes
Cooking time: 12 minutes
Servings: 4

Ingredients:

- ¾ pound round steak, cut into strips
- 1 pound broccoli florets
- 1/3 cup oyster sauce
- 2 teaspoons sesame oil

- 1 teaspoon soy sauce
- 1 teaspoon sugar
- 1/3 cup sherry
- 1 tablespoon olive oil
- 1 garlic clove, minced

Directions:

1. In a bowl, mix sesame oil with oyster sauce, soy sauce, sherry and sugar, stir well, add beef, toss and leave aside for 30 minutes.
2. Transfer beef to a pan that fits your air fryer, also add broccoli, garlic and oil, toss everything and cook at 380 degrees F for 12 minutes.
3. Divide among plates and serve.
4. Enjoy!

Nutrition Values: calories 330, fat 12, fiber 7, carbs 23, protein 23

292. PROVENCAL PORK

Preparation time: 10 minutes
Cooking time: 15 minutes
Servings: 2

Ingredients:

- 1 red onion, sliced
- 1 yellow bell pepper, cut into strips
- 1 green bell pepper, cut into strips
- Salt and black pepper to the taste
- 2 teaspoons Provencal herbs
- ½ tablespoon mustard
- 1 tablespoon olive oil
- 7 ounces pork tenderloin

Directions:

1. In a baking dish that fits your air fryer, mix yellow bell pepper with green bell pepper, onion, salt, pepper, Provencal herbs and half of the oil and toss well.
2. Season pork with salt, pepper, mustard and the rest of the oil, toss well and add to veggies.
3. Introduce everything in your air fryer, cook at 370 degrees F for 15 minutes, divide among plates and serve.
4. Enjoy!

Nutrition Values: calories 300, fat 8, fiber 7,

carbs 21, protein 23

293. BEEF STRIPS WITH SNOW PEAS AND MUSHROOMS

Preparation time: 10 minutes
Cooking time: 22 minutes
Servings: 2

Ingredients:

- 2 beef steaks, cut into strips
- Salt and black pepper to the taste
- 7 ounces snow peas
- 8 ounces white mushrooms, halved
- 1 yellow onion, cut into rings
- 2 tablespoons soy sauce
- 1 teaspoon olive oil

Directions:

1. In a bowl, mix olive oil with soy sauce, whisk, add beef strips and toss.
2. In another bowl, mix snow peas, onion and mushrooms with salt, pepper and the oil, toss well, put in a pan that fits your air fryer and cook at 350 degrees F for 16 minutes.
3. Add beef strips to the pan as well and cook at 400 degrees F for 6 minutes more.
4. Divide everything on plates and serve.
5. Enjoy!

Nutrition Values: calories 235, fat 8, fiber 2, carbs 22, protein 24

294. GARLIC LAMB CHOPS

Preparation time: 10 minutes
Cooking time: 10 minutes
Servings: 4

Ingredients:

- 3 tablespoons olive oil
- 8 lamb chops
- Salt and black pepper to the taste
- 4 garlic cloves, minced
- 1 tablespoon oregano, chopped
- 1 tablespoon coriander, chopped

Directions:

1. In a bowl, mix oregano with salt, pepper, oil, garlic and lamb chops and toss to coat.

2. Transfer lamb chops to your air fryer and cook at 400 degrees F for 10 minutes.
3. Divide lamb chops on plates and serve with a side salad.
4. Enjoy!

Nutrition Values: calories 231, fat 7, fiber 5, carbs 14, protein 23

295. CRISPY LAMB

Preparation time: 10 minutes
Cooking time: 30 minutes
Servings: 4

Ingredients:

- 1 tablespoon bread crumbs
- 2 tablespoons macadamia nuts, toasted and crushed
- 1 tablespoon olive oil
- 1 garlic clove, minced
- 28 ounces rack of lamb
- Salt and black pepper to the taste
- 1 egg,
- 1 tablespoon rosemary, chopped

Directions:

1. In a bowl, mix oil with garlic and stir well.
2. Season lamb with salt, pepper and brush with the oil.
3. In another bowl, mix nuts with breadcrumbs and rosemary.
4. Put the egg in a separate bowl and whisk well.
5. Dip lamb in egg, then in macadamia mix, place them in your air fryer's basket, cook at 360 degrees F and cook for 25 minutes, increase heat to 400 degrees F and cook for 5 minutes more.
6. Divide among plates and serve right away.
7. Enjoy!

Nutrition Values: calories 230, fat 2, fiber 2, carbs 10, protein 12

296. INDIAN PORK

Preparation time: 35 minutes
Cooking time: 10 minutes
Servings: 4

Ingredients:

- 1 teaspoon ginger powder

- 2 teaspoons chili paste
- 2 garlic cloves, minced
- 14 ounces pork chops, cubed
- 1 shallot, chopped
- 1 teaspoon coriander, ground
- 7 ounces coconut milk
- 2 tablespoons olive oil
- 3 ounces peanuts, ground
- 3 tablespoons soy sauce
- Salt and black pepper to the taste

Directions:

1. In a bowl, mix ginger with 1 teaspoon chili paste, half of the garlic, half of the soy sauce and half of the oil, whisk, add meat, toss and leave aside for 10 minutes.
2. Transfer meat to your air fryer's basket and cook at 400 degrees F for 12 minutes, turning halfway.
3. Meanwhile, heat up a pan with the rest of the oil over medium high heat, add shallot, the rest of the garlic, coriander, coconut milk, the rest of the peanuts, the rest of the chili paste and the rest of the soy sauce, stir and cook for 5 minutes.
4. Divide pork on plates, spread coconut mix on top and serve.
5. Enjoy!

Nutrition Values: calories 423, fat 11, fiber 4, carbs 42, protein 18

297. LAMB AND CREAMY BRUSSELS SPROUTS

Preparation time: 10 minutes
Cooking time: 1 hour and 10 minutes
Servings: 4

Ingredients:

- 2 pounds leg of lamb, scored
- 2 tablespoons olive oil
- 1 tablespoon rosemary, chopped
- 1 tablespoon lemon thyme, chopped
- 1 garlic clove, minced
- 1 and ½ pounds Brussels sprouts, trimmed
- 1 tablespoon butter, melted
- ½ cup sour cream

- Salt and black pepper to the taste

Directions:

1. Season leg of lamb with salt, pepper, thyme and rosemary, brush with oil, place in your air fryer's basket, cook at 300 degrees F for 1 hour, transfer to a plate and keep warm.
2. In a pan that fits your air fryer, mix Brussels sprouts with salt, pepper, garlic, butter and sour cream, toss, put in your air fryer and cook at 400 degrees F for 10 minutes.
3. Divide lamb on plates, add Brussels sprouts on the side and serve.
4. Enjoy!

Nutrition Values: calories 440, fat 23, fiber 0, carbs 2, protein 49

298. BEEF FILLETS WITH GARLIC MAYO

Preparation time: 10 minutes
Cooking time: 40 minutes
Servings: 8

Ingredients:

- 1 cup mayonnaise
- 1/3 cup sour cream
- 2 garlic cloves, minced
- 3 pounds beef fillet
- 2 tablespoons chives, chopped
- 2 tablespoons mustard
- 2 tablespoons mustard
- ¼ cup tarragon, chopped
- Salt and black pepper to the taste

Directions:

1. Season beef with salt and pepper to the taste, place in your air fryer, cook at 370 degrees F for 20 minutes, transfer to a plate and leave aside for a few minutes.
2. In a bowl, mix garlic with sour cream, chives, mayo, some salt and pepper, whisk and leave aside.
3. In another bowl, mix mustard with Dijon mustard and tarragon, whisk, add beef, toss, return to your air fryer and cook at 350 degrees F for 20 minutes more.
4. Divide beef on plates, spread garlic mayo

on top and serve.
5. Enjoy!

Nutrition Values: calories 400, fat 12, fiber 2, carbs 27, protein 19

299. MUSTARD MARINATED BEEF

Preparation time: 10 minutes
Cooking time: 45 minutes
Servings: 6

Ingredients:

- 6 bacon strips
- 2 tablespoons butter
- 3 garlic cloves, minced
- Salt and black pepper to the taste
- 1 tablespoon horseradish
- 1 tablespoon mustard
- 3 pounds beef roast
- 1 and ¾ cup beef stock
- ¾ cup red wine

Directions:

1. In a bowl, mix butter with mustard, garlic, salt, pepper and horseradish, whisk and rub beef with this mix.
2. Arrange bacon strips on a cutting board, place beef on top, fold bacon around beef, transfer to your air fryer's basket, cook at 400 degrees F for 15 minutes and transfer to a pan that fits your fryer.
3. Add stock and wine to beef, introduce pan in your air fryer and cook at 360 degrees F for 30 minutes more.
4. Carve beef, divide among plates and serve with a side salad.
5. Enjoy!

Nutrition Values: calories 500, fat 9, fiber 4, carbs 29, protein 36

300. CREAMY PORK

Preparation time: 10 minutes
Cooking time: 22 minutes
Servings: 6

Ingredients:

- 2 pounds pork meat, boneless and cubed
- 2 yellow onions, chopped

- 1 tablespoon olive oil
- 1 garlic clove, minced
- 3 cups chicken stock
- 2 tablespoons sweet paprika
- Salt and black pepper to the taste
- 2 tablespoons white flour
- 1 and ½ cups sour cream
- 2 tablespoons dill, chopped

Directions:

1. In a pan that fits your air fryer, mix pork with salt, pepper and oil, toss, introduce in your air fryer and cook at 360 degrees F for 7 minutes.
2. Add onion, garlic, stock, paprika, flour, sour cream and dill, toss and cook at 370 degrees F for 15 minutes more.
3. Divide everything on plates and serve right away.
4. Enjoy!

Nutrition Values: calories 300, fat 4, fiber 10, carbs 26, protein 34

VEGETABLES

301. SPINACH AND CREAM CHEESE MIX

Preparation time: 5 minutes
Cooking time: 8 minutes
Servings: 4

Ingredients:

- 14 ounces baby spinach
- 1 tablespoon olive oil
- 2 tablespoons milk
- 3 ounces cream cheese, softened
- Salt and black pepper to taste
- 1 yellow onion, chopped

Directions:

1. In a pan that fits your air fryer, mix all ingredients and toss gently.
2. Place the pan in the air fryer and cook at 260 degrees F for 8 minutes.
3. Divide between plates and serve.

Nutrition Values: calories 190, fat 4, fiber 2, carbs 13, protein 9

302. BALSAMIC ASPARAGUS

Preparation time: 5 minutes
Cooking time: 5 minutes
Servings: 4

Ingredients:

- 1 asparagus bunch, trimmed and halved
- Salt and black pepper to taste
- 2 tablespoons lime juice
- 2 tablespoons olive oil
- 2 teaspoons balsamic vinegar
- 1 teaspoon oregano, dried

Directions:

1. In a bowl, combine all ingredients and toss.
2. Put the asparagus in your air fryer's basket and cook at 400 degrees F for 5 minutes.
3. Divide the asparagus between plates and serve.

Nutrition Values: calories 190, fat 3, fiber 6,

carbs 8, protein 4

303. CHEESY ASPARAGUS

Preparation time: 5 minutes
Cooking time: 6 minutes
Servings: 6

Ingredients:

- 14 ounces asparagus, trimmed
- 8 ounces cream cheese, softened
- 16 ounces cheddar cheese, grated
- ½ cup sour cream
- 3 garlic cloves, minced
- 1 teaspoon garlic powder

Directions:

1. In a pan that fits your air fryer, the mix asparagus with the cream cheese, sour cream, garlic powder, and garlic; toss.
2. Sprinkle the cheddar cheese on top, and then place the pan in the fryer.
3. Cook at 400 degrees F for 6 minutes.
4. Divide between plates and serve.

Nutrition Values: calories 191, fat 8, fiber 2, carbs 12, protein 8

304. SIMPLE FENNEL MIX

Preparation time: 10 minutes
Cooking time:12 minutes
Servings: 2

Ingredients:

- 2 fennel bulbs, trimmed and halved
- A drizzle of olive oil
- 2 garlic cloves, minced
- 1 tablespoon lime juice
- 1 teaspoon sweet paprika

Directions:

1. In a bowl, combine all ingredients and toss.
2. Put the fennel in your air fryer's basket and cook at 400 degrees F for 12 minutes.
3. Divide between plates and serve.

Nutrition Values: calories 131, fat 4, fiber 7,

carbs 10, protein 8

305. BEETS AND CAPERS

Preparation time: 5 minutes
Cooking time: 20 minutes
Servings: 4

Ingredients:

- 4 beets, peeled and cut into wedges
- 2 tablespoons balsamic vinegar
- 1 tablespoon cilantro, chopped
- Salt and black pepper to taste
- 1 tablespoon olive oil
- 2 tablespoons capers

Directions:

1. Put the beet wedges in your air fryer's basket and cook at 400 degrees F for 20 minutes.
2. Transfer the beet wedges to a salad bowl, and then add the remaining ingredients.
3. Toss, serve, and enjoy.

Nutrition Values: calories 70, fat 1, fiber 1, carbs 6, protein 4

306. SESAME SEED BEETS MIX

Preparation time: 10 minutes
Cooking time: 20 minutes
Servings: 6

Ingredients:

- 6 beets, peeled and quartered
- Salt and black pepper to taste
- 1 tablespoon sesame seeds, toasted
- 1 tablespoon red wine vinegar
- 1 tablespoon olive oil

Directions:

1. Put the beets in your air fryer's basket and cook at 400 degrees F for 20 minutes.
2. Transfer the beets to a bowl, and add all remaining ingredients.
3. Toss and serve.

Nutrition Values: calories 100, fat 2, fiber 4, carbs 7, protein 5

307. BEETS AND KALE MIX

Preparation time: 5 minutes
Cooking time: 20 minutes

Servings: 4

Ingredients:

- 1½ pounds beets, peeled and quartered
- 1 tablespoon olive oil
- 2 tablespoons balsamic vinegar
- ½ cup orange juice
- Salt and black pepper to taste
- 2 scallions, chopped
- 2 cups kale leaves

Directions:

1. Put the beets in your air fryer's basket and cook at 400 degrees F for 15 minutes.
2. Add the kale leaves and cook for another 5 minutes.
3. Transfer the beets and kale to a bowl and add all remaining ingredients.
4. Toss, serve, and enjoy.

Nutrition Values: calories 151, fat 2, fiber 3, carbs 9, protein 4

308. BEET AND TOMATO SALAD

Preparation time: 5 minutes
Cooking time: 25 minutes
Servings: 6

Ingredients:

- 8 small beets, trimmed, peeled and cut into wedges
- 1 red onion, sliced
- 1 tablespoon balsamic vinegar
- Salt and black pepper to taste
- 1 pint mixed cherry tomatoes, halved
- 2 ounces pecans, chopped
- 2 tablespoons olive oil

Directions:

1. Put the beets in your air fryer's basket, and add the salt, pepper, and 1 tablespoon of the oil.
2. Cook at 400 degrees F for 15 minutes.
3. Transfer the beets to a pan that fits your air fryer, and add the onions, tomatoes, pecans, and remaining 1 tablespoon of the oil; toss well.
4. Cook at 400 degrees F for 10 more minutes.
5. Divide between plates and serve.

Nutrition Values: calories 144, fat 7, fiber 5, carbs 8, protein 6

309. CAULIFLOWER MIX

Preparation time: 5 minutes
Cooking time: 7 minutes
Servings: 4

Ingredients:

- 1 cauliflower head, florets separated
- 1 tablespoon peanut oil
- 6 garlic cloves, minced
- 1 tablespoon Chinese rice wine vinegar
- Salt and black pepper to taste

Directions:

1. Mix all ingredients in a bowl.
2. Put the mixture in the fryer and cook at 400 degrees F for 7 minutes.
3. Divide between plates and serve.

Nutrition Values: calories 141, fat 3, fiber 4, carbs 4, protein 2

310. BROCCOLI AND TOMATOES

Preparation time: 5 minutes
Cooking time: 7 minutes
Servings: 4

Ingredients:

- 1 broccoli head, florets separated
- Salt and black pepper to taste
- 6 cherry tomatoes, halved
- ¼ cup scallions, chopped
- 1 tablespoon olive oil

Directions:

1. Put the broccoli florets in your air fryer's basket, and add the salt, pepper, and ½ tablespoon of the oil; toss well.
2. Cook at 380 degrees F for 7 minutes.
3. Transfer the broccoli to a bowl, and add the tomatoes, scallions, salt, pepper, and the remaining ½ tablespoon of oil.
4. Toss and serve.

Nutrition Values: calories 111, fat 4, fiber 4, carbs 9, protein 2

311. TERIYAKI CAULIFLOWER

Preparation Time: 20 min

Servings: 4

Nutrition Values: Calories: 147; Carbs: 18.2g; Fat: 7.1g; Protein: 3.4g

Ingredients

- 1 big cauliflower head, cut into florets
- ½ cup soy sauce
- 3 tbsp brown sugar
- 1 tsp sesame oil
- ⅓ cup water
- ½ chili powder
- 2 cloves garlic, chopped
- 1 tsp cornstarch

Directions

1. In a measuring cup, whisk soy sauce, sugar, sesame oil, water, chili powder, garlic and cornstarch, until smooth. In a bowl, add cauliflower, and pour teriyaki sauce over the top; toss with hands until well-coated.
2. Take the cauliflower to the Air fryer's basket and cook for 14 minutes at 340 F, turning once halfway through. When ready, check if the cauliflower is cooked but not too soft. Serve with rice and edamame beans!

312. SWEET POTATO FRENCH FRIES

Preparation Time: 30 min
Servings: 4

Nutrition Values: Calories: 176; Carbs: 20.3g; Fat: 10.1g; Protein: 1.6g

Ingredients

- ½ tsp salt
- ½ tsp garlic powder
- ½ tsp chili powder
- ¼ tsp cumin
- 3 tbsp olive oil
- 3 sweet potatoes, cut into thick strips

Directions

1. In a bowl, mix salt, garlic powder, chili powder, and cumin, and whisk in oil. Coat the strips well in this mixture and arrange them in the Air fryer's basket, without

overcrowding. Cook for 20 minutes at 380 F, or until crispy.

Spicy Mixed Veggie Bites

Preparation Time: 1 hr 30 min
Servings: 13 to 16 bites

Nutrition Values: Calories: 160; Carbs: 3g; Fat: 8g; Protein: 3g

Ingredients

- 1 medium cauliflower, cut in florets
- 6 medium carrots, diced
- 1 medium broccoli, cut in florets
- 1 onion, diced
- ½ cup garden peas
- 2 leeks, sliced thinly
- 1 small zucchini, chopped
- ⅓ cup flour
- 1 tbsp garlic paste
- 2 tbsp olive oil
- 1 tbsp curry paste
- 2 tsp mixed spice
- 1 tsp coriander
- 1 tsp cumin powder
- 1 ½ cups milk
- 1 tsp ginger paste
- Salt and pepper to taste

Directions

1. In a pot, steam all vegetables, except the leek and courgette, for 10 minutes; set aside. Place a wok over medium heat, and add the onion, ginger, garlic and olive oil. Stir-fry until onions turn transparent. Add in leek, zucchini and curry paste. Stir and cook for 5 minutes. Add all spices and milk; stir and simmer for 10 minutes.
2. Once the sauce has reduced, add the steamed veggies; mix evenly. Transfer to a bowl and refrigerate for 1 hour. Remove the veggie base from the fridge and mold into bite sizes. Arrange the veggie bites in the fryer basket and cook at 350 F for 10 minutes. Once ready, serve warm with yogurt sauce.

313. BRUSSELS SPROUTS WITH GARLIC AIOLI

Preparation Time: 25 min
Servings: 4

Nutrition Values: Calories: 42; Carbs: 0g; Fat: 2.6g; Protein: 4.9g

Ingredients

- 1 lb brussels sprouts, trimmed and excess leaves removed
- Salt and pepper to taste
- 1 ½ tbsp olive oil
- 2 tsp lemon juice
- 1 tsp powdered chili
- 3 cloves garlic
- ¾ cup mayonnaise, whole egg
- 2 cups water

Directions

1. Place a skillet over medium heat on a stove top, add the garlic cloves with the peels on it and roast until lightly brown and fragrant. Remove the skillet and place a pot with water over the same heat; bring to a boil.
2. Using a knife, cut the brussels sprouts in halves lengthwise. Add to the boiling water to blanch for just 3 minutes. Drain through a sieve and set aside. Preheat the Air fryer to 350 F. Remove the garlic from the skillet to a plate; peel, crush and set aside. Add olive oil to the skillet and light the fire to medium heat on the stove top.
3. Stir in the brussels sprouts, season with pepper and salt; sauté for 2 minutes and turn off the heat. Pour the brussels sprouts in the fryer's basket and cook for 5 minutes.
4. Meanwhile, make the garlic aioli. In a bowl, add mayonnaise, crushed garlic, lemon juice, powdered chili, pepper and salt; mix well. Remove the brussels sprouts onto a serving bowl and serve with the garlic aioli.

314. CHEESY STUFFED PEPPERS

Preparation Time: 40 min
Servings: 4

Nutrition Values: Calories: 115; Carbs: 0g; Fat: 16g; Protein: 13g

Ingredients

- 4 green peppers
- Salt and pepper to taste
- ½ cup olive oil
- 1 red onion, chopped
- 1 large tomato, chopped
- ½ cup crumbled Goat cheese
- 3 cups cauliflower, chopped
- 2 tbsp grated Parmesan cheese
- 2 tbsp chopped basil
- 1 tbsp lemon zest

Directions

1. Preheat the Air Fryer to 350 F, and cut the peppers a quarter way from the head down and lengthwise. Remove the membrane and seeds. Season the peppers with pepper, salt, and drizzle olive oil over.
2. Place the pepper bottoms in the fryer's basket and cook them for 5 minutes at 350 F to soften a little bit.
3. In a mixing bowl, add the tomatoes, goat cheese, lemon zest, basil, and cauliflower; season with salt and pepper, and mix well. Remove the bottoms from the Air fryer to a flat surface and spoon the cheese mixture into them.
4. Sprinkle Parmesan on top of each and gently place in the basket; cook for 15 minutes. Serve warm.

315. CHEESY MUSHROOM AND CAULIFLOWER BALLS

Preparation Time: 50 min
Servings: 4

Nutrition Values: Calories: 115; Carbs: 4.1g; Fat: 8.6g; Protein: 5.6g

Ingredients

- ½ lb mushrooms, diced
- 3 tbsp olive oil
- 1 small red onion, chopped
- 3 cloves garlic, minced
- 3 cups cauliflower, chopped
- 2 tbsp chicken stock
- 1 cup breadcrumbs

- 1 cup Grana Padano cheese
- ¼ cup coconut oil
- 2 sprigs chopped fresh thyme
- Salt and pepper to taste

Directions

1. Place a skillet over medium heat on a stove top. Add olive oil, once heated, sauté garlic and onion, until translucent.
2. Add the mushrooms, stir-fry for 4 minutes; add the cauliflower and stir-fry for 5 minutes. Pour in the stock, thyme, and simmer until the cauliflower has absorbed the stock. Add Grana Padano cheese, pepper, and salt.
3. Stir and turn off the heat. Allow the mixture cool and make bite-size balls of the mixture. Place them in a plate and refrigerate for 30 minutes to harden. Preheat the Air Fryer to 350 F.
4. In a bowl, add the breadcrumbs and coconut oil and mix well. Remove the mushroom balls from the refrigerator, stir the breadcrumb mixture again, and roll the balls in the breadcrumb mixture.
5. Place the balls in the Air fryer's basket without overcrowding, and cook for 15 minutes, tossing every 5 minutes for an even cook. Repeat until all the mushroom balls are fried. Serve with sautéed zoodles and tomato sauce.

316. VEGETABLE CROQUETTES

Preparation Time: 1 hr 30 min
Servings: 3

Nutrition Values: Calories: 24; Carbs: 2.6g; Fat: 0.3g; Protein: 3.3g

Ingredients

- 1 lb red potatoes
- 2 cups water
- 1 ¼ cups milk
- Salt to taste
- 2 tsp + 3 tsp butter
- 2 tsp olive oil
- 2 red peppers, chopped
- ½ cup baby spinach, chopped
- 3 mushrooms, chopped

- 1/6 broccoli florets, chopped
- 1/6 cup sliced green onion
- ½ red onion, chopped
- 2 cloves garlic, minced
- 1 medium carrot, grated
- ⅓ cup flour
- 2 tbsp cornstarch
- 1 ½ cups breadcrumbs
- Cooking spray

Directions

1. Place the potatoes in a pot, add the water, and bring it to boil over medium heat on a stove top. Boil until tender and mashable. Drain the potatoes through a sieve and place them in a bowl.
2. Add the 2 teaspoons of butter, 1 cup of milk, and salt. Use a potato masher to mash well; set aside.
3. Place a skillet over medium heat on a stove top and melt the remaining butter. Add the onion, garlic, red peppers, broccoli, and mushrooms; stir-fry for 2 minutes. Add green onion and spinach, and cook until the spinach wilts.
4. Season with salt and stir. Turn the heat off and pour the veggie mixture into the potato mash. Use the potato masher to mash the veggies into the potatoes; allow cooling. Using your hands, form oblong balls of the mixture and place them on a baking sheet in a single layer. Refrigerate for 30 minutes.
5. In 3 separate bowls, add breadcrumbs in one, flour in another, and cornstarch, remaining milk and salt in a third bowl. Mix cornstarch, salt and 1 tbsp of water. Remove the patties from the fridge. Preheat the fryer to 390 F.
6. Dredge each veggie mold in flour, then in the cornstarch mixture, and then in the breadcrumbs. Place the patties in batches in a single layer in the basket without overlapping. Spray with olive oil and cook for 2 minutes. Flip, spray them with cooking spray and cook for more 3 minutes. Remove to a wire rack and serve with tomato sauce.

317. CURRIED CAULIFLOWER FLORETS

Preparation Time: 34 min
Servings: 4

Nutrition Values: Calories: 123; Carbs: 2g; Fat: 11g; Protein: 5g

Ingredients

- 1 large cauliflower head
- Salt to taste
- 1 ½ tbsp curry powder
- ½ cup olive oil
- ⅓ cup fried pine nuts

Directions

1. Preheat the Air Fryer to 390 F, and mix the pine nuts and 1 tsp of olive oil, in a medium bowl. Pour them in the air fryer's basket and cook for 2 minutes; remove to cool.
2. Place the cauliflower on a cutting board. Use a knife to cut them into 1-inch florets. Place them in a large mixing bowl. Add the curry powder, salt, and the remaining olive oil; mix well. Place the cauliflower florets in the fryer's basket in 2 batches, and cook each batch for 10 minutes. Remove the curried florets onto a serving platter, sprinkle with the pine nuts, and toss. Serve the florets with tomato sauce or as a side to a meat dish.

318. ROASTED ROSEMARY SQUASH

Preparation Time: 30 min
Servings: 2

Nutrition Values: Calories: 123; Carbs: 25.7g; Fat: 0.2g; Protein: 1.3g

Ingredients

- 1 butternut squash
- 1 tbsp dried rosemary
- Cooking spray
- Salt to season

Directions

1. Place the butternut squash on a cutting board and peel it; cut it in half and remove

the seeds. Cut the pulp into wedges and season with salt.

2. Preheat the Air Fryer to 350 F, spray the squash wedges with cooking spray and sprinkle with rosemary. Grease the fryer's basket with cooking spray and place the wedges inside it without overlapping. Slide the fryer basket back in and cook for 20 minutes, flipping once halfway through. Serve with maple syrup and goat cheese.

319. EGGPLANT GRATIN WITH MOZZARELLA CRUST

Preparation Time: 30 min
Servings: 2 to 3

Nutrition Values: Calories: 317; Carbs: 2g; Fat: 16.83g; Protein: 12g

Ingredients

- 1 cup cubed eggplant
- ¼ cup chopped red pepper
- ¼ cup chopped green pepper
- ¼ cup chopped onion
- ⅓ cup chopped tomatoes
- 1 clove garlic, minced
- 1 tbsp sliced pimiento-stuffed olives
- 1 tsp capers
- ¼ tsp dried basil
- ¼ tsp dried marjoram
- Salt and pepper to taste
- Cooking spray
- ¼ cup grated mozzarella cheese
- 1 tbsp breadcrumbs

Directions

1. Preheat the Air Fryer to 300 F, and in a bowl, add the eggplant, green pepper, red pepper, onion, tomatoes, olives, garlic, basil marjoram, capers, salt, and pepper. Lightly grease a baking dish with the olive oil cooking spray.
2. Ladle the eggplant mixture into the baking dish and level it using the vessel. Sprinkle the mozzarella cheese on top and cover with the breadcrumbs. Place the dish in the Air Fryer and cook for 20 minutes. Serve with rice.

320. THREE VEG BAKE

Preparation Time: 30 min
Servings: 3

Nutrition Values: Calories: 50; Carbs: 4g; Fat: 2g; Protein: 2g

Ingredients

- 3 turnips, sliced
- 1 large red onion, cut into rings
- 1 large zucchini, sliced
- Salt and pepper to taste
- 2 cloves garlic, crushed
- 1 bay leaf, cut in 6 pieces
- 1 tbsp olive oil
- Cooking spray

Directions

1. Place the turnips, onion, and zucchini in a bowl. Toss with olive oil and season with salt and pepper.
2. Preheat the Air Fryer to 330 F, and place the veggies into a baking pan that fits in the Air fryer. Slip the bay leaves in the different parts of the slices and tuck the garlic cloves in between the slices.
3. Insert the pan in the Air fryer's basket and cook for 15 minutes. Serve warm with as a side to a meat dish or salad.

321. EASY ROAST WINTER VEGETABLE DELIGHT

Preparation Time: 30 min
Servings: 2

Nutrition Values: Calories: 50; Carbs: 5g; Fat: 3g; Protein: 2g

Ingredients

- 1 parsnip, peeled and sliced in a 2-inch thickness
- 1 cup chopped butternut squash
- 2 small red onions, cut in wedges
- 1 cup chopped celery
- 1 tbsp chopped fresh thyme
- Salt and pepper to taste
- 2 tsp olive oil

Directions

1. Preheat the Air Fryer to 200 F, and in a bowl, add turnip, squash, red onions, celery, thyme, pepper, salt, and olive oil; mix well. Pour the vegetables into the fryer's basket and cook for 16 minutes, tossing once halfway through.

322. POTATO, EGGPLANT, AND ZUCCHINI CHIPS

Preparation Time: 45 min
Servings: 4

Nutrition Values: Calories: 120; Carbs: 6g; Fat: 3.5g; Protein: 3g

Ingredients

- 1 large eggplant
- 5 potatoes
- 3 zucchinis
- ½ cup cornstarch
- ½ cup water
- ½ cup olive oil
- Salt to season

Directions

1. Preheat the Air Fryer to 390 F, and cut the eggplant and zucchini in long 3-inch strips. Peel and cut the potatoes into 3-inch strips; set aside. In a bowl, stir in cornstarch, water, salt, pepper, oil, eggplants, zucchini, and potatoes.
2. Place one-third of the veggie strips in the fryer's basket and cook them for 12 minutes. Once ready, transfer them to a serving platter. Repeat the cooking process for the remaining veggie strips. Serve warm.

323. STUFFED MUSHROOMS WITH BACON & CHEESE

Preparation Time: 20 min
Servings: 3 to 4

Nutrition Values: Calories: 67; Carbs: 0.2g; Fat: 3.5g; Protein: 2.7g

Ingredients

- 14 small button mushrooms
- 1 clove garlic, minced
- alt and pepper to taste
- 4 slices bacon, chopped
- ¼ cup grated Cheddar cheese
- 1 tbsp olive oil
- 1 tbsp chopped parsley

Directions

1. Preheat the Air Fryer to 390 F, and in a bowl, add the oil, bacon, cheddar cheese, parsley, salt, pepper, and garlic. Mix well with a spoon. Cut the stalks of the mushroom off and fill each cap with the bacon mixture.
2. Press the bacon mixture into the caps to avoid from falling off. Place the stuffed mushrooms in the fryer's basket and cook at 390 F for 8 minutes. Once golden and crispy, plate them and serve with a green salad.

324. TOMATO SANDWICHES WITH FETA AND PESTO

Preparation Time: 60 min
Servings: 2

Nutrition Values: Calories: 41; Carbs: 5g; Fat: 4g; Protein: 2g

Ingredients

- 1 heirloom tomato
- 1 -4- ozblock Feta cheese
- 1 small red onion, thinly sliced
- 1 clove garlic
- Salt to taste
- 2 tsp + ¼ cup olive oil
- 1 ½ tbsp toasted pine nuts
- ¼ cup chopped parsley
- ¼ cup grated Parmesan cheese
- ¼ cup chopped basil

Directions

1. Add basil, pine nuts, garlic and salt to a food processor. Process while adding the ¼ cup of olive oil slowly. Once the oil is finished, pour the basil pesto into a bowl and refrigerate for 30 minutes. Preheat the Air fryer to 390 F.
2. Slice the feta cheese and tomato into ½ inch circular slices. Use a kitchen towel to pat the tomatoes dry. Remove the pesto

from the fridge and use a tablespoon to spread some pesto on each slice of tomato. Top with a slice of feta cheese. Add the onion and remaining olive oil in a bowl and toss. Spoon on top of feta cheese.

3. Place the tomato in the fryer's basket and cook for 12 minutes. Remove to a serving platter, sprinkle lightly with salt and top with the remaining pesto. Serve with a side of rice or lean meat.

4. Italian Style Tofu

325. PREPARATION TIME: 30 MIN

Servings: 2

Nutrition Values: Calories: 87; Carbs: 3.4g; Fat: 4.4g; Protein: 10g

Ingredients

- 6 oz extra firm tofu
- pepper to season
- 1 tbsp vegetable broth
- 1 tbsp soy sauce
- ⅓ tsp dried oregano
- ⅓ tsp garlic powder
- ⅓ tsp dried basil
- ⅓ tsp onion powder

Directions

1. Place the tofu on a cutting board, and cut it into 3 lengthwise slices with a knife. Line a side of the cutting board with paper towels, place the tofu on it and cover with paper towel. Use your hands to press the tofu gently until as much liquid has been extracted from it.

2. Remove the paper towels and use a knife to chop the tofu into 8 cubes; set aside. In another bowl, add the soy sauce, vegetable broth, oregano, basil, garlic powder, onion powder, and black pepper; mix well with a spoon.

3. Pour the spice mixture on the tofu, stir the tofu until well coated; set aside to marinate for 10 minutes. Preheat the Air Fryer to 390 F, and arrange the tofu in the fryer's basket, in a single layer; cook for 10 minutes, flipping it at the 6-minute mark.

Remove to a plate and serve with green salad.

326. TWO-CHEESE VEGETABLE FRITTATA

Preparation Time: 35 min
Servings: 2

Nutrition Values: Calories: 203; Carbs: 9.3g; Fat: 15.2g; Protein: 6.4g

Ingredients

- 1 cup baby spinach
- ⅓ cup sliced mushrooms
- 1 large zucchini, sliced with a 1-inch thickness
- 1 small red onion, sliced
- ¼ cup chopped chives
- ¼ lb asparagus, trimmed and sliced thinly
- 2 tsp olive oil
- 4 eggs, cracked into a bowl
- ⅓ cup milk
- Salt and pepper to taste
- ⅓ cup grated Cheddar cheese
- ⅓ cup crumbled Feta cheese

Directions

1. Preheat the Air Fryer to 320 F and line a 6 x 6 inches baking dish with parchment paper; set aside. In the egg bowl, add milk, salt, and pepper; beat evenly. Place a skillet over medium heat on a stove top, and heat olive oil.

2. Add the asparagus, zucchini, onion, mushrooms, and baby spinach; stir-fry for 5 minutes. Pour the veggies into the baking dish and top with the egg mixture. Sprinkle feta and cheddar cheese over and place in the Air Fryer.

3. Cook for 15 minutes. Remove the baking dish and garnish with fresh chives.

327. NUTTY PUMPKIN WITH BLUE CHEESE

Preparation Time: 30 min / Serve: 1

Nutrition Values: Calories: 495; Carbs: 29g; Fat: 27g; Protein: 9g

Ingredients

- ½ small pumpkin
- 2 oz blue cheese , cubed
- 2 tbsp pine nuts
- 1 tbsp olive oil
- ½ cup baby spinach, packed
- 1 spring onion, sliced
- 1 radish, thinly sliced
- 1 tsp vinegar

Directions

1. Preheat the Air fryer to 330 F, and place the pine nuts in a baking dish to toast them for 5 minutes; set aside. Peel the pumpkin and chop it into small pieces. Place in the baking dish and toss with the olive oil. Increase the temperature to 390 F and cook the pumpkin for 20 minutes.
2. Place the pumpkin in a serving bowl. Add baby spinach, radish and spring onion; toss with the vinegar. Stir in the cubed blue cheese and top with the toasted pine nuts, to serve.

328. CHILI BEAN BURRITOS

Preparation Time: 30 min
Servings: 6

Nutrition Values: Calories: 248; Carbs: 25g; Fat: 8.7g; Protein: 9g

Ingredients

- 6 tortillas
- 1 cup grated cheddar cheese
- 1 can -8 ozbeans
- 1 tsp seasoning, any kind

Directions

1. Preheat the Air fryer to 350 F, and mix the beans with the seasoning. Divide the bean mixture between the tortillas and top with cheddar cheese. Roll the burritos and arrange them on a lined baking dish.
2. Place in the Air fryer and cook for 5 minutes, or to your liking.

329. VEGGIE MEATBALLS

Preparation Time: 30 min
Servings: 3

Nutrition Values: Calories: 288; Carbs: 32g;

Fat: 21g; Protein: 6g

Ingredients

- 2 tbsp olive oil
- 2 tbsp soy sauce
- 1 tbsp flax meal
- 2 cups cooked chickpeas
- ½ cup sweet onion, diced
- ½ cup grated carrots
- ½ cup roasted cashews
- Juice of 1 lemon
- ½ tsp turmeric
- 1 tsp cumin
- 1 tsp garlic powder
- 1 cup rolled oats

Directions

1. Combine the oil, onions, and carrots into a baking dish and cook them in the air fryer for 6 minutes at 350 F.
2. Meanwhile, ground the oats and cashews in a food processor. Place them in a large bowl. Process the chickpeas with the lemon juice and soy sauce, until smooth. Add them to the bowl as well.
3. Add onions and carrots to the bowl with chickpeas. Stir in the remaining ingredients; mix until fully incorporated. Make meatballs out of the mixture. Increase the temperature to 370 degrees F and cook for 12 minutes.

330. EGGPLANT CHEESEBURGER

Preparation Time: 10 min / Serve: 1

Nutrition Values: Calories: 399: Carbs: 21g; Fat: 17g; Protein: 8g

Ingredients

- 1 hamburger bun
- 2-inch eggplant slice, cut along the round axis
- 1 mozzarella slice
- 1 red onion cut into 3 rings
- 1 lettuce leaf
- ½ tbsp tomato sauce
- 1 pickle, sliced

Directions

1. Preheat the air fryer to 330 F, and place the eggplant slice to roast for 6 minutes. Place the mozzarella slice on top of the eggplant and cook for 30 more seconds. Spread the tomato sauce on one half of the bun.
2. Place the lettuce leaf on top of the sauce. Place the cheesy eggplant on top of the lettuce. Top with onion rings and pickles, and then with the other bun half and enjoy.

331. CHEESY BROCCOLI WITH EGGS

Preparation Time: 15 min
Servings: 4

Nutrition Values: Calories: 265: Carbs: 19g; Fat: 23g; Protein: 26g

Ingredients

- 1 lb broccoli
- 4 eggs
- 1 cup cheese , shredded
- 1 cup cream
- 1 pinch nutmeg
- 1 tsp ginger powder
- salt and pepper to taste

Directions

1. Steam the broccoli for 5 minutes. Then drain them and add 1 egg, cream, nutmeg, ginger, salt and pepper. Butter small ramekins and spread the mixture. Sprinkle the shredded cheese on top. Cook for 10 minutes at 280 F.

332. AIR-FRIED SWEET POTATO

Preparation Time: 30min
Servings: 4

Nutrition Values: Calories: 111; Carbs: 12.3g; Fat: 3.8g; Protein: 8.9g

Ingredients

- ½ tsp salt
- ½ tsp garlic powder
- ½ tsp cayenne pepper
- ¼ tsp cumin
- 3 tbsp olive oil

- 3 sweet potatoes, cut into ½-inch thick wedges
- A handful of chopped fresh parsley
- Sea salt

Directions

1. In a bowl, mix salt, garlic powder, chili powder, and cumin. Whisk in oil, and coat the potatoes. Arrange in the Air fryer, without overcrowding, and cook for 20 minutes at 380 F; toss regularly to get the crispy on all sides. Sprinkle with parsley and sea salt, and serve!

333. CRUNCHY PARMESAN ZUCCHINI

Preparation Time: 40 min
Servings: 4

Nutrition Values: Calories: 369: Carbs: 14g; Fat: 12g; Protein: 9.5g

Ingredients

- 4 small zucchini cut lengthwise
- ½ cup grated Parmesan cheese
- ½ cup breadcrumbs
- ¼ cup melted butter
- ¼ cup chopped parsley
- 4 garlic cloves, minced
- Salt and pepper, to taste

Directions

2. Preheat the Air fryer to 350 F, and in a bowl, mix the breadcrumbs, Parmesan, garlic, and parsley. Season with salt and pepper, to taste; stir in the melted butter. Arrange the zucchinis with the cut side up.
3. Spread the mixture onto the zucchini evenly. Place half of the zucchinis in the air fryer and cook for 13 minutes.
4. Increase the temperature to 370 F, and cook for 3 more minutes for extra crunchiness. Repeat, and serve hot.

334. SPINACH AND FETA CRESCENT TRIANGLES

Preparation Time: 20 min
Servings: 4

Nutrition Values: Calories: 178; Carbs: 10.8g;

Fat: 11.9g; Protein: 8g

Ingredients

- 14 oz store-bought crescent dough
- 1 cup steamed spinach
- 1 cup crumbled feta cheese
- ¼ tsp garlic powder
- 1 tsp chopped oregano
- ¼ tsp salt

Directions

1. Preheat the Air fryer to 350 F, and roll the dough onto a lightly floured flat surface. Combine the feta, spinach, oregano, salt, and garlic powder together in a bowl. Cut the dough into 4 equal pieces.
2. Divide the spinach/feta mixture between the dough pieces. Make sure to place the filling in the center. Fold the dough and secure with a fork. Place onto a lined baking dish, and then in the Air fryer. Cook for 12 minutes, until lightly browned.

335. FETA CHEESE TRIANGLES

Preparation Time: 20 min
Servings: 4

Nutrition Values: Calories: 254; Carbs: 21g; Fat: 19g; Protein: 21g

Ingredients

- 4 oz feta cheese
- 2 sheets filo pastry
- 1 egg yolk
- 2 tbsp parsley, finely chopped
- 1 scallion, finely chopped
- 2 tbsp olive oil
- salt and black pepper

Directions

1. In a large bowl, beat the yolk and mix with the cheese, the chopped parsley and scallion. Season with salt and black pepper. Cut each filo sheet in three parts or strips. Put a teaspoon of the feta mixture on the bottom.
2. Roll the strip in a spinning spiral way until the filling of the inside mixture is completely wrapped in a triangle. Preheat

the Air Fryer to 360 F, and brush the surface of the filo with oil. Place up to 5 triangles in the Air frier's basket and cook for 5 minutes. Lower the temperature to 330 F, cook for 3 more minutes or until golden brown.

336. EGGPLANT CAVIAR

Preparation Time: 20 min
Servings: 3

Nutrition Values: Calories: 125; Carbs: 12g; Fat: 3g; Protein: 2g

Ingredients

- 3 medium eggplants
- ½ red onion, chopped and blended
- 2 tbsp balsamic vinegar
- 1 tbsp olive oil
- salt

Directions

1. Arrange the eggplants in the basket and cook them for 15 minutes at 380 F. Remove them and let them cool. Then cut the eggplants in half, lengthwise, and empty their insides with a spoon.
2. Blend the onion in a blender. Put the inside of the eggplants in the blender and process everything. Add the vinegar, olive oil and salt, then blend again. Serve cool with bread and tomato sauce or ketchup.

337. SPINACH PIE

Preparation time: 10 minutes
Cooking time: 15 minutes
Servings: 4

Ingredients:

- 7 ounces flour
- 2 tablespoons butter
- 7ounces spinach
- 1 tablespoon olive oil
- 2 eggs
- 2 tablespoons milk
- 3 ounces cottage cheese
- Salt and black pepper to the taste
- 1 yellow onion, chopped

Directions:

1. In your food processor, mix flour with butter, 1 egg, milk, salt and pepper, blend well, transfer to a bowl, knead, cover and leave for 10 minutes.
2. Heat up a pan with the oil over medium high heat, add onion and spinach, stir and cook for 2 minutes.
3. Add salt, pepper, the remaining egg and cottage cheese, stir well and take off heat.
4. Divide dough in 4 pieces, roll each piece, place on the bottom of a ramekin, add spinach filling over dough, place ramekins in your air fryer's basket and cook at 360 degrees F for 15 minutes.
5. Serve warm,
6. Enjoy!

Nutrition Values: calories 250, fat 12, fiber 2, carbs 23, protein 12

338. BALSAMIC ARTICHOKES

Preparation time: 10 minutes
Cooking time: 7 minutes
Servings: 4

Ingredients:

- 4 big artichokes, trimmed
- Salt and black pepper to the taste
- 2 tablespoons lemon juice
- ¼ cup extra virgin olive oil
- 2 teaspoons balsamic vinegar
- 1 teaspoon oregano, dried
- 2 garlic cloves, minced

Directions:

1. Season artichokes with salt and pepper, rub them with half of the oil and half of the lemon juice, put them in your air fryer and cook at 360 degrees F for 7 minutes.
2. Meanwhile, in a bowl, mix the rest of the lemon juice with vinegar, the remaining oil, salt, pepper, garlic and oregano and stir very well.
3. Arrange artichokes on a platter, drizzle the balsamic vinaigrette over them and serve.
4. Enjoy!

Nutrition Values: calories 200, fat 3, fiber 6, carbs 12, protein 4

339. CHEESY ARTICHOKES

Preparation time: 10 minutes
Cooking time: 6 minutes
Servings: 6

Ingredients:

- 14 ounces canned artichoke hearts
- 8 ounces cream cheese
- 16 ounces parmesan cheese, grated
- 10 ounces spinach
- ½ cup chicken stock
- 8 ounces mozzarella, shredded
- ½ cup sour cream
- 3 garlic cloves, minced
- ½ cup mayonnaise
- 1 teaspoon onion powder

Directions:

1. In a pan that fits your air fryer, mix artichokes with stock, garlic, spinach, cream cheese, sour cream, onion powder and mayo, toss, introduce in your air fryer and cook at 350 degrees F for 6 minutes.
2. Add mozzarella and parmesan, stir well and serve.
3. Enjoy!

Nutrition Values: calories 261, fat 12, fiber 2, carbs 12, protein 15

340. ARTICHOKES AND SPECIAL SAUCE

Preparation time: 10 minutes
Cooking time: 6 minutes
Servings: 2

Ingredients:

- 2 artichokes, trimmed
- A drizzle of olive oil
- 2 garlic cloves, minced
- 1 tablespoon lemon juice
- For the sauce:
- ¼ cup coconut oil
- ¼ cup extra virgin olive oil
- 3 anchovy fillets
- 3 garlic cloves

Directions:

1. In a bowl, mix artichokes with oil, 2 garlic cloves and lemon juice, toss well, transfer

to your air fryer, cook at 350 degrees F for 6 minutes and divide among plates.

2. In your food processor, mix coconut oil with anchovy, 3 garlic cloves and olive oil, blend very well, drizzle over artichokes and serve.

3. Enjoy!

Nutrition Values: calories 261, fat 4, fiber 7, carbs 20, protein 12

341. BEET SALAD AND PARSLEY DRESSING

Preparation time: 10 minutes
Cooking time: 14 minutes
Servings: 4

Ingredients:

- 4 beets
- 2 tablespoons balsamic vinegar
- A bunch of parsley, chopped
- Salt and black pepper to the taste
- 1 tablespoon extra virgin olive oil
- 1 garlic clove, chopped
- 2 tablespoons capers

Directions:

1. Put beets in your air fryer and cook them at 360 degrees F for 14 minutes.
2. Meanwhile, in a bowl, mix parsley with garlic, salt, pepper, olive oil and capers and stir very well.
3. Transfer beets to a cutting board, leave them to cool down, peel them, slice put them in a salad bowl.
4. Add vinegar, drizzle the parsley dressing all over and serve.
5. Enjoy!

Nutrition Values: calories 70, fat 2, fiber 1, carbs 6, protein 4

342. BEETS AND BLUE CHEESE SALAD

Preparation time: 10 minutes
Cooking time: 14 minutes
Servings: 6

Ingredients:

- 6 beets, peeled and quartered

- Salt and black pepper to the taste
- ¼ cup blue cheese, crumbled
- 1 tablespoon olive oil

Directions:

1. Put beets in your air fryer, cook them at 350 degrees F for 14 minutes and transfer them to a bowl.
2. Add blue cheese, salt, pepper and oil, toss and serve.
3. Enjoy!

Nutrition Values: calories 100, fat 4, fiber 4, carbs 10, protein 5

343. BEETS AND ARUGULA SALAD

Preparation time: 10 minutes
Cooking time: 10 minutes
Servings: 4

Ingredients:

- 1 and ½ pounds beets, peeled and quartered
- A drizzle of olive oil
- 2 teaspoons orange zest, grated
- 2 tablespoons cider vinegar
- ½ cup orange juice
- 2 tablespoons brown sugar
- 2 scallions, chopped
- 2 teaspoons mustard
- 2 cups arugula

Directions:

1. Rub beets with the oil and orange juice, place them in your air fryer and cook at 350 degrees F for 10 minutes.
2. Transfer beet quarters to a bowl, add scallions, arugula and orange zest and toss.
3. In a separate bowl, mix sugar with mustard and vinegar, whisk well, add to salad, toss and serve.
4. Enjoy!

Nutrition Values: calories 121, fat 2, fiber 3, carbs 11, protein 4

344. BEET, TOMATO AND GOAT CHEESE MIX

Preparation time: 30 minutes
Cooking time: 14 minutes
Servings: 8

Ingredients:

- 8 small beets, trimmed, peeled and halved
- 1 red onion, sliced
- 4 ounces goat cheese, crumbled
- 1 tablespoon balsamic vinegar
- Salt and black pepper to the taste
- 2 tablespoons sugar
- 1 pint mixed cherry tomatoes, halved
- 2 ounces pecans
- 2 tablespoons olive oil

Directions:

1. Put beets in your air fryer, season them with salt and pepper, cook at 350 degrees F for 14 minutes and transfer to a salad bowl.
2. Add onion, cherry tomatoes and pecans and toss.
3. In another bowl, mix vinegar with sugar and oil, whisk well until sugar dissolves and add to salad.
4. Also add goat cheese, toss and serve.
5. Enjoy!

Nutrition Values: calories 124, fat 7, fiber 5, carbs 12, protein 6

345. BROCCOLI SALAD

Preparation time: 10 minutes
Cooking time: 8 minutes
Servings: 4

Ingredients:

- 1 broccoli head, florets separated
- 1 tablespoon peanut oil
- 6 garlic cloves, minced
- 1 tablespoon Chinese rice wine vinegar
- Salt and black pepper to the taste

Directions:

1. In a bowl, mix broccoli with salt, pepper and half of the oil, toss, transfer to your air fryer and cook at 350 degrees F for 8 minutes, shaking the fryer halfway.
2. Transfer broccoli to a salad bowl, add the rest of the peanut oil, garlic and rice

vinegar, toss really well and serve.
3. Enjoy!

Nutrition Values: calories 121, fat 3, fiber 4, carbs 4, protein 4

346. BRUSSELS SPROUTS AND TOMATOES MIX

Preparation time: 5 minutes
Cooking time: 10 minutes
Servings: 4

Ingredients:

- 1 pound Brussels sprouts, trimmed
- Salt and black pepper to the taste
- 6 cherry tomatoes, halved
- ¼ cup green onions, chopped
- 1 tablespoon olive oil

Directions:

1. Season Brussels sprouts with salt and pepper, put them in your air fryer and cook at 350 degrees F for 10 minutes.
2. Transfer them to a bowl, add salt, pepper, cherry tomatoes, green onions and olive oil, toss well and serve.
3. Enjoy!

Nutrition Values: calories 121, fat 4, fiber 4, carbs 11, protein 4

347. ARTICHOKES AND MAYONNAISE MIX WITH PARMESAN

Preparation Time: 20 minutes
Servings: 6

Ingredients:

- canned artichoke hearts - 14 ounces
- A drizzle of olive oil
- parmesan cheese - 16 ounces, grated
- garlic cloves - 3, minced
- mayonnaise - ½ cup
- garlic powder - 1 teaspoon

Directions:

1. Pour the artichokes with the oil, garlic, and garlic powder in a pan that fits right into your fryer, mix properly and toss well.

2. Put the pan in the fryer and cook at a temperature of 350 o F for 15 minutes.
3. Let the mix cool down, then add the mayo, and toss well to coat.
4. Cut into different plates, then sprinkle the parmesan on top, and serve right away.

Nutrition Values:

calories 200, fat 11, fiber 3, carbs 9, protein 4

348. COCONUT ARTICHOKES RECIPE

Preparation Time: 20 minutes
Servings: 2

Ingredients:

- Artichokes - 2, washed, trimmed and halved
- garlic cloves - 2, minced
- Coconut - ¼ cup, shredded
- Lemon Juice - 1
- coconut oil - 1 tablespoon, melted

Directions:

1. Mix the artichokes with the garlic, oil, and lemon juice in a bowl; and toss well to ensure it is well coated.
2. Transfer them artichokes to the air fryer and cook at a temperature of 360 o F. Do this for 15 minutes.
3. Cut the artichokes into different plates, then sprinkle the coconut as toppings, and serve.
4. Enjoy your meal!

Nutrition Values:

calories 213, fat 8, fiber 6, carbs 13, protein 6

349. SEASONED WRAPPED ASPARAGUS RECIPE

Preparation Time: 10 minutes
Servings: 4

Ingredients:

- asparagus spears - 8, trimmed
- prosciutto slices - 8 ounces
- A pinch of salt and black pepper

Directions:

1. First, wrap the asparagus with slices of

prosciutto; then add salt and pepper to taste.
2. Introduce all of it to an air fryer's basket and cook at a temperature of 400 o F for about 5 minutes.
3. Cut into different plates and serve.

Nutrition Values:

calories 100, fat 2, fiber 5, carbs 8, protein 4

350. SEASONED CAJUN ASPARAGUS MIX

Preparation Time: 10 minutes
Servings: 4

Ingredients:

- extra virgin olive oil - 1 teaspoon
- asparagus - 1 bunch, trimmed
- Cajun seasoning - ½ tablespoon

Directions:

1. Mix the asparagus with the oil and Cajun seasoning in a clean bowl; coat the asparagus properly.
2. Move the asparagus to your air fryer and cook at a temperature of 400 o F for about 5 minutes.
3. Cut all of it into different plates and serve.

Nutrition Values:

calories 151, fat 3, fiber 4, carbs 9, protein 4

351. SEASONED SQUASH SALAD

Preparation Time: 17 minutes
Servings: 4

Ingredients:

- butternut squash - 1, cubed
- balsamic vinegar - 2 tablespoons
- cilantro - 1 bunch, chopped
- Salt and black pepper to taste
- olive oil - 1 tablespoon

Directions:

1. Place the squash in the air fryer, then sprinkle a pinch of salt and pepper to taste. Add oil to the mix and toss well to coat.
2. Cook at a temperature of 400 o F for about 15 minutes.

3. Move the squash to a clean bowl, before adding the vinegar and cilantro. Toss the mix well.
4. Serve away and enjoy your meal!

Nutrition Values:

calories 151, fat 4, fiber 7, carbs 11, protein 8

352. YUMMY AND CREAMY SQUASH MIX

Preparation Time: 17 minutes
Servings: 6

Ingredients:

- big butternut squash - 1, roughly cubed
- sour cream - 1 cup
- Salt and black pepper to taste
- Parsley - 1 tablespoon, chopped
- A drizzle of olive oil

Directions:

1. Place the squash in the air fryer, then add the salt and pepper as seasoning. Ensure to rub with oil.
2. Cook at a temperature of 400 o F for about 15 minutes.
3. Then move the squash to a clean bowl before adding the cream and the parsley.
4. Toss well to coat before serving.

Nutrition Values:

calories 200, fat 7, fiber 6, carbs 11, protein 7

353. ORANGE CARROTS MIX

Preparation Time: 20 minutes
Servings: 4

Ingredients:

- baby carrots - 1½ pounds
- orange zest - 2 teaspoons
- cider vinegar - 2 tablespoons
- orange juice - ½ cup
- A handful of parsley, chopped
- A drizzle of olive oil

Directions:

1. Place the baby carrots in your clean air fryer's basket, followed by addition of the orange zest and oil,. Ensure that you rub the carrots well.

2. Cook at a temperature of 350 o F for 15 minutes.
3. Move the carrots to a clean bowl, before adding the vinegar and orange as well as juice, and parsley.
4. Toss well to coat, serve away, and enjoy your meal!

Nutrition Values:

calories 151, fat 6, fiber 6, carbs 11, protein 5

354. TOMATO SALAD MIX

Preparation Time: 10 minutes
Servings: 8

Ingredients:

- red onion - 1, sliced
- feta cheese - 2 ounces, crumbled
- Salt and black pepper to taste
- mixed cherry tomatoes - 1 pint, halved
- pecans - 2 ounces
- olive oil - 2 tablespoons

Directions:

1. Mix the tomatoes with the salt, pepper, onions, and the oil in your air fryer.
2. Cook at a temperature of 400 o F for 5 minutes.
3. Move to a bowl before adding the pecans and the cheese.
4. Toss well to coat and serve away.

Nutrition Values:

calories 151, fat 4, fiber 6, carbs 9, protein 4

355. HOT TOMATO AND GREEN BEANS SALAD

Preparation Time: 11 minutes
Servings: 4

Ingredients:

- green beans - 1 pound, trimmed and halved
- green onions - 2, chopped
- canned green chilies - 5 ounces, chopped
- jalapeno pepper - 1, chopped
- A drizzle of olive oil
- chili powder - 2 teaspoons
- garlic powder - 1 teaspoon

- Salt and black pepper to taste
- cherry tomatoes - 8, halved

Directions:

1. Put every single ingredient in a pan that fits perfectly into your air fryer, then mix and toss properly.
2. Introduce the pan to the fryer and cook at a temperature of 400 o F for a little above 5 minutes.
3. Cut the mix into different plates and serve while the meal is still hot.

Nutrition Values:

calories 200, fat 4, fiber 7, carbs 12, protein 6

356. BELL PEPPERS AND KALE MIX

Preparation Time: 20 minutes
Servings: 4

Ingredients:

- red bell peppers - 2, cut into strips
- green bell peppers - 2, cut into strips
- kale leaves - ½ pound
- Salt and black pepper to taste
- yellow onions - 2, roughly chopped
- veggie stock - ¼ cup
- tomato sauce - 2 tablespoons

Directions:

1. Put all of the ingredients in a pan that fits right into your air fryer; then mix well.
2. Transfer the pan to the fryer and cook at a temperature of 360 o F for 15 minutes.
3. Cut into different plates, serve your meal, and enjoy!

Nutrition Values:

calories 161, fat 7, fiber 6, carbs 12, protein 7

357. SEASONED GARLIC PARSNIPS

Preparation Time: 20 minutes
Servings: 4

Ingredients:

- Parsnips - 1 pound, cut into chunks
- olive oil - 1 tablespoon

- garlic cloves - 6, minced
- balsamic vinegar - 1 tablespoon
- Salt and black pepper to taste

Directions:

1. Put all of the ingredients in a bowl and mix properly.
2. Transfer them to the air fryer and cook at a temperature of 380 o F for 15 minutes.
3. Cut into different plates and serve away.

Nutrition Values:

calories 121, fat 3, fiber 6, carbs 12, protein 6

358. BROCCOLI AND POMEGRANATE TOPPINGS

Preparation Time: 12 minutes
Servings: 4

Ingredients:

- broccoli head - 1, florets separated
- Salt and black pepper to taste
- Pomegranate - 1, seeds separated
- A drizzle of olive oil

Directions:

1. Mix the broccoli with the salt, pepper, and oil in a bowl; toss well to coat.
2. Introduce the florets to your air fryer and cook at a temperature of 400 o F for a little above 5 minutes.
3. Cut into different plates, sprinkle the pomegranate seeds all over the dish, and serve away.

Nutrition Values:

calories 141, fat 3, fiber 4, carbs 11, protein 4

359. HOT BACON CAULIFLOWER

Preparation Time: 12 minutes
Servings: 4

Ingredients:

- cauliflower head - 1, florets separated
- olive oil - 1 tablespoon
- Salt and black pepper to taste
- Bacon - ½ cup, cooked and chopped
- tablespoons dill - 2, chopped

Directions:

1. Place the cauliflower in the air fryer; then add the salt and pepper to taste, followed by oil. Ensure to toss well to coat.
2. Cook at a temperature of 400 o F for about 15 minutes.
3. Cut the cauliflower into different plates, then sprinkle the bacon and the dill as toppings.
4. Serve right away.

Nutrition Values:

calories 200, fat 7, fiber 5, carbs 17, protein 7

360. HOT BUTTER BROCCOLI

Preparation Time: 11 minutes
Servings: 4

Ingredients:

- broccoli head - 1, florets separated
- lime juice - 1 tablespoon
- Salt and black pepper to taste
- Butter - 2 tablespoons, melted

Directions:

1. Mix all of the ingredients, gently and thoroughly, in a bowl
2. Place the broccoli mixture in your air fryer and cook at a temperature of 400 o F for a little above 5 minutes.
3. Serve while it is still hot.

Nutrition Values:

calories 151, fat 4, fiber 7, carbs 12, protein 6

361. NEW POTATOES MIX WITH TOPPINGS

Preparation Time: 20 minutes
Servings: 4

Ingredients:

- new potatoes - 1 pound, halved
- Salt and black pepper to taste
- Butter - 1½ tablespoons, melted
- Dill - 1 tablespoon, chopped

Directions:

1. Place the potatoes in your air fryer's basket, then add the salt and pepper to taste, as well as butter; toss well to coat.
2. Cook at a temperature of 400 o F for 15

minutes.
3. Cut into different plates, then sprinkle the dill as topping and serve.

Nutrition Values:

calories 171, fat 5, fiber 6, carbs 15, protein 8

362. SEASONED NAPA CABBAGE MIX

Preparation Time: 17 minutes
Servings: 4

Ingredients:

- napa cabbage - 1, shredded
- yellow onion - 1, chopped
- 2 tablespoons tomato sauce
- Nutmeg - ¼ teaspoon, ground
- Salt and black pepper to taste
- Parsley - 1 tablespoon, chopped

Directions:

1. Put every ingredient in a pan that fits right into your air fryer and mix well.
2. Put the pan in the fryer and cook at a temperature of 300 o F for close to 15 minutes.
3. Divide into different plates and serve right away.

Nutrition Values:

calories 154, fat 4, fiber 4, carbs 12, protein 5

363. BUTTER CABBAGE

Preparation Time: 17 minutes
Servings: 8

Ingredients:

- green cabbage head - 1, shredded
- butter - ¼ cup, melted
- sweet paprika - 1 tablespoon
- dill - 1 tablespoon, chopped

Directions:

1. Mix every ingredient in a pan that fits right into your air fryer.
2. Put the pan in the fryer and cook at a temperature of 320 o F for 12 minutes.
3. Divide into different plates, serve right away, and enjoy!

Nutrition Values:

calories 181, fat 4, fiber 6, carbs 15, protein 5

364. TURMERIC KALE RECIPE

Preparation Time: 17 minutes
Servings: 2

Ingredients:

- Butter - 3 tablespoons, melted
- kale leaves - 2 cups
- Salt and black pepper to taste
- yellow onion - ½ cup, chopped
- turmeric powder - 2 teaspoons

Directions:

1. Put all of the ingredients in a pan that fits right into your air fryer and mix properly.
2. Place the pan in the fryer and cook at a temperature of 250 o F for about 15 minutes.
3. Cut into different plates and serve.

Nutrition Values:

calories 151, fat 4, fiber 5, carbs 15, protein 6

365. SPICY CABBAGE MIX

Preparation Time: 17 minutes
Servings: 4

Ingredients:

- green cabbage head - 1, shredded
- olive oil - 1 tablespoon
- cayenne pepper - 1 teaspoon
- A pinch of salt and black pepper
- sweet paprika - 2 teaspoons

Directions:

1. Place all the ingredients in a pan that fits your fryer, and mix.
2. Put the pan in the fryer and cook at a temperature of 320 o F for about 15 minutes.
3. Cut into different plates and serve immediately.

Nutrition Values:

calories 124, fat 6, fiber 6, carbs 16, protein 7

366. EASY CELERY ROOT RECIPE

Preparation Time: 20 minutes
Servings: 4

Ingredients:

- celery root - 2 cups, roughly cubed
- A pinch of salt and black pepper
- Butter - ½ tablespoon, melted

Directions:

1. Place all the ingredients in your air fryer and toss well to coat
2. Cook at a temperature of 350 o F for 15 minutes.
3. Cut into different plates and serve right away.

Nutrition Values:

calories 124, fat 1, fiber 4, carbs 6, protein 6

367. SEASONED MAPLE GLAZED CORN

Preparation Time: 11 minutes
Servings: 4

Ingredients:

- ears of corn - 4
- maple syrup - 1 tablespoon
- Black pepper to taste
- Butter - 1 tablespoon, melted

Directions:

1. Mix the black pepper, butter, and the maple syrup in a clean bowl.
2. Rub the corn with the mixture, and then place it in your air fryer.
3. Cook at a temperature of 390 o F for a little above 5 minutes.
4. Cut the corn into different plates and serve.

Nutrition Values:

calories 100, fat 2, fiber 3, carbs 8, protein 3

368. SEASONED DILL CORN

Preparation Time: 11 minutes
Servings: 4

Ingredients:

- ears of corn - 4
- Salt and black pepper to taste
- Butter - 2 tablespoons, melted
- Dill - 2 tablespoon, chopped

Directions:

1. Mix the salt, pepper, and the butter in a bowl.
2. Pour butter mixture on the corn and rub, and then put it in your air fryer.
3. Cook at a temperature of390 o F for a little above 5 minutes.
4. Cut the corn into different plates, sprinkle the dill as topping, and then serve right away.

Nutrition Values:

calories 100, fat 2, fiber 5, carbs 9, protein 6

369. SEASONED BROCCOLI CASSEROLE

Preparation Time: 20 minutes
Servings: 4

Ingredients:

*   Butter - 2 tablespoons, melted
*   broccoli florets - 6 cups
*   garlic cloves - 2, minced
*   chicken stock - 1 cup
*   Salt and black pepper to taste
*   fettuccine pasta - 1 pound, cooked
*   green onions - 2, chopped
*   parmesan cheese - 1 tablespoon, grated
*   tomatoes -3, chopped

Directions:

1. Grease a baking dish with butter; the baking dish that fits your air fryer.
2. Add the broccoli, garlic, stock, salt, pepper, pasta, onions, and tomatoes; toss well to coat and ensure to toss gently.
3. Move the dish in the fryer and cook at a temperature of 390 o F for 15 minutes.
4. Sprinkle the parmesan as toppings, divide all into different plates, and serve.

Nutrition Values:

calories 151, fat 6, fiber 5, carbs 12, protein 4

370. SEASONED MUSTARD GREENS MIX

Preparation Time: 17 minutes
Servings: 6

Ingredients:

*   collard greens - 1 pound, trimmed
*   bacon - ¼ pound, cooked and chopped
*   A drizzle of olive oil
*   Salt and black pepper to taste
*   veggie stock - ½ cup

Directions:

1. Pour every ingredient to the pan that fits your air fryer and mix well.
2. Move the pan to the fryer and cook at a temperature of 260 o F for about 15 minutes.
3. Divide all of the mix into different plates and serve.

Nutrition Values:

calories 161, fat 4, fiber 5, carbs 14, protein 3

371. CHERRY TOMATOES SKEWERS RECIPE

Preparation Time: 36 Minutes
Servings: 4

Ingredients:

*   3 tbsp. balsamic vinegar
*   3 garlic cloves; minced
*   1 tbsp. thyme; chopped
*   24 cherry tomatoes
*   2 tbsp. olive oil
*   Salt and black pepper to the taste
*   For the dressing:
*   2 tbsp. balsamic vinegar
*   Salt and black pepper to the taste
*   4 tbsp. olive oil

Directions:

1. In a bowl; mix 2 tbsp. oil with 3 tbsp. vinegar, 3 garlic cloves, thyme, salt and black pepper and whisk well.
2. Add tomatoes, toss to coat and leave aside for 30 minutes
3. Arrange 6 tomatoes on one skewer and repeat with the rest of the tomatoes.
4. Introduce them in your air fryer and cook at 360 °F, for 6 minutes
5. In another bowl, mix 2 tbsp. vinegar with salt, pepper and 4 tbsp. oil and whisk well. Arrange tomato skewers on plates and

serve with the dressing drizzled on top.

Nutrition Values: Calories: 140; Fat: 1; Fiber: 1; Carbs: 2; Protein: 7

372. EGGPLANT AND GARLIC SAUCE RECIPE

Preparation Time: 20 Minutes
Servings: 4

Ingredients:

- 2 tbsp. olive oil
- 2 garlic cloves; minced
- 1 tbsp. ginger; grated
- 1 tbsp. soy sauce
- 3 eggplants; halved and sliced
- 1 red chili pepper; chopped.
- 1 green onion stalk; chopped.
- 1 tbsp. balsamic vinegar

Directions:

1. Heat up a pan that fits your air fryer with the oil over medium high heat, add eggplant slices and cook for 2 minutes
2. Add chili pepper, garlic, green onions, ginger, soy sauce and vinegar, introduce in your air fryer and cook at 320 °F, for 7 minutes. Divide among plates and serve.

Nutrition Values: Calories: 130; Fat: 2; Fiber: 4; Carbs: 7; Protein: 9

373. STUFFED BABY PEPPERS RECIPE

Preparation Time: 16 Minutes
Servings: 4

Ingredients:

- 12 baby bell peppers; cut into halves lengthwise
- 1 lb. shrimp; cooked, peeled and deveined
- 1/4 tsp. red pepper flakes; crushed
- 6 tbsp. jarred basil pesto
- 1 tbsp. lemon juice
- 1 tbsp. olive oil
- Salt and black pepper to the taste
- A handful parsley; chopped

Directions:

1. In a bowl; mix shrimp with pepper flakes, pesto, salt, black pepper, lemon juice, oil and parsley, whisk very well and stuff bell pepper halves with this mix
2. Place them in your air fryer and cook at 320 °F, for 6 minutes; Arrange peppers on plates and serve.

Nutrition Values: Calories: 130; Fat: 2; Fiber: 1; Carbs: 3; Protein: 15

374. BEET SALAD AND PARSLEY DRESSING RECIPE

Preparation Time: 24 Minutes
Servings: 4

Ingredients:

- 4 beets
- 2 tbsp. balsamic vinegar
- A bunch of parsley; chopped
- 1 tbsp. extra virgin olive oil
- 1 garlic clove; chopped
- 2 tbsp. capers
- Salt and black pepper to the taste

Directions:

1. Put beets in your air fryer and cook them at 360 °F, for 14 minutes.
2. Meanwhile; in a bowl, mix parsley with garlic, salt, pepper, olive oil and capers and stir very well
3. Transfer beets to a cutting board, leave them to cool down, peel them, slice put them in a salad bowl
4. Add vinegar, drizzle the parsley dressing all over and serve.

Nutrition Values: Calories: 70; Fat: 2; Fiber: 1; Carbs: 6; Protein: 4

375. HERBED EGGPLANT AND ZUCCHINI MIX RECIPE

Preparation Time: 18 Minutes
Servings: 4

Ingredients:

- 1 eggplant; roughly cubed
- 3 zucchinis; roughly cubed
- 2 tbsp. lemon juice

- 1 tsp. thyme; dried
- Salt and black pepper to the taste
- 1 tsp. oregano; dried
- 3 tbsp. olive oil

Directions:

1. Put eggplant in a dish that fits your air fryer, add zucchinis, lemon juice, salt, pepper, thyme, oregano and olive oil, toss, introduce in your air fryer and cook at 360 °F, for 8 minutes
2. Divide among plates and serve right away.

Nutrition Values: Calories: 152; Fat: 5; Fiber: 7; Carbs: 19; Protein: 5

376. PEPPERS STUFFED WITH BEEF RECIPE

Preparation Time: 65 Minutes
Servings: 4

Ingredients:

- 1-pound beef; ground
- 1 tsp. coriander; ground
- 1 onion; chopped
- 3 garlic cloves; minced
- 1/2 tsp. turmeric powder
- 1 tbsp. hot curry powder
- 2 tbsp. olive oil
- 1 tbsp. ginger; grated
- 1/2 tsp. cumin; ground
- Salt and black pepper to the taste
- 1 egg
- 4 bell peppers; cut into halves and seeds removed
- 1/3 cup raisins
- 1/3 cup walnuts; chopped

Directions:

1. Heat up a pan with the oil over medium high heat, add onion; stir and cook for 4 minutes.
2. Add garlic and beef; stir and cook for 10 minutes
3. Add coriander, ginger, cumin, curry powder, salt, pepper, turmeric, walnuts and raisins; stir take off heat and mix with the egg.
4. Stuff pepper halves with this mix,

introduce them in your air fryer and cook at 320 °F, for 20 minutes. Divide among plates and serve

Nutrition Values: Calories: 170; Fat: 4; Fiber: 3; Carbs: 7; Protein: 12

377. BEETS AND BLUE CHEESE SALAD RECIPE

Preparation Time: 24 Minutes
Servings: 6

Ingredients:

- 6 beets; peeled and quartered
- 1/4 cup blue cheese; crumbled
- 1 tbsp. olive oil
- Salt and black pepper to the taste

Directions:

1. Put beets in your air fryer, cook them at 350 °F, for 14 minutes and transfer them to a bowl.
2. Add blue cheese, salt, pepper and oil, toss and serve

Nutrition Values: Calories: 100; Fat: 4; Fiber: 4; Carbs: 10; Protein: 5

378. RADISH HASH RECIPE

Preparation Time: 17 Minutes
Servings: 4

Ingredients:

- 1/2 tsp. onion powder
- 1/3 cup parmesan; grated
- 4 eggs
- 1 lb. radishes; sliced
- 1/2 tsp. garlic powder
- Salt and black pepper to the taste

Directions:

1. In a bowl; mix radishes with salt, pepper, onion and garlic powder, eggs and parmesan and stir well
2. Transfer radishes to a pan that fits your air fryer and cook at 350 °F, for 7 minutes
3. Divide hash on plates and serve.

Nutrition Values: Calories: 80; Fat: 5; Fiber: 2; Carbs: 5; Protein: 7

379. FLAVORED FRIED TOMATOES RECIPE

Preparation Time: 25 Minutes
Servings: 8

Ingredients:

- 1 jalapeno pepper; chopped
- 4 garlic cloves; minced
- 1/2 tsp. oregano; dried
- 1/4 cup basil; chopped.
- 2 lbs. cherry tomatoes; halved
- Salt and black pepper to the taste
- 1/4 cup olive oil
- 1/2 cup parmesan; grated

Directions:

1. In a bowl; mix tomatoes with garlic, jalapeno, season with salt, pepper and oregano and drizzle the oil, toss to coat, introduce in your air fryer and cook at 380 °F, for 15 minutes
2. Transfer tomatoes to a bowl, add basil and parmesan, toss and serve.

Nutrition Values: Calories: 140; Fat: 2; Fiber: 2; Carbs: 6; Protein: 8

380. MEXICAN PEPPERS RECIPE

Preparation Time: 35 Minutes
Servings: 4

Ingredients:

- 4 bell peppers; tops cut off and seeds removed
- 1/2 cup tomato juice
- 1/4 cup yellow onion; chopped
- 1/4 cup green peppers; chopped.
- 2 cups tomato sauce
- 2 tbsp. jarred jalapenos; chopped.
- 4 chicken breasts
- 1 cup tomatoes; chopped
- Salt and black pepper to the taste
- 2 tsp. onion powder
- 1/2 tsp. red pepper; crushed
- 1 tsp. chili powder
- 1/2 tsp. garlic powder
- 1 tsp. cumin; ground

Directions:

1. In a pan that fits your air fryer, mix chicken breasts with tomato juice, jalapenos, tomatoes, onion, green peppers, salt, pepper, onion powder, red pepper, chili powder, garlic powder, oregano and cumin; stir well, introduce in your air fryer and cook at 350 °F, for 15 minutes
2. Shred meat using 2 forks; stir, stuff bell peppers with this mix, place them in your air fryer and cook at 320 °F, for 10 minutes more. Divide stuffed peppers on plates and serve

Nutrition Values: Calories: 180; Fat: 4; Fiber: 3; Carbs: 7; Protein: 14

381. BALSAMIC ARTICHOKES RECIPE

Preparation Time: 17 Minutes
Servings: 4

Ingredients:

- 4 big artichokes; trimmed
- 2 tbsp. lemon juice
- 2 tsp. balsamic vinegar
- 1 tsp. oregano; dried
- 1/4 cup extra virgin olive oil
- 2 garlic cloves; minced
- Salt and black pepper to the taste

Directions:

1. Season artichokes with salt and pepper, rub them with half of the oil and half of the lemon juice, put them in your air fryer and cook at 360 °F, for 7 minutes
2. Meanwhile; in a bowl, mix the rest of the lemon juice with vinegar, the remaining oil, salt, pepper, garlic and oregano and stir very well
3. Arrange artichokes on a platter, drizzle the balsamic vinaigrette over them and serve.

Nutrition Values: Calories: 200; Fat: 3; Fiber: 6; Carbs: 12; Protein: 4

382. BEETS AND ARUGULA SALAD TIME RECIPE

Preparation Time: 20 Minutes

Servings: 4

Ingredients:

- 1 ½ lbs. beets; peeled and quartered
- 2 tbsp. brown sugar
- 2 scallions; chopped
- 2 tsp. mustard
- A drizzle of olive oil
- 2 tsp. orange zest; grated
- 2 tbsp. cider vinegar
- 1/2 cup orange juice
- 2 cups arugula

Directions:

1. Rub beets with the oil and orange juice, place them in your air fryer and cook at 350 °F, for 10 minutes
2. Transfer beet quarters to a bowl, add scallions, arugula and orange zest and toss
3. In a separate bowl, mix sugar with mustard and vinegar, whisk well, add to salad, toss and serve.

Nutrition Values: Calories: 121; Fat: 2; Fiber: 3; Carbs: 11; Protein: 4

383. SESAME MUSTARD GREENS RECIPE

Preparation Time: 21 Minutes
Servings: 4

Ingredients:

- 2 garlic cloves; minced
- 3 tbsp. veggie stock
- 1/4 tsp. dark sesame oil
- 1 lb. mustard greens; torn
- 1 tbsp. olive oil
- 1/2 cup yellow onion; sliced
- Salt and black pepper to the taste

Directions:

1. Heat up a pan that fits your air fryer with the oil over medium heat, add onions; stir and brown them for 5 minutes.
2. Add garlic, stock, greens, salt and pepper; stir, introduce in your air fryer and cook at 350 °F, for 6 minutes. Add sesame oil, toss to coat, divide among plates and serve

Nutrition Values: Calories: 120; Fat: 3; Fiber:

1; Carbs: 3; Protein: 7

384. GARLIC TOMATOES RECIPE

Preparation Time: 25 Minutes
Servings: 4

Ingredients:

- 4 garlic cloves; crushed
- 1 lb. mixed cherry tomatoes
- 3 thyme springs; chopped.
- 1/4 cup olive oil
- Salt and black pepper to the taste

Directions:

1. In a bowl; mix tomatoes with salt, black pepper, garlic, olive oil and thyme, toss to coat, introduce in your air fryer and cook at 360 °F, for 15 minutes. Divide tomatoes mix on plates and serve

Nutrition Values: Calories: 100; Fat: 0; Fiber: 1; Carbs: 1; Protein: 6

385. BROCCOLI AND TOMATOES FRIED STEW RECIPE

Preparation Time: 30 Minutes
Servings: 4

Ingredients:

- 28 oz. canned tomatoes; pureed
- 1 broccoli head; florets separated
- 2 tsp. coriander seeds
- 1 tbsp. olive oil
- 1 yellow onion; chopped
- A pinch of red pepper; crushed
- 1 small ginger piece; chopped
- 1 garlic clove; minced
- Salt and black pepper to the taste

Directions:

1. Heat up a pan that fits your air fryer with the oil over medium heat, add onions, salt, pepper and red pepper; stir and cook for 7 minutes
2. Add ginger, garlic, coriander seeds, tomatoes and broccoli; stir, introduce in your air fryer and cook at 360 °F, for 12 minutes. Divide into bowls and serve.

Nutrition Values: Calories: 150; Fat: 4; Fiber:

2; Carbs: 7; Protein: 12

386. CHEESY ARTICHOKES RECIPE

Preparation Time: 16 Minutes
Servings: 6

Ingredients:

- 14 oz. canned artichoke hearts
- 8 oz. cream cheese
- 8 oz. mozzarella; shredded
- 1/2 cup sour cream
- 3 garlic cloves; minced
- 16 oz. parmesan cheese; grated
- 10 oz. spinach
- 1/2 cup chicken stock
- 1/2 cup mayonnaise
- 1 tsp. onion powder

Directions:

1. In a pan that fits your air fryer, mix artichokes with stock, garlic, spinach, cream cheese, sour cream, onion powder and mayo, toss, introduce in your air fryer and cook at 350 °F, for 6 minutes
2. Add mozzarella and parmesan; stir well and serve.

Nutrition Values: Calories: 261; Fat: 12; Fiber: 2; Carbs: 12; Protein: 15

387. STUFFED EGGPLANTS RECIPE

Preparation Time: 40 Minutes
Servings: 4

Ingredients:

- 4 small eggplants; halved lengthwise
- 1/2 cup cauliflower; chopped.
- 1 tsp. oregano; chopped
- 1/2 cup parsley; chopped
- Salt and black pepper to the taste
- 10 tbsp. olive oil
- 2 ½ lbs. tomatoes; cut into halves and grated
- 1 green bell pepper; chopped.
- 1 yellow onion; chopped
- 1 tbsp. garlic; minced

- 3 oz. feta cheese; crumbled

Directions:

1. Season eggplants with salt, pepper and 4 tbsp. oil, toss, put them in your air fryer and cook at 350 °F, for 16 minutes.
2. Meanwhile; heat up a pan with 3 tbsp. oil over medium high heat, add onion; stir and cook for 5 minutes.
3. Add bell pepper, garlic and cauliflower; stir, cook for 5 minutes; take off heat, add parsley, tomato, salt, pepper, oregano and cheese and whisk everything
4. Stuff eggplants with the veggie mix, drizzle the rest of the oil over them, put them in your air fryer and cook at 350 °F, for 6 minutes more. Divide among plates and serve right away

Nutrition Values: Calories: 240; Fat: 4, fiber, 2; Carbs: 19; Protein: 2

388. FRIED ASPARAGUS RECIPE

Preparation Time: 25 Minutes
Servings: 4

Ingredients:

- 2 lbs. fresh asparagus; trimmed
- 1/2 tsp. oregano; dried
- 1/4 tsp. red pepper flakes
- 1/4 cup olive oil
- Salt and black pepper to the taste
- 1 tsp. lemon zest
- 4 oz. feta cheese; crumbled
- 4 garlic cloves; minced
- 2 tbsp. parsley; finely chopped.
- Juice from 1 lemon

Directions:

1. In a bowl; mix oil with lemon zest, garlic, pepper flakes and oregano and whisk.
2. Add asparagus, cheese, salt and pepper, toss, transfer to your air fryer's basket and cook at 350 °F, for 8 minutes.
3. Divide asparagus on plates, drizzle lemon juice and sprinkle parsley on top and serve

Nutrition Values: Calories: 162; Fat: 13; Fiber: 5; Carbs: 12; Protein: 8

389. COLLARD GREENS MIX

RECIPE

Preparation Time: 20 Minutes
Servings: 4

Ingredients:

- 1 bunch collard greens; trimmed
- 2 tbsp. olive oil
- 2 tbsp. tomato puree
- 1 tbsp. balsamic vinegar
- 1 tsp. sugar
- 1 yellow onion; chopped
- 3 garlic cloves; minced
- Salt and black pepper to the taste

Directions:

1. In a dish that fits your air fryer, mix oil, garlic, vinegar, onion and tomato puree and whisk
2. Add collard greens, salt, pepper and sugar, toss, introduce in your air fryer and cook at 320 °F, for 10 minutes. Divide collard greens mix on plates and serve

Nutrition Values: Calories: 121; Fat: 3; Fiber: 3; Carbs: 7; Protein: 3

390. SPANISH GREENS RECIPE

Preparation Time: 18 Minutes
Servings: 4

Ingredients:

- 1 apple; cored and chopped.
- 1 yellow onion; sliced
- 1/4 cup pine nuts; toasted
- 1/4 cup balsamic vinegar
- 3 tbsp. olive oil
- 1/4 cup raisins
- 6 garlic cloves; chopped
- 5 cups mixed spinach and chard
- Salt and black pepper to the taste
- A pinch of nutmeg

Directions:

1. Heat up a pan that fits your air fryer with the oil over medium high heat, add onion; stir and cook for 3 minutes
2. Add apple, garlic, raisins, vinegar, mixed spinach and chard, nutmeg, salt and pepper; stir, introduce in preheated air fryer and cook at 350 °F, for 5 minutes
3. Divide among plates, sprinkle pine nuts on top and serve.

Nutrition Values: Calories: 120; Fat: 1; Fiber: 2; Carbs: 3; Protein: 6

391. STUFFED TOMATOES RECIPE

Preparation Time: 25 Minutes
Servings: 4

Ingredients:

- 4 tomatoes; tops cut off and pulp scooped and chopped.
- 1 yellow onion; chopped.
- 1 tbsp. butter
- 2 tbsp. celery; chopped
- 1/2 cup mushrooms; chopped.
- 1 tbsp. bread crumbs
- 1 cup cottage cheese
- Salt and black pepper to the taste
- 1/4 tsp. caraway seeds
- 1 tbsp. parsley; chopped

Directions:

1. Heat up a pan with the butter over medium heat, melt it, add onion and celery; stir and cook for 3 minutes.
2. Add tomato pulp and mushrooms; stir and cook for 1 minute more
3. Add salt, pepper, crumbled bread, cheese, caraway seeds and parsley; stir, cook for 4 minutes more and take off heat.
4. Stuff tomatoes with this mix, place them in your air fryer and cook at 350 °F, for 8 minutes. Divide stuffed tomatoes on plates and serve

Nutrition Values: Calories: 143; Fat: 4; Fiber: 6; Carbs: 4; Protein: 4

392. ZUCCHINI MIX RECIPE

Preparation Time: 24 Minutes
Servings: 6

Ingredients:

- 6 zucchinis; halved and then sliced
- 3 garlic cloves; minced
- 2 oz. parmesan; grated

- 3/4 cup heavy cream
- Salt and black pepper to the taste
- 1 tbsp. butter
- 1 tsp. oregano; dried
- 1/2 cup yellow onion; chopped

Directions:

1. Heat up a pan that fits your air fryer with the butter over medium high heat, add onion; stir and cook for 4 minutes
2. Add garlic, zucchinis, oregano, salt, pepper and heavy cream, toss, introduce in your air fryer and cook at 350 °F, for 10 minutes. Add parmesan; stir, divide among plates and serve.

Nutrition Values: Calories: 160; Fat: 4; Fiber: 2; Carbs: 8; Protein: 8

393. BROCCOLI HASH RECIPE

Preparation Time: 38 Minutes
Servings: 2

Ingredients:

- 10 oz. mushrooms; halved
- 1 broccoli head; florets separated
- 1 garlic clove; minced
- 1 tbsp. balsamic vinegar
- 1 avocado; peeled and pitted
- A pinch of red pepper flakes
- 1 yellow onion; chopped.
- 1 tbsp. olive oil
- Salt and black pepper
- 1 tsp. basil; dried

Directions:

1. In a bowl; mix mushrooms with broccoli, onion, garlic and avocado.
2. In another bowl, mix vinegar, oil, salt, pepper and basil and whisk well
3. Pour this over veggies, toss to coat, leave aside for 30 minutes; transfer to your air fryer's basket and cook at 350 °F, for 8 minutes; Divide among plates and serve with pepper flakes on top

Nutrition Values: Calories: 182; Fat: 3; Fiber: 3; Carbs: 5; Protein: 8

GRILLED MEAT

394. GRILLED LAMB WITH HERBED SALT

Servings: 8
Cooking Time: 1 hour 20 minutes

Ingredients:

- 4 pounds boneless leg of lamb, cut into 2-inch chunks
- 2 ½ tablespoons herb salt
- 2 tablespoons olive oil

Directions:

1. Preheat the air fryer at 3900F.
2. Place the grill pan accessory in the air fryer.
3. Season the meat with the herb salt and brush with olive oil.
4. Grill the meat for 20 minutes per batch.
5. Make sure to flip the meat every 10 minutes for even cooking.

Nutrition Values:

Calories: 347; Carbs: 0g; Protein: 46.6g; Fat: 17.8g

395. DELICIOUS DRY RUBBED FLANK STEAK

Servings: 3
Cooking Time: 45 minutes

Ingredients:

- 2 tablespoons sugar
- 1 tablespoon chili powder
- 1 tablespoon paprika
- 2 teaspoons salt
- 2 teaspoons black pepper
- 1 teaspoon garlic powder
- 1 teaspoon mustard powder
- ½ teaspoon coriander
- ½ teaspoon ground cumin
- 1 ½ pounds flank steak

Directions:

1. Preheat the air fryer at 3900F.
2. Place the grill pan accessory in the air fryer.
3. In a small bowl, combine all the spices and rub all over the flank steak.
4. Place on the grill and cook for 15 minutes per batch.
5. Make sure to flip the meat every 8 minutes for even grilling.

Nutrition Values:

Calories: 330; Carbs: 10.2g; Protein:50 g; Fat:12.1 g

396. GRILLED LEG OF LAMB WITH MINT YOGURT

Servings: 6
Cooking Time: 1 hour

Ingredients:

- 1 cup rosemary leaves
- ¾ cup peeled garlic cloves, crushed
- 2 tablespoons olive oil
- 3 pounds lamb shanks, boned removed and sliced into 2-inch chunks
- 1 tablespoon lemon zest
- Salt and pepper to taste
- 2 cups Greek yogurt
- 1 cup fresh mint, chopped
- 1 tablespoon lemon juice

Directions:

1. Place in the Ziploc bag the rosemary leaves, garlic cloves, olive oil, lamb shanks, and lemon zest. Season with salt and pepper to taste.
2. Allow to marinate for 30 minutes in the fridge.
3. Preheat the air fryer at 3900F.
4. Place the grill pan accessory in the air fryer.
5. Place the lamb shanks and garlic on the grill pan and cook for 20 minutes per batch.
6. Flip the meat every 10 minutes.
7. Meanwhile, mix together the Greek yogurt, fresh mint, and lemon juice. Season with salt and pepper to taste.

8. Serve the lamb shanks with the mint yogurt

Nutrition Values:

Calories: 443; Carbs: 9.6g; Protein: 63.9g; Fat: 16.5g

397. GRILLED STEAK WITH BEET SALAD

Servings: 6
Cooking Time: 45 minutes

Ingredients:

- 1-pound tri-tip, sliced
- 2 tablespoons olive oil
- Salt and pepper to taste
- 1 bunch scallions, chopped
- 1 bunch arugula, torn
- 3 beets, peeled and sliced thinly
- 3 tablespoons balsamic vinegar

Directions:

1. Preheat the air fryer at 3900F.
2. Place the grill pan accessory in the air fryer.
3. Season the tri-tip with salt and pepper. Drizzle with oil.
4. Grill for 15 minutes per batch.
5. Meanwhile, prepare the salad by tossing the rest of the ingredients in a salad bowl.
6. Toss in the grilled tri-trip and drizzle with more balsamic vinegar.

Nutrition Values:

Calories: 221; Carbs: 20.7g; Protein: 17.2g; Fat: 7.7g

398. GRILLED SWEET AND SOUR SOY PORK BELLY

Servings: 4
Cooking Time: 60 minutes

Ingredients:

- 2 pounds pork belly
- ¼ cup lemon juice
- ½ cup soy sauce
- 3 tablespoons brown sugar
- 2 tablespoons hoisin sauce
- Salt and pepper to taste

- 3-star anise
- 1 bay leaf

Directions:

1. Place all ingredients in a Ziploc bag and allow to marinate in the fridge for at least 2 hours.
2. Preheat the air fryer at 3900F.
3. Place the grill pan accessory in the air fryer.
4. Grill the pork for at least 20 minutes per batch.
5. Make sure to flip the pork every 10 minutes.
6. Chop the pork before serving and garnish with green onions.

Nutrition Values:

Calories: 1301; Carbs: 15.5g; Protein:24 g; Fat: 126.4g

399. TEXAS RODEO-STYLE BEEF

Servings: 6
Cooking Time: 1 hour

Ingredients:

- 3 pounds beef steak sliced
- Salt and pepper to taste
- 2 onion, chopped
- ½ cup honey
- ½ cup ketchup
- 1 clove of garlic, minced
- 1 tablespoon chili powder
- ½ teaspoon dry mustard

Directions:

1. Place all ingredients in a Ziploc bag and allow to marinate in the fridge for at least 2 hours.
2. Preheat the air fryer at 3900F.
3. Place the grill pan accessory in the air fryer.
4. Grill the beef for 15 minutes per batch making sure that you flip it every 8 minutes for even grilling.
5. Meanwhile, pour the marinade on a saucepan and allow to simmer over medium heat until the sauce thickens.
6. Baste the beef with the sauce before serving.

Nutrition Values:

Calories: 542; Carbs: 49g; Protein: 37g; Fat: 22g

400. MUSTARD-MARINATED FLANK STEAK

Servings: 3
Cooking Time: 45 minutes

Ingredients:

- 1 ¼ pounds beef flank steak
- ½ teaspoon black pepper
- 1 cup Italian salad dressing
- ½ cup yellow mustard
- Salt to taste

Directions:

1. Place all ingredients in a Ziploc bag and allow to marinate in the fridge for at least 2 hours.
2. Preheat the air fryer at 3900F.
3. Place the grill pan accessory in the air fryer.
4. Grill for 15 minutes per batch making sure to flip the meat halfway through the cooking time.

Nutrition Values:

Calories: 576; Carbs: 3.1g; Protein:35 g; Fat: 47g

401. GRILLED RUM BEEF RIBEYE STEAK

Servings: 4
Cooking Time: 50 minutes

Ingredients:

- 2 pounds bone-in ribeye steak
- 2 tablespoons extra virgin olive oil
- Salt and black pepper to taste
- ½ cup rum

Directions:

1. Place all ingredients in a Ziploc bag and allow to marinate in the fridge for at least 2 hours.
2. Preheat the air fryer at 3900F.
3. Place the grill pan accessory in the air fryer.
4. Grill for 25 minutes per piece.
5. Halfway through the cooking time, flip the

meat for even grilling.

Nutrition Values:

Calories: 394; Carbs: 0.1g; Protein: 48.9g; Fat: 21.5g

402. ORIENTAL GRILLED FAMILY STEAK

Servings: 3
Cooking Time: 50 minutes

Ingredients:

- 1/3 cup soy sauce
- 1/3 cup dry sherry
- 1 tablespoon brown sugar
- ½ teaspoon dry mustard
- 1 clove of garlic, minced
- 1 ½ pounds beef top round steak
- 2 green onions, chopped

Directions:

1. Place all ingredients except for the green onions in a Ziploc bag and allow to marinate in the fridge for at least 2 hours.
2. Preheat the air fryer at 3900F.
3. Place the grill pan accessory in the air fryer. Add meat and cover top with foil.
4. Grill for 50 minutes.
5. Halfway through the cooking time, flip the meat for even grilling.
6. Meanwhile, pour the marinade into a saucepan and simmer for 10 minutes until the sauce thickens.
7. Baste the meat with the sauce and garnish with green onions before serving.

Nutrition Values:

Calories: 170; Carbs: 3g; Protein: 28g; Fat: 5g

403. TANDOORI SPICED SIRLOIN

Servings: 3
Cooking Time: 25 minutes

Ingredients:

- 1 ½ pounds boneless beef top loin steak
- ½ cup low-fat yogurt
- ¼ cup mint, chopped
- 3 tablespoons lemon juice
- 6 cloves of garlic, minced

- 2 teaspoons curry powder
- 2 teaspoons paprika
- Salt and pepper to taste

Directions:

1. Place all ingredients except for the green onions in a Ziploc bag and allow to marinate in the fridge for at least 2 hours.
2. Preheat the air fryer at 3900F.
3. Place the grill pan accessory in the air fryer.
4. Grill for 25 to 30 minutes.
5. Flip the steaks halfway through the cooking time for even grilling.

Nutrition Values:

Calories: 596; Carbs: 8.9g; Protein: 70.5g; Fat: 30.9g

404. RIBEYE STEAK WITH PEACHES

Servings: 2
Cooking Time: 45 minutes

Ingredients:

- 1-pound T-bone steak
- 1 tablespoon paprika
- 2 teaspoons lemon pepper seasoning
- ¼ cup balsamic vinegar
- 1 cup peach puree
- Salt and pepper to taste
- 1 teaspoon thyme

Directions:

1. Place all ingredients in a Ziploc bag and allow to marinate in the fridge for at least 2 hours.
2. Preheat the air fryer at 3900F.
3. Place the grill pan accessory in the air fryer.
4. Grill for 20 minutes and flip the meat halfway through the cooking time.

Nutrition Values:

Calories: 570; Carbs: 35.7g; Protein: 47g; Fat: 26.5g

405. KANSAS CITY RIBS

Servings: 2
Cooking Time: 50 minutes

Ingredients:

- 1-pound pork ribs, small
- 1 tablespoon brown sugar
- 1 teaspoon dry mustard
- ¼ teaspoon cayenne pepper
- 2 cloves of garlic
- 1 cup ketchup
- ¼ cup molasses
- ¼ cup apple cider vinegar
- 1 tablespoon Worcestershire sauce
- 1 tablespoon liquid smoke seasoning, hickory
- Salt and pepper to taste

Directions:

1. Place all ingredients in a Ziploc bag and allow to marinate in the fridge for at least 2 hours.
2. Preheat the air fryer at 3900F.
3. Place the grill pan accessory in the air fryer.
4. Grill meat for 25 minutes per batch.
5. Flip the meat halfway through the cooking time.
6. Pour the marinade in a saucepan and allow to simmer until the sauce thickens.
7. Pour glaze over the meat before serving.

Nutrition Values:

Calories: 634; Carbs: 32g; Protein: 32g; Fat: 42g

406. GRILLED STEAK CUBES WITH CHARRED ONIONS

Servings: 3
Cooking Time: 40 minutes

Ingredients:

- 1-pound boneless beef sirloin, cut into cubes
- 1 cup red onions, cut into wedges
- Salt and pepper to taste
- 1 tablespoon dry mustard
- 1 tablespoon olive oil

Directions:

1. Preheat the air fryer at 3900F.
2. Place the grill pan accessory in the air fryer.

3. Toss all ingredients in a bowl and mix until everything is coated with the seasonings.
4. Place on the grill pan and cook for 40 minutes.
5. Halfway through the cooking time, give a stir to cook evenly.

Nutrition Values:

Calories: 260; Carbs: 5.2g; Protein: 35.7g; Fat: 10.7g

407. TRIP TIP ROAST WITH GRILLED AVOCADO

Servings: 4
Cooking Time: 50 minutes

Ingredients:

*   1 teaspoon onion powder
*   1 teaspoon garlic powder
*   1-pound beef tri-tip
*   ½ cup red wine vinegar
*   3 tablespoons olive oil
*   3 avocadoes, seeded and sliced

Directions:

1. In a Ziploc bag, place all ingredients except for the avocado slices.
2. Allow to marinate in the fridge for 2 hours.
3. Preheat the air fryer at 3300F.
4. Place the grill pan accessory in the air fryer.
5. Grill the avocado for 2 minutes while the beef is marinating. Set aside.
6. After two hours, grill the beef for 50 minutes. Flip the beef halfway through the cooking time.
7. Serve the beef with grilled avocadoes

Nutrition Values:

Calories: 515; Carbs: 8g; Protein: 33g; Fat: 39g

408. BOURBON GRILLED BEEF

Servings: 4
Cooking Time: 60 minutes

Ingredients:

*   2 pounds beef steak, pounded
*   ¼ cup bourbon

*   ¼ cup barbecue sauce
*   1 tablespoon Worcestershire sauce
*   Salt and pepper to taste

Directions:

1. Place all ingredients in a Ziploc bag and allow to marinate in the fridge for at least 2 hours.
2. Preheat the air fryer at 3900F.
3. Place the grill pan accessory in the air fryer.
4. Place on the grill pan and cook for 20 minutes per batch.
5. Halfway through the cooking time, give a stir to cook evenly.
6. Meanwhile, pour the marinade on a saucepan and allow to simmer until the sauce thickens.
7. Serve beef with the bourbon sauce.

Nutrition Values:

Calories: 346; Carbs: 9.8g; Protein: 48.2g; Fat: 12.6g

409. PAPRIKA BEEF FLANK STEAK

Servings: 4
Cooking Time: 40 minutes

Ingredients:

*   1 ¼ pounds beef flank steak, sliced thinly
*   Salt and pepper to taste
*   3 tablespoons paprika powder
*   1 tablespoon cayenne pepper
*   1 tablespoon garlic powder
*   1 tablespoon onion powder
*   1 red bell pepper, julienned
*   1 yellow bell pepper, julienned
*   3 tablespoons olive oil

Directions:

1. Preheat the air fryer at 3900F.
2. Place the grill pan accessory in the air fryer.
3. In a bowl, toss all ingredients to coat everything with the seasonings.
4. Place on the grill pan and cook for 40 minutes.
5. Make sure to stir every 10 minutes for

even cooking.

Nutrition Values:

Calories: 334; Carbs: 9.8g; Protein: 32.5g; Fat: 18.2g

410. ESPRESSO-RUBBED STEAK

Servings: 3
Cooking Time: 50 minutes

Ingredients:

- 2 teaspoons chili powder
- Salt and pepper to taste
- 1 teaspoon instant espresso powder
- ½ teaspoon garlic powder
- 1 ½ pounds beef flank steak
- 2 tablespoons olive oil

Directions:

1. Preheat the air fryer at 3900F.
2. Place the grill pan accessory in the air fryer.
3. Make the dry rub by mixing the chili powder, salt, pepper, espresso powder, and garlic powder.
4. Rub all over the steak and brush with oil.
5. Place on the grill pan and cook for 40 minutes.
6. Halfway through the cooking time, flip the beef to cook evenly.

Nutrition Values:

Calories: 249; Carbs: 4g; Protein: 20g; Fat: 17g

411. NEW YORK BEEF STRIPS

Servings: 4
Cooking Time: 50 minutes

Ingredients:

- 4 boneless beef top loin steaks
- Salt and pepper to taste
- 2 tablespoons butter, softened
- 2 pounds crumbled blue cheese
- 2 tablespoons cream cheese
- 1 tablespoon pine nuts, toasted

Directions:

1. Preheat the air fryer at 3900F.
2. Place the grill pan accessory in the air fryer.

3. Season the beef with salt and pepper. Brush all sides with butter.
4. Grill for 25 minutes per batch making sure to flip halfway through the cooking time.
5. Slice the beef and serve with blue cheese, cream cheese and pine nuts.

Nutrition Values:

Calories: 682; Carbs: 1g; Protein: 75g; Fat: 42g

412. PERFECT YET SIMPLE GRILLED STEAK

Servings: 2
Cooking Time: 50 minutes

Ingredients:

- 2 large ribeye strip steaks
- Salt and pepper to taste
- 1 teaspoon liquid smoke seasoning, hickory

Directions:

1. Preheat the air fryer at 3900F.
2. Place the grill pan accessory in the air fryer.
3. Season the beef with salt, pepper, and liquid seasoning.
4. Grill for 25 minutes per batch.
5. Flip the meat halfway through the cooking time for even browning.

Nutrition Values:

Calories: 476; Carbs: 7g; Protein: 49g; Fat: 28g

413. SMOKED BEEF CHUCK

Servings: 6
Cooking Time: 1 hour and 30 minutes

Ingredients:

- 3 pounds beef chuck roll, scored with knife
- 2 ounces black peppercorns
- 3 tablespoons salt
- 2 tablespoons olive oil

Directions:

1. Preheat the air fryer at 3900F.
2. Place the grill pan accessory in the air fryer.
3. Season the beef chuck roll with black

peppercorns and salt.

4. Brush with olive oil and cover top with foil.
5. Grill for 1 hour and 30 minutes.
6. Flip the beef every 30 minutes for even grilling on all sides.

Nutrition Values:

Calories: 360; Carbs: 1.4g; Protein: 46.7g; Fat: 18g

414. SOUS VIDE SMOKED BRISKET

Servings: 6
Cooking Time: 1 hour

Ingredients:

- 3 pounds flat-cut brisket
- ¼ teaspoon liquid smoke
- Salt and pepper to taste
- 1 cup dill pickles

Directions:

1. Preheat the air fryer at 3900F.
2. Place the grill pan accessory in the air fryer.
3. Season the brisket with liquid smoke, salt, and pepper.
4. Place on the grill pan and cook for 30 minutes per batch.
5. Flip the meat halfway through cooking time for even grilling.
6. Serve with dill pickles.

Nutrition Values:

Calories: 309; Carbs: 1.2g; Protein: 49g; Fat:12 g

415. SKIRT STEAK WITH MOJO MARINADE

Servings: 4
Cooking Time: 60 minutes

Ingredients:

- 2 pounds skirt steak, trimmed from excess fat
- 2 tablespoons lime juice
- ¼ cup orange juice
- 2 tablespoons olive oil
- 4 cloves of garlic, minced
- 1 teaspoon ground cumin

- Salt and pepper to taste

Directions:

1. Place all ingredients in a mixing bowl and allow to marinate in the fridge for at least 2 hours
2. Preheat the air fryer at 3900F.
3. Place the grill pan accessory in the air fryer.
4. Grill for 15 minutes per batch and flip the beef every 8 minutes for even grilling.
5. Meanwhile, pour the marinade on a saucepan and allow to simmer for 10 minutes or until the sauce thickens.
6. Slice the beef and pour over the sauce.

Nutrition Values:

Calories: 568; Carbs: 4.7g; Protein: 59.1g; Fat: 34.7g

416. DIJON-MARINATED SKIRT STEAK

Servings: 2
Cooking Time: 40 minutes

Ingredients:

- ¼ cup Dijon mustard
- 1-pound skirt steak, trimmed
- 2 tablespoons champagne vinegar
- 1 tablespoon rosemary leaves
- Salt and pepper to taste

Directions:

1. Place all ingredients in a Ziploc bag and marinate in the fridge for 2 hours.
2. Preheat the air fryer at 3900F.
3. Place the grill pan accessory in the air fryer.
4. Grill the skirt steak for 20 minutes per batch.
5. Flip the beef halfway through the cooking time.

Nutrition Values:

Calories: 516; Carbs: 4.2g; Protein: 60.9g; Fat: 28.4g

417. GRILLED CARNE ASADA STEAK

Servings: 2

Cooking Time: 50 minutes

Ingredients:

- 2 slices skirt steak
- 1 dried ancho chilies, chopped
- 1 chipotle pepper, chopped
- 2 tablespoons of fresh lemon juice
- 2 tablespoons olive oil
- 3 cloves of garlic, minced
- 1 tablespoons soy sauce
- 2 tablespoons Asian fish sauce
- 1 tablespoon cumin
- 1 tablespoon coriander seeds
- 2 tablespoons brown sugar

Directions:

1. Place all ingredients in a Ziploc bag and marinate in the fridge for 2 hours.
2. Preheat the air fryer at 3900F.
3. Place the grill pan accessory in the air fryer.
4. Grill the skirt steak for 20 minutes.
5. Flip the steak every 10 minutes for even grilling.

Nutrition Values:

Calories: 697; Carbs: 10.2g; Protein:62.7 g; Fat: 45g

418. CHIMICHURRI-STYLE STEAK

Servings: 6
Cooking Time: 60 minutes

Ingredients:

- 3 pounds steak
- Salt and pepper to taste
- 1 cup commercial chimichurri

Directions:

1. Place all ingredients in a Ziploc bag and marinate in the fridge for 2 hours.
2. Preheat the air fryer at 3900F.
3. Place the grill pan accessory in the air fryer.
4. Grill the skirt steak for 20 minutes per batch.
5. Flip the steak every 10 minutes for even grilling.

Nutrition Values:

Calories: 507; Carbs: 2.8g; Protein: 63g; Fat: 27g

419. STRIP STEAK WITH CUCUMBER YOGURT SAUCE

Servings: 2
Cooking Time: 50 minutes

Ingredients:

- 2 New York strip steaks
- Salt and pepper to taste
- 3 tablespoons olive oil
- 1 cucumber, seeded and chopped
- 1 cup Greek yogurt
- ½ cup parsley, chopped

Directions:

1. Preheat the air fryer at 3900F.
2. Place the grill pan accessory in the air fryer.
3. Season the strip steaks with salt and pepper. Drizzle with oil.
4. Grill the steak for 20 minutes per batch and make sure to flip the meat every 10 minutes for even grilling.
5. Meanwhile, combine the cucumber, yogurt, and parsley.
6. Serve the beef with the cucumber yogurt.

Nutrition Values:

Calories: 460; Carbs: 5.2g; Protein: 50.8g; Fat: 26.3g

SNACKS

420. PORK BITES

Preparation time: 10 minutes
Cooking time: 15 minutes
Servings: 4

Ingredients:

- 2 teaspoons garlic powder
- 2 eggs
- Salt and black pepper to taste
- ¾ cup panko breadcrumbs
- ¾ cup coconut, shredded
- A drizzle of olive oil
- 1 pound ground pork

Directions:

1. In a bowl, mix coconut with panko and stir well.
2. In another bowl, mix the pork, salt, pepper, eggs, and garlic powder, and then shape medium meatballs out of this mix.
3. Dredge the meatballs in the coconut mix, place them in your air fryer's basket, introduce in the air fryer, and cook at 350 degrees F for 15 minutes.
4. Serve and enjoy!

Nutrition Values: calories 192, fat 4, fiber 2, carbs 14, protein 6

421. BANANA CHIPS

Preparation time: 5 minutes
Cooking time: 5 minutes
Servings: 8

Ingredients:

- ¼ cup peanut butter, soft
- 1 banana, peeled and sliced into 16 pieces
- 1 tablespoon vegetable oil

Directions:

1. Put the banana slices in your air fryer's basket and drizzle the oil over them.
2. Cook at 360 degrees F for 5 minutes.
3. Transfer to bowls and serve them dipped in peanut butter.

Nutrition Values: calories 100, fat 4, fiber 1,
carbs 10, protein 4

422. LEMONY APPLE BITES

Preparation time: 5 minutes
Cooking time: 5 minutes
Servings: 4

Ingredients:

- 3 big apples, cored, peeled and cubed
- 2 teaspoons lemon juice
- ½ cup caramel sauce

Directions:

1. In your air fryer, mix all the ingredients; toss well.
2. Cook at 340 degrees F for 5 minutes.
3. Divide into cups and serve as a snack.

Nutrition Values: calories 180, fat 4, fiber 3, carbs 10, protein 3

423. ZUCCHINI BALLS

Preparation time: 10 minutes
Cooking time: 12 minutes
Servings: 8

Ingredients:

- Cooking spray
- ½ cup dill, chopped
- 1 egg
- ½ cup white flour
- Salt and black pepper to taste
- 2 garlic cloves, minced
- 3 zucchinis, grated

Directions:

1. In a bowl, mix all the ingredients and stir.
2. Shape the mix into medium balls and place them into your air fryer's basket.
3. Cook at 375 degrees F for 12 minutes, flipping them halfway.
4. Serve them as a snack right away.

Nutrition Values: calories 120, fat 1, fiber 2, carbs 5, protein 3

424. BASIL AND CILANTRO

CRACKERS

Preparation time: 10 minutes
Cooking time: 16 minutes
Servings: 6

Ingredients:

- ½ teaspoon baking powder
- Salt and black pepper to taste
- 1¼ cups flour
- 1 garlic clove, minced
- 2 tablespoons basil, minced
- 2 tablespoons cilantro, minced
- 4 tablespoons butter, melted

Directions:

1. Add all of the ingredients to a bowl and stir until you obtain a dough.
2. Spread this on a lined baking sheet that fits your air fryer.
3. Place the baking sheet in the fryer at 325 degrees F and cook for 16 minutes.
4. Cool down, cut, and serve.

Nutrition Values: calories 171, fat 9, fiber 1, carbs 8, protein 4

425. BALSAMIC ZUCCHINI SLICES

Preparation time: 5 minutes
Cooking time: 50 minutes
Servings: 6

Ingredients:

- 3 zucchinis, thinly sliced
- Salt and black pepper to taste
- 2 tablespoons avocado oil
- 2 tablespoons balsamic vinegar

Directions:

1. Add all of the ingredients to a bowl and mix.
2. Put the zucchini mixture in your air fryer's basket and cook at 220 degrees F for 50 minutes.
3. Serve as a snack and enjoy!

Nutrition Values: calories 40, fat 3, fiber 7, carbs 3, protein 7

426. TURMERIC CARROT CHIPS

Preparation time: 5 minutes
Cooking time: 25 minutes
Servings: 4

Ingredients:

- 4 carrots, thinly sliced
- Salt and black pepper to taste
- ½ teaspoon turmeric powder
- ½ teaspoon chaat masala
- 1 teaspoon olive oil

Directions:

1. Place all ingredients in a bowl and toss well.
2. Put the mixture in your air fryer's basket and cook at 370 degrees F for 25 minutes, shaking the fryer from time to time.
3. Serve as a snack.

Nutrition Values: calories 161, fat 1, fiber 2, carbs 5, protein 3

427. CHIVES RADISH SNACK

Preparation time: 5 minutes
Cooking time: 10 minutes
Servings: 4

Ingredients:

- 16 radishes, sliced
- A drizzle of olive oil
- Salt and black pepper to taste
- 1 tablespoon chives, chopped

Directions:

1. In a bowl, mix the radishes, salt, pepper, and oil; toss well.
2. Place the radishes in your air fryer's basket and cook at 350 degrees F for 10 minutes.
3. Divide into bowls and serve with chives sprinkled on top.

Nutrition Values: calories 100, fat 1, fiber 2, carbs 4, protein 1

428. LENTILS SNACK

Preparation time: 5 minutes
Cooking time: 12 minutes
Servings: 4

Ingredients:

- 15 ounces canned lentils, drained

- ½ teaspoon cumin, ground
- 1 tablespoon olive oil
- 1 teaspoon sweet paprika
- Salt and black pepper to taste

Directions:

1. Place all ingredients in a bowl and mix well.
2. Transfer the mixture to your air fryer and cook at 400 degrees F for 12 minutes.
3. Divide into bowls and serve as a snack -or a side, or appetizer!.

Nutrition Values: calories 151, fat 1, fiber 6, carbs 10, protein 6

429. AIR FRIED CORN

Preparation time: 5 minutes
Cooking time: 10 minutes
Servings: 4

Ingredients:

- 2 tablespoons corn kernels
- 2½ tablespoons butter

Directions:

1. In a pan that fits your air fryer, mix the corn with the butter.
2. Place the pan in the fryer and cook at 400 degrees F for 10 minutes.
3. Serve as a snack and enjoy!

Nutrition Values: calories 70, fat 2, fiber 2, carbs 7, protein 3

430. SALMON TARTS

Preparation Time: 20 min
Servings: 15

Nutrition Values: Calories: 415; Carbs: 43g; Fat: 23g; Protein: 10g

Ingredients

- 15 mini tart cases
- 4 eggs, lightly beaten
- ½ cup heavy cream
- Salt and black pepper
- 3 oz smoked salmon
- 6 oz cream cheese, divided into 15 pieces
- 6 fresh dill

Directions

1. Mix together eggs and cream in a pourable measuring container. Arrange the tarts into the air fryer. Pour in mixture into the tarts, about halfway up the side and top with a piece of salmon and a piece of cheese. Cook for 10 minutes at 340 F, regularly check to avoid overcooking. Sprinkle dill and serve chilled.

431. PARMESAN CRUSTED PICKLES

Preparation Time: 35 min
Servings: 4

Nutrition Values: Calories 335; Carbs 34g; Fat 14g; Protein 17g

Ingredients

- 3 cups Dill Pickles, sliced, drained
- 2 eggs
- 2 tsp water
- 1 cup Grated Parmesan cheese
- 1 ½ cups breadcrumbs, smooth
- black pepper to taste
- Cooking spray

Directions

1. Add the breadcrumbs and black pepper to a bowl and mix well; set aside. In another bowl, crack the eggs and beat with the water. Set aside. Add the cheese to a separate bowl; set aside. Preheat the Air Fryer to 400 F.
2. Pull out the fryer basket and spray it lightly with cooking spray. Dredge the pickle slices it in the egg mixture, then in breadcrumbs and then in cheese. Place them in the fryer without overlapping.
3. Slide the fryer basket back in and cook for 4 minutes. Turn them and cook for further for 5 minutes, until crispy. Serve with a cheese dip.

432. BREADED MUSHROOMS

Preparation Time: 55 min
Servings: 4

Nutrition Values: Calories 487; Carbs 49g; Fat 22g; Protein 31g

Ingredients

- 1 lb small Button mushrooms, cleaned
- 2 cups breadcrumbs
- 2 eggs, beaten
- Salt and pepper to taste
- 2 cups Parmigiano Reggiano cheese, grated

Directions

1. Preheat the Air Fryer to 360 F. Pour the breadcrumbs in a bowl, add salt and pepper and mix well. Pour the cheese in a separate bowl and set aside. Dip each mushroom in the eggs, then in the crumbs, and then in the cheese.
2. Slide out the fryer basket and add 6 to 10 mushrooms. Cook them for 20 minutes, in batches, if needed. Serve with cheese dip.

433. CHEESY STICKS WITH SWEET THAI SAUCE

Preparation Time: 2 hrs 20 min
Servings: 4

Nutrition Values: Calories 158; Carbs 14g; Fat 7g; Protein 9g

Ingredients

- 12 mozzarella string cheese
- 2 cups breadcrumbs
- 3 eggs
- 1 cup sweet thai sauce
- 4 tbsp skimmed milk

Directions

1. Pour the crumbs in a medium bowl. Crack the eggs into another bowl and beat with the milk. One after the other, dip each cheese sticks in the egg mixture, in the crumbs, then egg mixture again and then in the crumbs again.
2. Place the coated cheese sticks on a cookie sheet and freeze for 1 to 2 hours. Preheat the Air Fryer to 380 F. Arrange the sticks in the fryer without overcrowding. Cook for 5 minutes, flipping them halfway through cooking to brown evenly. Cook in batches. Serve with a sweet thai sauce.

434. BACON WRAPPED AVOCADOS

Preparation Time: 40 min
Servings: 6

Nutrition Values: Calories 193; Carbs 10g; Fat 16g; Protein 4g

Ingredients

- 12 thick strips bacon
- 3 large avocados, sliced
- ⅓ tsp salt
- ⅓ tsp chili powder
- ⅓ tsp cumin powder

Directions

1. Stretch the bacon strips to elongate and use a knife to cut in half to make 24 pieces. Wrap each bacon piece around a slice of avocado from one end to the other end. Tuck the end of bacon into the wrap. Arrange on a flat surface and season with salt, chili and cumin on both sides.
2. Arrange 4 to 8 wrapped pieces in the fryer and cook at 350 F for 8 minutes, or until the bacon is browned and crunchy, flipping halfway through to cook evenly. Remove onto a wire rack and repeat the process for the remaining avocado pieces.

435. HOT CHICKEN WINGETTES

Preparation Time: 45 min
Servings: 3

Nutrition Values: Calories 563; Carbs 2g; Fat 28g; Protein 35g

Ingredients

- 15 chicken wingettes
- Salt and pepper to taste
- ⅓ cup hot sauce
- ⅓ cup butter
- ½ tbsp vinegar

Directions

1. Preheat the Air Fryer to 360 F. Season the wingettes with pepper and salt. Add them to the air fryer and cook for 35 minutes. Toss every 5 minutes. Once ready, remove them into a bowl. Over low heat, melt the butter in a saucepan. Add the vinegar and

hot sauce. Stir and cook for a minute.

2. Turn the heat off. Pour the sauce over the chicken. Toss to coat well. Transfer the chicken to a serving platter.Serve with a side of celery strips and blue cheese dressing.

436. BACON & CHICKEN WRAPPED JALAPENOS

Preparation Time: 40 min
Servings: 4

Nutrition Values: Calories 244; Carbs 13g; Fat 12.8g; Protein 9.3g

Ingredients

- 8 Jalapeno peppers, halved lengthwise and seeded
- 4 chicken breasts, butterflied and halved
- 6 oz cream cheese
- 6 oz Cheddar cheese
- 16 slices bacon
- 1 cup breadcrumbs
- Salt and pepper to taste
- 2 eggs
- Cooking spray

Directions

1. Season the chicken with pepper and salt on both sides. In a bowl, add cream cheese, cheddar, a pinch of pepper and salt. Mix well. Take each jalapeno and spoon in the cheese mixture to the brim. On a working board, flatten each piece of chicken and lay 2 bacon slices each on them. Place a stuffed jalapeno on each laid out chicken and bacon set, and wrap the jalapenos in them.
2. Preheat the air fryer to 350 F. Add the eggs to a bowl and pour the breadcrumbs in another bowl. Also, set a flat plate aside. Take each wrapped jalapeno and dip it into the eggs and then in the breadcrumbs. Place them on the flat plate. Lightly grease the fryer basket with cooking spray. Arrange 4-5 breaded jalapenos in the basket, and cook for 7 minutes.
3. Prepare a paper towel lined plate; set

aside. Once the timer beeps, open the fryer, turn the jalapenos, and cook further for 4 minutes. Once ready, remove them onto the paper towel lined plate. Repeat the cooking process for the remaining jalapenos. Serve with a sweet dip for an enhanced taste.

437. MOUTH-WATERING SALAMI STICKS

Preparation Time: 2 hrs 10 min
Servings: 3

Nutrition Values: Calories 428; Carbs 12g; Fat 16g; Protein 42g

Ingredients

- 1 lb ground beef
- 3 tbsp sugar
- A pinch garlic powder
- A pinch chili powder
- Salt to taste
- 1 tsp liquid smoke

Directions

1. Place the meat, sugar, garlic powder, chili powder, salt and liquid smoke in a bowl. Mix with a spoon. Mold out 4 sticks with your hands, place them on a plate, and refrigerate for 2 hours. Cook at 350 F. for 10 minutes, flipping once halfway through.

438. CARROT CRISPS

Preparation Time: 20 min
Servings: 2

Nutrition Values: Calories 35; Carbs 8g; Fat 3g; Protein 1g

Ingredients

- 3 large carrots, washed and peeled
- Salt to taste
- Cooking spray

Directions

2. Using a mandolin slicer, slice the carrots very thinly heightwise. Put the carrot strips in a bowl and season with salt to taste. Grease the fryer basket lightly with cooking spray, and add the carrot strips.

Cook at 350 F for 10 minutes, stirring once halfway through.

439. CALAMARI WITH OLIVES

Preparation Time: 25 min
Servings: 3

Nutrition Values: Calories 128; Carbs 0g; Fat 3g; Protein 22g

Ingredients

- ½ lb calamari rings
- ½ piece coriander, chopped
- 2 strips chili pepper, chopped
- 1 tbsp olive oil
- 1 cup pimiento-stuffed green olives, sliced
- Salt and black pepper to taste

Directions

1. In a bowl, add rings, chili pepper, salt, black pepper, oil, and coriander. Mix and let marinate for 10 minutes. Pour the calamari into an oven-safe bowl, that fits into the fryer basket.
2. Slide the fryer basket out, place the bowl in it, and slide the basket back in. Cook for 15 minutes stirring every 5 minutes using a spoon, at 400 F. After 15 minutes, and add in the olives.
3. Stir, close and continue to cook for 3 minutes. Once ready, transfer to a serving platter. Serve warm with a side of bread slices and mayonnaise.

440. SWEET MIXED NUTS

Preparation Time: 25 min
Servings: 5

Nutrition Values: Calories 147; Carbs 10g; Fat 12g; Protein 3g

Ingredients

- ½ cup pecans
- ½ cup walnuts
- ½ cup almonds
- A pinch cayenne pepper
- 2 tbsp sugar
- 2 tbsp egg whites
- 2 tsp cinnamon
- Cooking spray

Directions

1. Add the pepper, sugar, and cinnamon to a bowl and mix well; set aside. In another bowl, mix in the pecans, walnuts, almonds, and egg whites. Add the spice mixture to the nuts and give it a good mix. Lightly grease the fryer basket with cooking spray.
2. Pour in the nuts, and cook them for 10 minutes. Stir the nuts using a wooden vessel, and cook for further for 10 minutes. Pour the nuts in the bowl. Let cool before crunching on them.

441. CHEESY ONION RINGS

Preparation Time: 20 min
Servings: 3

Nutrition Values: Calories 205; Carbs 14g; Fat 11g; Protein 12g

Ingredients

- 1 onion, peeled and sliced into 1-inch rings
- ¾ cup Parmesan cheese
- 2 medium eggs, beaten
- 1 tsp garlic powder
- A pinch of salt
- 1 cup flour
- 1 tsp paprika powder

Directions

1. Add the eggs to a bowl; set aside In another bowl, add cheese, garlic powder, salt, flour, and paprika. Mix with a spoon. Dip each onion ring in egg, then in the cheese mixture, in the egg again and finally in the cheese mixture.
2. Add the rings to the basket and cook them for 8 minutes at 350 F. Remove onto a serving platter and serve with a cheese or tomatoes dip.

442. CHEESY SAUSAGE BALLS

Preparation Time: 50 min
Servings: 8

Nutrition Values: Calories 456; Carbs 23g; Fat 36g; Protein 36g

Ingredients

- 1 ½ lb ground sausages
- 2 ¼ cups Cheddar cheese, shredded
- 1 ½ cup flour
- ¾ tsp baking soda
- 4 eggs
- ¾ cup sour cream
- 1 tsp dried oregano
- 1 tsp smoked paprika
- 2 tsp garlic powder
- ½ cup liquid coconut oil

Directions

1. In a pan over medium heat, add the sausages and brown for 3-4 minutes. Drain the excess fat and set aside. In a bowl, sift in baking soda, and flour. Set aside. In another bowl, add eggs, sour cream, oregano, paprika, coconut oil, and garlic powder. Whisk to combine well. Combine the egg and flour mixtures using a spatula.

2. Add the cheese and sausages. Fold in and let it sit for 5 minutes to thicken. Rub your hands with coconut oil and mold out bite-size balls out of the batter. Place them on a tray, and refrigerate for 15 minutes. Then, add them in the air fryer, without overcrowding. Cook for 10 minutes per round, at 400 F, in batches if needed.

443. CRUSTED COCONUT SHRIMP

Preparation Time: 30 min
Servings: 5

Nutrition Values: Calories 149; Carbs 7g; Fat 2g; Protein 18g

Ingredients

- 1 lb jumbo shrimp, peeled and deveined
- ¾ cup shredded coconut
- 1 tbsp maple syrup
- ½ cup breadcrumbs
- ⅓ cup cornstarch
- ½ cup milk

Directions

1. Pour the cornstarch in a zipper bag, add shrimp, zip the bag up and shake

vigorously to coat with the cornstarch. Mix the syrup and milk in a bowl and set aside. In a separate bowl, mix the breadcrumbs and shredded coconut. Open the zipper bag and remove each shrimp while shaking off excess starch.

2. Dip each shrimp in the milk mixture and then in the crumbs mixture while pressing loosely to trap enough crumbs and coconut. Place the coated shrimp in the fryer without overcrowding. Cook 12 minutes at 350 F, flipping once halfway through. Cook until golden brown. Serve with a coconut based dip.

444. QUICK CHEESE STICKS

Preparation Time: 5 min
Servings: 12

Nutrition Values: Calories 256; Carbs 8g; Fat 21g; Protein 16g

Ingredients

- 6 -6 ozbread cheese
- 2 tbsp butter
- 2 cups panko crumbs

Directions

1. Put the butter in a bowl and melt in the microwave, for 2 minutes; set aside. With a knife, cut the cheese into equal sized sticks. Brush each stick with butter and dip into panko crumbs. Arrange the cheese sticks in a single layer on the fryer basket. Cook at 390 F for 10 minutes. Flip them halfway through, to brown evenly; serve warm.

445. SPICY CHEESE LINGS

Preparation Time: 25 min
Servings: 3

Nutrition Values: Calories 225; Carbs 35g; Fat 5.6g; Protein 8g

Ingredients

- 4 tbsp grated cheese + extra for rolling
- 1 cup flour + extra for kneading
- ¼ tsp chili powder
- ½ tsp baking powder
- 3 tsp butter

- A pinch of salt
- Water

Directions

1. In a bowl, mix in the cheese, flour, baking powder, chili powder, butter, and salt. The mixture should be crusty. Add some drops of water and mix well to get a dough. Remove the dough on a flat surface.
2. Rub some extra flour in your palms and on the surface, and knead the dough for a while. Using a rolling pin, roll the dough out into a thin sheet. With a pastry cutter, cut the dough into your desired lings' shape. Add the cheese lings in the basket, and cook for 6 minutes at 350 F, flipping once halfway through.

446. RADISH CHIPS

Preparation Time: 30 min
Servings: 4

Nutrition Values: Calories 25; Carbs 0.2g; Fat 2g; Protein 0.1g

Ingredients

- 10 radishes, leaves removed and cleaned
- Salt to season
- Water
- Cooking spray

Directions

1. Using a mandolin, slice the radishes thinly. Place them in a pot and cover them with water. Heat the pot on a stovetop, and bring to boil, until the radishes are translucent, for 4 minutes. After 4 minutes, drain the radishes through a sieve; set aside. Grease the fryer basket with cooking spray.
2. Add in the radish slices and cook for 8 minutes, flipping once halfway through. Cook until golden brown, at 400 F. Meanwhile, prepare a paper towel-lined plate. Once the radishes are ready, transfer them to the paper towel-lined plate. Season with salt, and serve with ketchup or garlic mayo.

447. ZUCCHINI PARMESAN

CHIPS

Preparation Time: 20 min
Servings: 3

Nutrition Values: Calories 268; Carbs 13g; Fat 16g; Protein 17g

Ingredients

- 3 medium zucchinis
- 1 cup breadcrumbs
- 2 eggs, beaten
- 1 cup grated Parmesan cheese
- Salt and pepper to taste
- 1 tsp smoked paprika
- Cooking spray

Directions

1. With a mandolin cutter, slice the zucchinis thinly. Use paper towels to press out excess liquid. In a bowl, add crumbs, salt, pepper, cheese, and paprika. Mix well and set aside. Set a wire rack or tray aside. Dip each zucchini slice in egg and then in the cheese mix while pressing to coat them well.
2. Place them on the wire rack. Spray the coated slices with oil. Put the slices in the fryer basket in a single layer without overlapping. Cook at 350 F for 8 minutes for each batch. Serve sprinkled with salt and with a spicy dip.

448. PAPRIKA CHICKEN NUGGETS

Preparation Time: 1 hr 20 min
Servings: 4

Nutrition Values: Calories 548; Carbs 51g; Fat 23g; Protein 49g

Ingredients

- 2 chicken breasts, bones removed
- 2 tbsp paprika
- 2 cups milk
- 2 eggs
- 4 tsp onion powder
- 1 ½ tsp garlic powder
- Salt and pepper to taste
- 1 cups flour

- 2 cups breadcrumbs
- Cooking spray

Directions

1. Cut the chicken into 1-inch chunks. In a bowl, mix in paprika, onion, garlic, salt, pepper, flour, and breadcrumbs. In another bowl, crack the eggs, add the milk and beat them together. Prepare a tray. Dip each chicken chunk in the egg mixture, place them on the tray, and refrigerate for 1 hour.
2. Preheat the Air Fryer to 370 F. Roll each chunk in the crumb mixture. Place the crusted chicken in the fryer's basket. Spray with cooking spray. Cook for 8 minutes at 360 F, flipping once halfway through. Serve with a tomato dip or ketchup. Yum!

449. COOL CHICKEN CROQUETTES

Preparation Time: 20 min
Servings: 4

Nutrition Values: Calories: 230; Carbs: 10g; Fat: 12g; Protein: 9g

Ingredients

- 4 chicken breasts
- 1 whole egg
- Salt and pepper to taste
- 1 cup oats, crumbled
- ½ tsp garlic powder
- 1 tbsp parsley
- 1 tbsp thyme

Directions

1. Preheat your Air Fryer to 360 degrees F. Pulse chicken breast in a processor food until well blended. Add seasoning to the chicken alongside garlic, parsley, thyme and mix well. In a bowl, add beaten egg and beat until the yolk is mixed.
2. In a separate bowl, add crumbled oats. Form croquettes using the chicken mixture and dip in beaten egg, and finally in oats until coated. Place the nuggets in your fryer's cooking basket. Cook for 10 minutes, making sure to keep shaking the basket after every 5 minutes.

450. HERBED CROUTONS WITH BRIE CHEESE

Preparation Time: 20 min / Serve: 1

Nutrition Values: Calories: 20; Carbs: 1.5g; Fat: 1.3g; Protein: 0.5g

Ingredients

- 2 tbsp olive oil
- 1 tbsp french herbs
- 7 oz brie cheese, chopped
- 2 slices bread, halved

Directions

1. Preheat your Air Fryer to 340 degrees F. Using a bowl, mix oil with herbs. Dip the bread slices in the oil mixture to coat. Place the coated slices on a flat surface. Lay the brie cheese on the slices. Place the slices into your air fryer's basket and cook for 7 minutes. Once the bread is ready, cut into cubes.

451. CHEESY BACON FRIES

Preparation Time: 25 min
Servings: 4

Nutrition Values: Calories: 447; Carbs: 44g; Fat: 28g; Protein: 5g

Ingredients

- 2 large russet potatoes, cut strips
- 5 slices bacon, chopped
- 2 tbsp vegetable oil
- 2½ cups Cheddar cheese, shredded
- 3 oz melted cream cheese
- Salt and pepper to taste
- ¼ cup scallions, chopped

Directions

2. Boil salted water in a large sized pot. Add potatoes to the salted water and allow to boil for 4 minutes until blanched. Strain the potatoes in a colander and rinse thoroughly with cold water to remove starch from the surface. Dry them with a kitchen towel. Preheat your Air Fryer to 400 F.
3. Add chopped bacon to your Air Fryer's cooking basket and cook for 4 minutes

until crispy, making sure to give the basket a shake after 2 minutes; set aside. Add dried potatoes to the cooking basket and drizzle oil on top to coat. Cook for 25 minutes, shaking the basket every 5 minutes. Season with salt and pepper after 12 minutes.

4. Once cooked, transfer the fries to an 8-inch pan. In a bowl, mix 2 cups of cheddar cheese with cream cheese. Pour over the potatoes and add in crumbled bacon. Place the pan into the air fryer's cooking basket and cook for 5 more minutes at 340 F. Sprinkle chopped scallions on top and serve with your desired dressing.

452. CHILI CHEESE BALLS

Preparation Time: 50 min
Servings: 6

Nutrition Values: Calories 395; Carbs 45g; Fat 13g; Protein 23g

Ingredients

- 2 cups crumbled Cottage cheese
- 2 cups grated Parmesan cheese
- 2 red potatoes, peeled and chopped
- 1 medium onion, finely chopped
- 1 ½ tsp red chili flakes
- 1 green chili, finely chopped
- Salt to taste
- 4 tbsp chopped coriander leaves
- 1 cup flour
- 1 cup breadcrumbs
- Water

Directions

1. Place the potatoes in a pot, add water and bring them to boil over medium heat for 25 to 30 minutes until soft. Turn off the heat, drain the potatoes through a sieve, and place in a bowl. With a potato masher, mash the potatoes and leave to cool.

2. Add the cottage cheese, Parmesan cheese, onion, red chili flakes, green chili, salt, coriander, and flour to the potato mash. Use a wooden spoon to mix the ingredients well, then, use your hands to mold out bite-size balls. Pour the crumbs

in a bowl and roll each cheese ball lightly in it.

3. Place them on a tray. Put 8 to 10 cheese balls in the fryer basket, and cook for 15 minutes at 350 F. Repeat the cooking process for the remaining cheese balls. Serve with tomato-basil dip.

453. JUICY PICKLED CHIPS

Preparation Time: 20 min
Servings: 3

Nutrition Values: Calories: 140; Carbs: 17g; Fat: 7g; Protein: 2g

Ingredients

- 36 sweet pickle chips
- 1 cup buttermilk
- 3 tbsp smoked paprika
- 2 cups flour
- ¼ cup cornmeal
- Salt and black pepper to taste

Directions

1. Preheat your Air Fryer to 400 F. Using a bowl mix flour, paprika, pepper, salt, cornmeal and powder. Place pickles in buttermilk and set aside for 5 minutes. Dip the pickles in the spice mixture and place them in the air fryer's cooking basket. Cook for 10 minutes.

454. COCONUT CHICKEN BITES

Preparation time: 10 minutes
Cooking time: 13 minutes
Servings: 4

Ingredients:

- 2 teaspoons garlic powder
- 2 eggs
- Salt and black pepper to the taste
- ¾ cup panko bread crumbs
- ¾ cup coconut, shredded
- Cooking spray
- 8 chicken tenders

Directions:

2. In a bowl, mix eggs with salt, pepper and garlic powder and whisk well.
3. In another bowl, mix coconut with panko

and stir well.

4. Dip chicken tenders in eggs mix and then coat in coconut one well.
5. Spray chicken bites with cooking spray, place them in your air fryer's basket and cook them at 350 degrees F for 10 minutes.
6. Arrange them on a platter and serve as an appetizer.
7. Enjoy!

Nutrition Values: calories 252, fat 4, fiber 2, carbs 14, protein 24

455. BUFFALO CAULIFLOWER SNACK

Preparation time: 10 minutes
Cooking time: 15 minutes
Servings: 4

Ingredients:

- 4 cups cauliflower florets
- 1 cup panko bread crumbs
- ¼ cup butter, melted
- ¼ cup buffalo sauce
- Mayonnaise for serving

Directions:

1. In a bowl, mix buffalo sauce with butter and whisk well.
2. Dip cauliflower florets in this mix and coat them in panko bread crumbs.
3. Place them in your air fryer's basket and cook at 350 degrees F for 15 minutes.
4. Arrange them on a platter and serve with mayo on the side.
5. Enjoy!

Nutrition Values: calories 241, fat 4, fiber 7, carbs 8, protein 4

456. BANANA SNACK

Preparation time: 10 minutes
Cooking time: 5 minutes
Servings: 8

Ingredients:

- 16 baking cups crust
- ¼ cup peanut butter
- ¾ cup chocolate chips

- 1 banana, peeled and sliced into 16 pieces
- 1 tablespoon vegetable oil

Directions:

1. Put chocolate chips in a small pot, heat up over low heat, stir until it melts and take off heat.
2. In a bowl, mix peanut butter with coconut oil and whisk well.
3. Spoon 1 teaspoon chocolate mix in a cup, add 1 banana slice and top with 1 teaspoon butter mix
4. Repeat with the rest of the cups, place them all into a dish that fits your air fryer, cook at 320 degrees F for 5 minutes, transfer to a freezer and keep there until you serve them as a snack.
5. Enjoy!

Nutrition Values: calories 70, fat 4, fiber 1, carbs 10, protein 1

457. POTATO SPREAD

Preparation time: 10 minutes
Cooking time: 10 minutes
Servings: 10

Ingredients:

- 19 ounces canned garbanzo beans, drained
- 1 cup sweet potatoes, peeled and chopped
- ¼ cup tahini
- 2 tablespoons lemon juice
- 1 tablespoon olive oil
- 5 garlic cloves, minced
- ½ teaspoon cumin, ground
- 2 tablespoons water
- A pinch of salt and white pepper

Directions:

1. Put potatoes in your air fryer's basket, cook them at 360 degrees F for 15 minutes, cool them down, peel, put them in your food processor and pulse well. basket,
2. Add sesame paste, garlic, beans, lemon juice, cumin, water and oil and pulse really well.
3. Add salt and pepper, pulse again, divide into bowls and serve.
4. Enjoy!

Nutrition Values: calories 200, fat 3, fiber 10, carbs 20, protein 11

458. MEXICAN APPLE SNACK

Preparation time: 10 minutes
Cooking time: 5 minutes
Servings: 4

Ingredients:

- 3 big apples, cored, peeled and cubed
- 2 teaspoons lemon juice
- ¼ cup pecans, chopped
- ½ cup dark chocolate chips
- ½ cup clean caramel sauce

Directions:

1. In a bowl, mix apples with lemon juice, stir and transfer to a pan that fits your air fryer.
2. Add chocolate chips, pecans, drizzle the caramel sauce, toss, introduce in your air fryer and cook at 320 degrees F for 5 minutes.
3. Toss gently, divide into small bowls and serve right away as a snack.
4. Enjoy!

Nutrition Values: calories 200, fat 4, fiber 3, carbs 20, protein 3

459. SHRIMP MUFFINS

Preparation time: 10 minutes
Cooking time: 26 minutes
Servings: 6

Ingredients:

- 1 spaghetti squash, peeled and halved
- 2 tablespoons mayonnaise
- 1 cup mozzarella, shredded
- 8 ounces shrimp, peeled, cooked and chopped
- 1 and ½ cups panko
- 1 teaspoon parsley flakes
- 1 garlic clove, minced
- Salt and black pepper to the taste
- Cooking spray

Directions:

1. Put squash halves in your air fryer, cook at 350 degrees F for 16 minutes, leave aside

to cool down and scrape flesh into a bowl.

2. Add salt, pepper, parsley flakes, panko, shrimp, mayo and mozzarella and stir well.
3. Spray a muffin tray that fits your air fryer with cooking spray and divide squash and shrimp mix in each cup.
4. Introduce in the fryer and cook at 360 degrees F for 10 minutes.
5. Arrange muffins on a platter and serve as a snack.
6. Enjoy!

Nutrition Values: calories 60, fat 2, fiber 0.4, carbs 4, protein 4

460. ZUCCHINI CAKES

Preparation time: 10 minutes
Cooking time: 12 minutes
Servings: 12

Ingredients:

- Cooking spray
- ½ cup dill, chopped
- 1 egg
- ½ cup whole wheat flour
- Salt and black pepper to the taste
- 1 yellow onion, chopped
- 2 garlic cloves, minced
- 3 zucchinis, grated

Directions:

1. In a bowl, mix zucchinis with garlic, onion, flour, salt, pepper, egg and dill, stir well, shape small patties out of this mix, spray them with cooking spray, place them in your air fryer's basket and cook at 370 degrees F for 6 minutes on each side.
2. Serve them as a snack right away.
3. Enjoy!

Nutrition Values: calories 60, fat 1, fiber 2, carbs 6, protein 2

461. CAULIFLOWER BARS

Preparation time: 10 minutes
Cooking time: 25 minutes
Servings: 12

Ingredients:

- 1 big cauliflower head, florets separated

- ½ cup mozzarella, shredded
- ¼ cup egg whites
- 1 teaspoon Italian seasoning
- Salt and black pepper to the taste

Directions:

1. Put cauliflower florets in your food processor, pulse well, spread on a lined baking sheet that fits your air fryer, introduce in the fryer and cook at 360 degrees F for 10 minutes.
2. Transfer cauliflower to a bowl, add salt, pepper, cheese, egg whites and Italian seasoning, stir really well, spread this into a rectangle pan that fits your air fryer, press well, introduce in the fryer and cook at 360 degrees F for 15 minutes more.
3. Cut into 12 bars, arrange them on a platter and serve as a snack
4. Enjoy!

Nutrition Values: calories 50, fat 1, fiber 2, carbs 3, protein 3

462. PESTO CRACKERS

Preparation time: 10 minutes
Cooking time: 17 minutes
Servings: 6

Ingredients:

- ½ teaspoon baking powder
- Salt and black pepper to the taste
- 1 and ¼ cups flour
- ¼ teaspoon basil, dried
- 1 garlic clove, minced
- 2 tablespoons basil pesto
- 3 tablespoons butter

Directions:

1. In a bowl, mix salt, pepper, baking powder, flour, garlic, cayenne, basil, pesto and butter and stir until you obtain a dough.
2. Spread this dough on a lined baking sheet that fits your air fryer, introduce in the fryer at 325 degrees F and bake for 17 minutes.
3. Leave aside to cool down, cut crackers and serve them as a snack.
4. Enjoy!

Nutrition Values: calories 200, fat 20, fiber 1, carbs 4, protein 7

463. PUMPKIN MUFFINS

Preparation time: 10 minutes
Cooking time: 15 minutes
Servings: 18

Ingredients:

- ¼ cup butter
- ¾ cup pumpkin puree
- 2 tablespoons flaxseed meal
- ¼ cup flour
- ½ cup sugar
- ½ teaspoon nutmeg, ground
- 1 teaspoon cinnamon powder
- ½ teaspoon baking soda
- 1 egg
- ½ teaspoon baking powder

Directions:

1. In a bowl, mix butter with pumpkin puree and egg and blend well.
2. Add flaxseed meal, flour, sugar, baking soda, baking powder, nutmeg and cinnamon and stir well.
3. Spoon this into a muffin pan that fits your fryer introduce in the fryer at 350 degrees F and bake for 15 minutes.
4. Serve muffins cold as a snack.
5. Enjoy!

Nutrition Values: calories 50, fat 3, fiber 1, carbs 2, protein 2

464. ZUCCHINI CHIPS

Preparation time: 10 minutes
Cooking time: 1 hour
Servings: 6

Ingredients:

- 3 zucchinis, thinly sliced
- Salt and black pepper to the taste
- 2 tablespoons olive oil
- 2 tablespoons balsamic vinegar

Directions:

1. In a bowl, mix oil with vinegar, salt and pepper and whisk well.
2. Add zucchini slices, toss to coat well,

introduce in your air fryer and cook at 200 degrees F for 1 hour.
3. Serve zucchini chips cold as a snack.
4. Enjoy!

Nutrition Values: calories 40, fat 3, fiber 7, carbs 3, protein 7

465. BEEF JERKY SNACK

Preparation time: 2 hours
Cooking time: 1 hour and 30 minutes
Servings: 6

Ingredients:

- 2 cups soy sauce
- ½ cup Worcestershire sauce
- 2 tablespoons black peppercorns
- 2 tablespoons black pepper
- 2 pounds beef round, sliced

Directions:

1. In a bowl, mix soy sauce with black peppercorns, black pepper and Worcestershire sauce and whisk well.
2. Add beef slices, toss to coat and leave aside in the fridge for 6 hours.
3. Introduce beef rounds in your air fryer and cook them at 370 degrees F for 1 hour and 30 minutes.
4. Transfer to a bowl and serve cold.
5. Enjoy!

Nutrition Values: calories 300, fat 12, fiber 4, carbs 3, protein 8

466. HONEY PARTY WINGS

Preparation time: 1 hour and 10 minutes
Cooking time: 12 minutes
Servings: 8

Ingredients:

- 16 chicken wings, halved
- 2 tablespoons soy sauce
- 2 tablespoons honey
- Salt and black pepper to the taste
- 2 tablespoons lime juice

Directions:

1. In a bowl, mix chicken wings with soy sauce, honey, salt, pepper and lime juice, toss well and keep in the fridge for 1 hour.

2. Transfer chicken wings to your air fryer and cook them at 360 degrees F for 12 minutes, flipping them halfway.
3. Arrange them on a platter and serve as an appetizer.
4. Enjoy!

Nutrition Values: calories 211, fat 4, fiber 7, carbs 14, protein 3

467. SALMON PARTY PATTIES

Preparation time: 10 minutes
Cooking time: 22 minutes
Servings: 4

Ingredients:

- 3 big potatoes, boiled, drained and mashed
- 1 big salmon fillet, skinless, boneless
- 2 tablespoons parsley, chopped
- 2 tablespoon dill, chopped
- Salt and black pepper to the taste
- 1 egg
- 2 tablespoons bread crumbs
- Cooking spray

Directions:

1. Place salmon in your air fryer's basket and cook for 10 minutes at 360 degrees F.
2. Transfer salmon to a cutting board, cool it down, flake it and put it in a bowl.
3. Add mashed potatoes, salt, pepper, dill, parsley, egg and bread crumbs, stir well and shape 8 patties out of this mix.
4. Place salmon patties in your air fryer's basket, spry them with cooking oil, cook at 360 degrees F for 12 minutes, flipping them halfway, transfer them to a platter and serve as an appetizer.
5. Enjoy!

Nutrition Values: calories 231, fat 3, fiber 7, carbs 14, protein 4

468. BANANA CHIPS

Preparation time: 10 minutes
Cooking time: 15 minutes
Servings: 4

Ingredients:

- 4 bananas, peeled and sliced

- A pinch of salt
- ½ teaspoon turmeric powder
- ½ teaspoon chaat masala
- 1 teaspoon olive oil

Directions:

1. In a bowl, mix banana slices with salt, turmeric, chaat masala and oil, toss and leave aside for 10 minutes.
2. Transfer banana slices to your preheated air fryer at 360 degrees F and cook them for 15 minutes flipping them once.
3. Serve as a snack.
4. Enjoy!

Nutrition Values: calories 121, fat 1, fiber 2, carbs 3, protein 3

469. SPRING ROLLS

Preparation time: 10 minutes
Cooking time: 25 minutes
Servings: 8

Ingredients:

- 2 cups green cabbage, shredded
- 2 yellow onions, chopped
- 1 carrot, grated
- ½ chili pepper, minced
- 1 tablespoon ginger, grated
- 3 garlic cloves, minced
- 1 teaspoon sugar
- Salt and black pepper to the taste
- 1 teaspoon soy sauce
- 2 tablespoons olive oil
- 10 spring roll sheets
- 2 tablespoons corn flour
- 2 tablespoons water

Directions:

1. Heat up a pan with the oil over medium heat, add cabbage, onions, carrots, chili pepper, ginger, garlic, sugar, salt, pepper and soy sauce, stir well, cook for 2-3 minutes, take off heat and cool down.
2. Cut spring roll sheets in squares, divide cabbage mix on each and roll them.
3. In a bowl, mix corn flour with water, stir well and seal spring rolls with this mix.
4. Place spring rolls in your air fryer's basket

and cook them at 360 degrees F for 10 minutes.
5. Flip roll and cook them for 10 minutes more.
6. Arrange on a platter and serve them as an appetizer.
7. Enjoy!

Nutrition Values: calories 214, fat 4, fiber 4, carbs 12, protein 4

DESSERTS

470. EASY CHEESECAKE RECIPE

Preparation Time: 25 Minutes
Servings: 15

Ingredients:

- 1 lb. cream cheese
- 1/2 tsp. vanilla extract
- 1 cup graham crackers; crumbled
- 2 tbsp. butter
- 2 eggs
- 4 tbsp. sugar

Directions:

1. In a bowl; mix crackers with butter.
2. Press crackers mix on the bottom of a lined cake pan, introduce in your air fryer and cook at 350 °F, for 4 minutes
3. Meanwhile; in a bowl, mix sugar with cream cheese, eggs and vanilla and whisk well.
4. Spread filling over crackers crust and cook your cheesecake in your air fryer at 310 °F, for 15 minutes. Leave cake in the fridge for 3 hours, slice and serve

Nutrition Values: Calories: 245; Fat: 12; Fiber: 1; Carbs: 20; Protein: 3

471. MACAROONS RECIPE

Preparation Time: 18 Minutes
Servings: 20

Ingredients:

- 2 tbsp. sugar
- 2 cup coconut; shredded
- 4 egg whites
- 1 tsp. vanilla extract

Directions:

1. In a bowl; mix egg whites with stevia and beat using your mixer
2. Add coconut and vanilla extract, whisk again, shape small balls out of this mix, introduce them in your air fryer and cook at 340 °F, for 8 minutes. Serve macaroons cold

Nutrition Values: Calories: 55; Fat: 6; Fiber: 1; Carbs: 2; Protein: 1

472. ORANGE CAKE RECIPE

Preparation Time: 42 Minutes
Servings: 12

Ingredients:

- 1 orange, peeled and cut into quarters
- 1 tsp. vanilla extract
- 6 eggs
- 2 tbsp. orange zest
- 4 oz. cream cheese
- 1 tsp. baking powder
- 9 oz. flour
- 2 oz. sugar+ 2 tbsp.
- 4 oz. yogurt

Directions:

1. In your food processor, pulse orange very well
2. Add flour, 2 tbsp. sugar, eggs, baking powder, vanilla extract and pulse well again.
3. Transfer this into 2 spring form pans, introduce each in your fryer and cook at 330 °F, for 16 minutes
4. Meanwhile; in a bowl, mix cream cheese with orange zest, yogurt and the rest of the sugar and stir well.
5. Place one cake layer on a plate, add half of the cream cheese mix, add the other cake layer and top with the rest of the cream cheese mix. Spread it well, slice and serve.

Nutrition Values: Calories: 200; Fat: 13; Fiber: 2; Carbs: 9; Protein: 8

473. BREAD DOUGH AND AMARETTO DESSERT RECIPE

Preparation Time: 22 Minutes
Servings: 12

Ingredients:

- 1 lb. bread dough

- 1 cup heavy cream
- 12 oz. chocolate chips
- 1 cup sugar
- 1/2 cup butter; melted
- 2 tbsp. amaretto liqueur

Directions:

1. Roll dough, cut into 20 slices and then cut each slice in halves.
2. Brush dough pieces with butter, sprinkle sugar, place them in your air fryer's basket after you've brushed it some butter, cook them at 350 °F, for 5 minutes; flip them, cook for 3 minutes more and transfer to a platter
3. Heat up a pan with the heavy cream over medium heat, add chocolate chips and stir until they melt. Add liqueur; stir again, transfer to a bowl and serve bread dippers with this sauce

Nutrition Values: Calories: 200; Fat: 1; Fiber: 0; Carbs: 6; Protein: 6

474. CARROT CAKE RECIPE

Preparation Time: 55 Minutes
Servings: 6

Ingredients:

- 5 oz. flour
- 3/4 tsp. baking powder
- 1/4 tsp. nutmeg; ground
- 1/2 tsp. baking soda
- 1/2 tsp. cinnamon powder
- 1/2 cup sugar
- 1/3 cup carrots; grated
- 1/3 cup pecans; toasted and chopped.
- 1/4 cup pineapple juice
- 1/2 tsp. allspice
- 1 egg
- 3 tbsp. yogurt
- 4 tbsp. sunflower oil
- 1/3 cup coconut flakes; shredded
- Cooking spray

Directions:

1. In a bowl; mix flour with baking soda and powder, salt, allspice, cinnamon and nutmeg and stir.

2. In another bowl, mix egg with yogurt, sugar, pineapple juice, oil, carrots, pecans and coconut flakes and stir well
3. Combine the two mixtures and stir well, pour this into a spring form pan that fits your air fryer which you've greased with some cooking spray, transfer to your air fryer and cook on 320 °F, for 45 minutes.
4. Leave cake to cool down, then cut and serve it.

Nutrition Values: Calories: 200; Fat: 6; Fiber: 20; Carbs: 22; Protein: 4

475. BANANA BREAD RECIPE

Preparation Time: 50 Minutes
Servings: 6

Ingredients:

- 3/4 cup sugar
- 1/3 cup butter
- 1/3 cup milk
- 1 tsp. vanilla extract
- 1 egg
- 2 bananas; mashed
- 1 tsp. baking powder
- 1 ½ cups flour
- 1/2 tsp. baking soda
- 1 ½ tsp. cream of tartar
- Cooking spray

Directions:

1. In a bowl; mix milk with cream of tartar, sugar, butter, egg, vanilla and bananas and stir everything.
2. In another bowl, mix flour with baking powder and baking soda
3. Combine the 2 mixtures; stir well, pour this into a cake pan greased with some cooking spray, introduce in your air fryer and cook at 320 °F, for 40 minutes. Take bread out, leave aside to cool down, slice and serve it.

Nutrition Values: Calories: 292; Fat: 7; Fiber: 8; Carbs: 28; Protein: 4

476. EASY GRANOLA RECIPE

Preparation Time: 45 Minutes
Servings: 4

Ingredients:

- 1 cup coconut; shredded
- 1/2 cup almonds
- 1/2 cup pecans; chopped.
- 2 tbsp. sugar
- 1/2 cup pumpkin seeds
- 1/2 cup sunflower seeds
- 2 tbsp. sunflower oil
- 1 tsp. nutmeg; ground
- 1 tsp. apple pie spice mix

Directions:

1. In a bowl; mix almonds and pecans with pumpkin seeds, sunflower seeds, coconut, nutmeg and apple pie spice mix and stir well
2. Heat up a pan with the oil over medium heat, add sugar and stir well.
3. Pour this over nuts and coconut mix and stir well
4. Spread this on a lined baking sheet that fits your air fryer, introduce in your air fryer and cook at 300 °F and bake for 25 minutes. Leave your granola to cool down, cut and serve.

Nutrition Values: Calories: 322; Fat: 7; Fiber: 8; Carbs: 12; Protein: 7

477. PEARS AND ESPRESSO CREAM RECIPE

Preparation Time: 40 Minutes
Servings: 4

Ingredients:

- 4 pears; halved and cored
- 2 tbsp. water
- 2 tbsp. lemon juice
- 1 tbsp. sugar
- 2 tbsp. butter

For the cream:

- 1 cup whipping cream
- 2 tbsp. espresso; cold
- 1 cup mascarpone
- 1/3 cup sugar

Directions:

1. In a bowl; mix pears halves with lemon juice, 1 tbsp. sugar, butter and water, toss well, transfer them to your air fryer and cook at 360 °F, for 30 minutes
2. Meanwhile; in a bowl, mix whipping cream with mascarpone, ⅓ cup sugar and espresso, whisk really well and keep in the fridge until pears are done.
3. Divide pears on plates, top with espresso cream and serve them

Nutrition Values: Calories: 211; Fat: 5; Fiber: 7; Carbs: 8; Protein: 7

478. BANANA CAKE RECIPE

Preparation Time: 40 Minutes
Servings: 4

Ingredients:

- 1 tbsp. butter; soft
- 1 egg
- 1/3 cup brown sugar
- 1 tsp. baking powder
- 1/2 tsp. cinnamon powder
- 2 tbsp. honey
- 1 banana; peeled and mashed
- 1 cup white flour
- Cooking spray

Directions:

1. Spray a cake pan with some cooking spray and leave aside.
2. In a bowl; mix butter with sugar, banana, honey, egg, cinnamon, baking powder and flour and whisk
3. Pour this into a cake pan greased with cooking spray, introduce in your air fryer and cook at 350 °F, for 30 minutes. Leave cake to cool down, slice and serve

Nutrition Values: Calories: 232; Fat: 4; Fiber: 1; Carbs: 34; Protein: 4

479. FRIED BANANAS RECIPE

Preparation Time: 25 Minutes
Servings: 4

Ingredients:

- 3 tbsp. butter
- 3 tbsp. cinnamon sugar
- 1 cup panko

- 2 eggs
- 8 bananas; peeled and halved
- 1/2 cup corn flour

Directions:

1. Heat up a pan with the butter over medium high heat, add panko; stir and cook for 4 minutes and then transfer to a bowl
2. Roll each in flour, eggs and panko mix, arrange them in your air fryer's basket, dust with cinnamon sugar and cook at 280 °F, for 10 minutes. Serve right away.

Nutrition Values: Calories: 164; Fat: 1; Fiber: 4; Carbs: 32; Protein: 4

480. COFFEE CHEESECAKES RECIPE

Preparation Time: 30 Minutes
Servings: 6

Ingredients:

For the cheesecakes:
- 2 tbsp. butter
- 3 eggs
- 1/3 cup sugar
- 8 oz. cream cheese
- 3 tbsp. coffee
- 1 tbsp. caramel syrup
- For the frosting:
- 3 tbsp. caramel syrup
- 8 oz. mascarpone cheese; soft
- 3 tbsp. butter
- 2 tbsp. sugar

Directions:

1. In your blender, mix cream cheese with eggs, 2 tbsp. butter, coffee, 1 tbsp. caramel syrup and 1/3 cup sugar and pulse very well, spoon into a cupcakes pan that fits your air fryer, introduce in the fryer and cook at 320 °F and bake for 20 minutes
2. Leave aside to cool down and then keep in the freezer for 3 hours. Meanwhile; in a bowl, mix 3 tbsp. butter with 3 tbsp. caramel syrup, 2 tbsp. sugar and mascarpone, blend well, spoon this over cheesecakes and serve them.

Nutrition Values: Calories: 254; Fat: 23; Fiber: 0; Carbs: 21; Protein: 5

481. TOMATO CAKE RECIPE

Preparation Time: 40 Minutes
Servings: 4

Ingredients:

- 1 ½ cups flour
- 1 tsp. cinnamon powder
- 1 cup tomatoes chopped
- 1/2 cup olive oil
- 1 tsp. baking powder
- 1 tsp. baking soda
- 3/4 cup maple syrup
- 2 tbsp. apple cider vinegar

Directions:

1. In a bowl; mix flour with baking powder, baking soda, cinnamon and maple syrup and stir well.
2. In another bowl, mix tomatoes with olive oil and vinegar and stir well
3. Combine the 2 mixtures; stir well, pour into a greased round pan that fits your air fryer, introduce in the fryer and cook at 360 °F, for 30 minutes. Leave cake to cool down, slice and serve.

Nutrition Values: Calories: 153; Fat: 2; Fiber: 1; Carbs: 25; Protein: 4

482. CHOCOLATE CAKE RECIPE

Preparation Time: 40 Minutes
Servings: 12

Ingredients:

- 3/4 cup white flour
- 3/4 cup whole wheat flour
- 1 tsp. baking soda
- 3/4 tsp. pumpkin pie spice
- 3/4 cup sugar
- 1/2 tsp. vanilla extract
- 2/3 cup chocolate chips
- 1 banana; mashed
- 1/2 tsp. baking powder
- 2 tbsp. canola oil
- 1/2 cup Greek yogurt
- 8 oz. canned pumpkin puree

- 1 egg
- Cooking spray

Directions:

1. In a bowl; mix white flour with whole wheat flour, salt, baking soda and powder and pumpkin spice and stir
2. In another bowl, mix sugar with oil, banana, yogurt, pumpkin puree, vanilla and egg and stir using a mixer
3. Combine the 2 mixtures, add chocolate chips; stir, pour this into a greased Bundt pan that fits your air fryer.
4. Introduce in your air fryer and cook at 330 °F, for 30 minutes
5. Leave the cake to cool down, before cutting and serving it.

Nutrition Values: Calories: 232; Fat: 7; Fiber: 7; Carbs: 29; Protein: 4

483. CINNAMON ROLLS AND CREAM CHEESE DIP RECIPE

Preparation Time: 2 hours 15 Minutes
Servings: 8

Ingredients:

- 1 lb. bread dough
- 3/4 cup brown sugar
- 1/4 cup butter; melted
- 1 ½ tbsp. cinnamon; ground
- For the cream cheese dip:
- 2 tbsp. butter
- 1 ¼ cups sugar
- 1/2 tsp. vanilla
- 4 oz. cream cheese

Directions:

1. Roll dough on a floured working surface; shape a rectangle and brush with 1/4 cup butter.
2. In a bowl; mix cinnamon with sugar; stir, sprinkle this over dough, roll dough into a log, seal well and cut into 8 pieces
3. Leave rolls to rise for 2 hours, place them in your air fryer's basket, cook at 350 °F, for 5 minutes; flip them, cook for 4 minutes more and transfer to a platter
4. In a bowl; mix cream cheese with butter, sugar and vanilla and whisk really well.

Serve your cinnamon rolls with this cream cheese dip.

Nutrition Values: Calories: 200; Fat: 1; Fiber: 0; Carbs: 5; Protein: 6

484. PUMPKIN COOKIES RECIPE

Preparation Time: 25 Minutes
Servings: 24

Ingredients:

- 2 ½ cups flour
- 1/2 tsp. baking soda
- 2 tbsp. butter
- 1 tsp. vanilla extract
- 1 tbsp. flax seed; ground
- 3 tbsp. water
- 1/2 cup pumpkin flesh; mashed
- 1/4 cup honey
- 1/2 cup dark chocolate chips

Directions:

1. In a bowl; mix flax seed with water; stir and leave aside for a few minutes.
2. In another bowl, mix flour with salt and baking soda
3. In a third bowl, mix honey with pumpkin puree, butter, vanilla extract and flaxseed.
4. Combine flour with honey mix and chocolate chips and stir
5. Scoop 1 tbsp. of cookie dough on a lined baking sheet that fits your air fryer, repeat with the rest of the dough, introduce them in your air fryer and cook at 350 °F, for 15 minutes.
6. Leave cookies to cool down and serve.

Nutrition Values: Calories: 140; Fat: 2; Fiber: 2; Carbs: 7; Protein: 10

485. APPLE BREAD RECIPE

Preparation Time: 50 Minutes
Servings: 6

Ingredients:

- 3 cups apples; cored and cubed
- 1 cup sugar
- 1 tbsp. baking powder
- 1 stick butter
- 1 tbsp. vanilla

- 2 eggs
- 1 tbsp. apple pie spice
- 2 cups white flour
- 1 cup water

Directions:

1. In a bowl mix egg with 1 butter stick, apple pie spice and sugar and stir using your mixer.
2. Add apples and stir again well
3. In another bowl, mix baking powder with flour and stir.
4. Combine the 2 mixtures; stir and pour into a spring form pan
5. Put spring form pan in your air fryer and cook at 320 °F, for 40 minutes Slice and serve.

Nutrition Values: Calories: 192; Fat: 6; Fiber: 7; Carbs: 14; Protein: 7

486. STRAWBERRY PIE RECIPE

Preparation Time: 30 Minutes
Servings: 12

Ingredients:

For the crust: y
- 1 cup coconut; shredded
- 1/4 cup butter
- 1 cup sunflower seeds

For the filling:
- 1 tsp. gelatin
- 8 oz. cream cheese
- 1/2 tbsp. lemon juice
- 1/4 tsp. stevia
- 4 oz. strawberries
- 2 tbsp. water
- 1/2 cup heavy cream
- 8 oz. strawberries; chopped for serving

Directions:

1. In your food processor, mix sunflower seeds with coconut, a pinch of salt and butter, pulse and press this on the bottom of a cake pan that fits your air fryer
2. Heat up a pan with the water over medium heat, add gelatin; stir until it dissolves, leave aside to cool down, add this to your food processor, mix with 4 oz.

strawberries, cream cheese, lemon juice and stevia and blend well
3. Add heavy cream; stir well and spread this over crust.
4. Top with 8 oz. strawberries, introduce in your air fryer and cook at 330 °F, for 15 minutes. Keep in the fridge until you serve it.

Nutrition Values: Calories: 234; Fat: 23; Fiber: 2; Carbs: 6; Protein: 7

487. BREAD PUDDING RECIPE

Preparation Time: 1 hour 10 Minutes
Servings: 4

Ingredients:

- 6 glazed doughnuts; crumbled
- 1 cup cherries
- 4 egg yolks
- 1/4 cup sugar
- 1/2 cup chocolate chips.
- 1 ½ cups whipping cream
- 1/2 cup raisins

Directions:

1. In a bowl; mix cherries with egg yolks and whipping cream and stir well.
2. In another bowl, mix raisins with sugar, chocolate chips and doughnuts and stir
3. Combine the 2 mixtures, transfer everything to a greased pan that fits your air fryer and cook at 310 °F, for 1 hour. Chill pudding before cutting and serving it

Nutrition Values: Calories: 302; Fat: 8; Fiber: 2; Carbs: 23; Protein: 10

488. CHOCOLATE AND POMEGRANATE BARS RECIPE

Preparation Time: 2 hours 10 Minutes
Servings: 6

Ingredients:

- 1/2 cup milk
- 1/2 cup almonds; chopped
- 1 tsp. vanilla extract
- 1 ½ cups dark chocolate; chopped
- 1/2 cup pomegranate seeds

Directions:

1. Heat up a pan with the milk over medium low heat, add chocolate; stir for 5 minutes; take off heat add vanilla extract, half of the pomegranate seeds and half of the nuts and stir

2. Pour this into a lined baking pan, spread, sprinkle a pinch of salt, the rest of the pomegranate arils and nuts, introduce in your air fryer and cook at 300 °F, for 4 minutes. Keep in the fridge for 2 hours before serving.

Nutrition Values: Calories: 68; Fat: 1; Fiber: 4; Carbs: 6; Protein: 1

489. LEMONY CHEESECAKE

Preparation Time: 80 min + chilling time
Servings: 8

Nutrition Values: Calories: 487; Carbs: 23g; Fat: 38g; Protein: 9.3g

Ingredients

- 8 oz graham crackers, crushed
- 4 oz butter, melted
- 16 oz plain cream cheese
- 3 eggs
- 3 tbsp sugar
- 1 tbsp vanilla extract
- Zest of 2 lemons

Directions

1. Line a cake tin, that fits in your Air fryer, with baking paper. Mix together the crackers and butter, and press at the bottom of the tin. In a bowl, add cream cheese, eggs, sugar, vanilla and lemon zest and beat with a hand mixer until well combined and smooth. Pour the mixture into the tin, on top of the cracker's base. Cook for 40-45 minutes at 350 F, checking it to ensure it's set but still a bit wobbly. Let cool, then refrigerate overnight.

490. BAKED APPLES

Preparation Time: 35 min
Servings: 2

Nutrition Values: Calories: 322; Carbs: 37g;

Fat: 19g; Protein: 3.8g

Ingredients

- 2 granny smith apples, cored, bottom intact
- 2 tbsp butter, cold
- 3 tbsp sugar
- 3 tbsp crushed walnuts
- 2 tbsp raisins
- 1 tsp cinnamon

Directions

1. In a bowl, add butter, sugar, walnuts, raisins and cinnamon; mix with fingers until you obtain a crumble. Arrange the apples in the Air fryer. Stuff the apples with the filling mixture. Cook for 30 minutes at 400 F.

491. DARK CHOCOLATE BROWNIES

Preparation Time: 35 min
Servings: 10

Nutrition Values: Calories: 513; Carbs: 32g; Fat: 55g; Protein: 7g

Ingredients

- 6 oz dark chocolate
- 6 oz butter
- ¾ cup white sugar
- 3 eggs
- 2 tsp vanilla extract
- ¾ cup flour
- ¼ cup cocoa powder
- 1 cup chopped walnuts
- 1 cup white chocolate chips

Directions

1. Line a pan inside your Air fryer with baking paper. In a saucepan, melt chocolate and butter over low heat. Do not stop stirring until you obtain a smooth mixture. Let cool slightly, whisk in eggs and vanilla. Sift flour and cocoa and stir to mix well. Sprinkle the walnuts over and add the white chocolate into the batter. Pour the batter into the pan and cook for 20 minutes at 340 F. Serve with raspberry

syrup and ice cream.

492. CHOCOLATE AND RASPBERRY CAKE

Preparation Time: 40 min
Servings: 8
Nutrition Values: Calories: 486; Carbs: 63g; Fat: 23.6g; Protein: 8.1g

Ingredients

- 1 ½ cups flour
- ⅓ cup cocoa powder
- 2 tsp baking powder
- ¾ cup white sugar
- ¼ cup brown sugar
- ⅔ cup butter
- 2 tsp vanilla extract
- 1 cup milk
- 1 tsp baking soda
- 2 eggs
- 1 cup freeze-dried raspberries
- 1 cup chocolate chips

Directions

1. Line a cake tin with baking powder. In a bowl, sift flour, cocoa and baking powder. Place the sugars, butter, vanilla, milk and baking soda into a microwave-safe bowl and heat for 60 seconds until the butter melts and the ingredients incorporate; let cool slightly. Whisk the eggs into the mixture.
2. Pour the wet ingredients into the dry ones, and fold to combine. Add in the raspberries and chocolate chips into the batter. Pour the batter into the tin and cook for 30 minutes at 350 F.

493. MOON PIE

Preparation Time: 10 min
Servings: 4

Nutrition Values: Calories: 305; Carbs: 44g; Fat: 13.4g; Protein: 4g

Ingredients

- 4 graham cracker sheets, snapped in half
- 8 large marshmallows
- 8 squares each of dark, milk and white chocolate

Directions

1. Arrange the cracker halves on a board. Put 2 marshmallows onto half of the graham cracker halves. Place 2 squares of chocolate onto the cracker with the marshmallows. Put the remaining crackers on top to create 4 sandwiches. Wrap each one in the baking paper so it resembles a parcel. Cook in the fryer for 5 minutes at 340 F.

494. APPLE CARAMEL RELISH

Preparation Time: 40 min
Servings: 4

Nutrition Values: Calories: 382; Carbs: 56g; Fat: 18g; Protein: 3.4g

Ingredients

- 1 vanilla box cake
- 2 apples, peeled, sliced
- 3 oz butter, melted
- ½ cup brown sugar
- 1 tsp cinnamon
- ½ cup flour
- 1 cup caramel sauce

Directions

1. Line a cake tin with baking paper. In a bowl, mix butter, sugar, cinnamon and flour until you obtain a crumbly texture. Prepare the cake mix according to the instructions -no baking. Pour the batter into the tin and arrange the apple slices on top. Spoon the caramel over the apples and add the crumble over the sauce. Cook in the Air fryer for 35 minutes at 360 F; make sure to check it halfway through, so it's not overcooked.

495. CHOCOLATE AND PEANUT BUTTER FONDANTS

Preparation Time: 25 minutes
Servings: 4

Nutrition Values: Calories: 157; Carbs: 4g; Fat: 4g; Protein: 0.9g

Ingredients

- ¾ cup dark chocolate
- ½ cup peanut butter, crunchy
- 2 tbsp butter, diced
- ¼ cup + ¼ cup sugar
- 4 eggs, room temperature
- ⅛ cup flour, sieved
- 1 tsp salt
- ¼ cup water
- Cooking spray

Directions

1. Make a salted praline to top the chocolate fondant. Add ¼ cup of sugar, 1 tsp of salt and water into a saucepan. Stir and bring it to a boil over low heat on a stove top. Simmer until the desired color is achieved and reduced.
2. Pour it into a baking tray and leave to cool and harden. Preheat the Air Fryer to 300 F. Place a pot of water over medium heat and place a heatproof bowl over it. Add the chocolate, butter, and peanut butter to the bowl.
3. Stir continuously until fully melted, combined, and smooth. Remove the bowl from the heat and allow to cool slightly. Add the eggs to the chocolate and whisk. Add the flour and remaining sugar; mix well.
4. Grease 4 small loaf pans with cooking spray and divide the chocolate mixture between them. Place 2 pans at a time in the basket and cook for 7 minutes. Remove them and serve the fondants with a piece of salted praline.

496. WHITE CHOCOLATE PUDDING

Preparation Time: 40 min
Servings: 2

Nutrition Values: Calories : 320; Carbs: 3.06g; Fat: 25g; Protein: 11g

Ingredients

- 3 oz white chocolate
- 4 large egg whites
- 2 large egg yolks, at room temperature
- ¼ cup sugar + more for garnishing

- 1 tbsp melted butter
- 1 tbsp unmelted butter
- ¼ tsp vanilla extract
- 1 ½ tbsp flour

Directions

1. Coat two 6-oz ramekins with melted butter. Add the sugar and swirl it in the ramekins to coat the butter. Pour out the remaining sugar and keep it. Melt the unmelted butter with the chocolate in a microwave; set aside.
2. In another bowl, beat the egg yolks vigorously. Add the vanilla and kept sugar; beat to incorporate fully. Add the chocolate mixture and mix well. Add the flour and mix it with no lumps.
3. Preheat the Air Fryer to 330 F, and whisk the egg whites in another bowl till it holds stiff peaks. Add ⅓ of the egg whites into the chocolate mixture; fold in gently and evenly. Share the mixture into the ramekins with ½ inch space left at the top. Place the ramekins in the fryer basket, close the Air Fryer and cook for 14 minutes.
4. Dust with the remaining sugar and serve.

497. LEMON CURD

Preparation Time: 30 min
Servings: 2

Nutrition Values: Calories : 60; Carbs: 0g; Fat: 6g; Protein: 2g

Ingredients

- 3 tbsp butter
- 3 tbsp sugar
- 1 egg
- 1 egg yolk
- ¾ lemon, juiced

Directions

1. Add sugar and butter in a medium ramekin and beat evenly. Add egg and yolk slowly while still whisking. the fresh yellow color will be attained. Add the lemon juice and mix. Place the bowl in the fryer basket and cook at 250 F for 6 minutes. Increase the temperature again to

320 F and cook for 15 minutes.

2. Remove the bowl onto a flat surface; use a spoon to check for any lumps and remove. Cover the ramekin with a plastic wrap and refrigerate overnight or serve immediately.

498. ALMOND MERINGUE COOKIES

Preparation Time: 145 min
Servings: 4

Nutrition Values: Calories : 215; Carbs: 35g; Fat: 1.6g; Protein: 7.6g

Ingredients

- 8 egg whites
- ½ tsp almond extract
- 1 ⅓ cups sugar
- ¼ tsp salt
- 2 tsp lemon juice
- 1 ½ tsp vanilla extract
- Melted dark chocolate to drizzle

Directions

1. In a mixing bowl, add egg whites, salt, and lemon juice. Beat using an electric mixer until foamy. Slowly add the sugar and continue beating until completely combined; add the almond and vanilla extracts. Beat until stiff peaks form and glossy.

2. Line a round baking sheet with parchment paper. Fill a piping bag with the meringue mixture and pipe as many mounds on the baking sheet as you can leaving 2-inch spaces between each mound.

3. Place the baking sheet in the fryer basket and bake at 250 F for 5 minutes. Reduce the temperature to 220 F and bake for 15 more minutes. Then, reduce the temperature once more to 190 F and cook for 15 minutes. Remove the baking sheet and let the meringues cool for 2 hours. Drizzle with the dark chocolate before serving.

499. CHOCOLATE BANANA SANDWICHES

Preparation Time: 30 min
Servings: 2

Nutrition Values: Calories: 240; Carbs: 26g; Fat: 9.1g; Protein: 12.3g

Ingredients

- 4 slices of brioche
- 1 tbsp butter, melted
- 6 oz milk chocolate, broken into chunks
- 1 banana, sliced

Directions

1. Brush the brioche slices with butter. Spread chocolate and banana on 2 brioche slices. Top with the remaining 2 slices to create 2 sandwiches. Arrange the sandwiches into your air fryer and cook for 14 minutes at 400 F, turning once halfway through. Slice in half and serve with vanilla ice cream.

500. CRÈME BRULEE

Preparation Time: 60 min
Servings: 3

Nutrition Values: Calories : 402; Carbs: 9.5g; Fat: 32.5g; Protein: 13.6g

Ingredients

- 1 cup whipped cream
- 1 cup milk
- 2 vanilla pods
- 10 egg yolks
- 4 tbsp sugar + extra for topping

Directions

1. In a pan, add the milk and cream. Cut the vanilla pods open and scrape the seeds into the pan with the vanilla pods also. Place the pan over medium heat on a stove top until almost boiled while stirring regularly. Turn off the heat. Add the egg yolks to a bowl and beat it. Add the sugar and mix well but not too frothy.

2. Remove the vanilla pods from the milk mixture; pour the mixture onto the eggs mixture while stirring constantly. Let it sit for 25 minutes. Fill 2 to 3 ramekins with the mixture. Place the ramekins in the fryer basket and cook them at 190 F for

50 minutes. Once ready, remove the ramekins and let sit to cool. Sprinkle the remaining sugar over and use a torch to melt the sugar, so it browns at the top.

501. THE MOST CHOCOLATY FUDGE

Preparation Time: 55 min
Servings: 8

Nutrition Values: Calories: 494; Carbs: 65.7g; Fat: 25.1g; Protein: 5.6g

Ingredients

- 1 cup sugar
- 7 oz flour
- 1 tbsp honey
- ¼ cup milk
- 1 tsp vanilla extract
- 1 oz cocoa powder
- 2 eggs
- 4 oz butter
- 1 orange, juice and zest
- Icing:
- 1 oz butter, melted
- 4 oz powdered sugar
- 1 tbsp brown sugar
- 1 tbsp milk
- 2 tsp honey

Directions

1. Preheat the Air fryer to 350 F, and in a bowl, mix the dry ingredients for the fudge. Mix the wet ingredients separately; combine the two mixtures gently. Transfer the batter to a prepared cake pan. Cook for 35 minutes. Meanwhile whisk together all icing ingredients. When the cake cools, coat with the icing. Let set before slicing.

502. WHITE CHOCOLATE CHIP COOKIES

Preparation Time: 30 min
Servings: 8

Nutrition Values: Calories: 167; Carbs: 21.3g; Fat: 11.3g; Protein: 0.7g

Ingredients

- 6 oz self-rising flour
- 3 oz brown sugar
- 2 oz white chocolate chips
- 1 tbsp honey
- 1 ½ tbsp milk
- 4 oz butter

Directions

1. Preheat the Air fryer to 350 F, and beat the butter and sugar until fluffy. Beat in the honey, milk, and flour. Gently fold in the chocolate chips. Drop spoonfuls of the mixture onto a prepared cookie sheet. Cook for 18 minutes.

503. WHITE FILLING COCONUT AND OAT COOKIES

Preparation Time: 30 min
Servings: 4

Nutrition Values: Calories: 477; Carbs: 73.8g; Fat: 16.8g; Protein: 7.4g

Ingredients

- 5 ½ oz flour
- 1 tsp vanilla extract
- 3 oz sugar
- ½ cup oats
- 1 small egg, beaten
- ¼ cup coconut flakes

Filling:

- 1 oz white chocolate, melted
- 2 oz butter
- 4 oz powdered sugar
- 1 tsp vanilla extract

Directions

1. Beat all the cookie ingredients, with an electric mixer, except the flour. When smooth, fold in the flour. Drop spoonfuls of the batter onto a prepared cookie sheet. Cook in the Air fryer at 350 F for 18 minutes; then let cool.
2. Meanwhile, prepare the filling by beating all ingredients together; spread the filling on half of the cookies. Top with the other halves to make cookie sandwiches.

504. TASTY BANANA CAKE

Preparation time: 10 minutes
Cooking time: 30 minutes
Servings: 4

Ingredients:

- 1 tablespoon butter, soft
- 1 egg
- 1/3 cup brown sugar
- 2 tablespoons honey
- 1 banana, peeled and mashed
- 1 cup white flour
- 1 teaspoon baking powder
- ½ teaspoon cinnamon powder
- Cooking spray

Directions:

1. Spray a cake pan with some cooking spray and leave aside.
2. In a bowl, mix butter with sugar, banana, honey, egg, cinnamon, baking powder and flour and whisk
3. Pour this into a cake pan greased with cooking spray, introduce in your air fryer and cook at 350 degrees F for 30 minutes.
4. Leave cake to cool down, slice and serve.
5. Enjoy!

Nutrition Values: calories 232, fat 4, fiber 1, carbs 34, protein 4

505. SIMPLE CHEESECAKE

Preparation time: 10 minutes
Cooking time: 15 minutes
Servings: 15

Ingredients:

- 1 pound cream cheese
- ½ teaspoon vanilla extract
- 2 eggs
- 4 tablespoons sugar
- 1 cup graham crackers, crumbled
- 2 tablespoons butter

Directions:

1. In a bowl, mix crackers with butter.
2. Press crackers mix on the bottom of a lined cake pan, introduce in your air fryer and cook at 350 degrees F for 4 minutes.
3. Meanwhile, in a bowl, mix sugar with cream cheese, eggs and vanilla and whisk

well.
4. Spread filling over crackers crust and cook your cheesecake in your air fryer at 310 degrees F for 15 minutes.
5. Leave cake in the fridge for 3 hours, slice and serve.
6. Enjoy!

Nutrition Values: calories 245, fat 12, fiber 1, carbs 20, protein 3

506. BREAD PUDDING

Preparation time: 10 minutes
Cooking time: 1 hour
Servings: 4

Ingredients:

- 6 glazed doughnuts, crumbled
- 1 cup cherries
- 4 egg yolks
- 1 and ½ cups whipping cream
- ½ cup raisins
- ¼ cup sugar
- ½ cup chocolate chips.

Directions:

1. In a bowl, mix cherries with egg yolks and whipping cream and stir well.
2. In another bowl, mix raisins with sugar, chocolate chips and doughnuts and stir.
3. Combine the 2 mixtures, transfer everything to a greased pan that fits your air fryer and cook at 310 degrees F for 1 hour.
4. Chill pudding before cutting and serving it.
5. Enjoy!

Nutrition Values: calories 302, fat 8, fiber 2, carbs 23, protein 10

507. BREAD DOUGH AND AMARETTO DESSERT

Preparation time: 10 minutes
Cooking time: 12 minutes
Servings: 12

Ingredients:

- 1 pound bread dough
- 1 cup sugar

- ½ cup butter, melted
- 1 cup heavy cream
- 12 ounces chocolate chips
- 2 tablespoons amaretto liqueur

Directions:

1. Roll dough, cut into 20 slices and then cut each slice in halves.
2. Brush dough pieces with butter, sprinkle sugar, place them in your air fryer's basket after you've brushed it some butter, cook them at 350 degrees F for 5 minutes, flip them, cook for 3 minutes more and transfer to a platter.
3. Heat up a pan with the heavy cream over medium heat, add chocolate chips and stir until they melt.
4. Add liqueur, stir again, transfer to a bowl and serve bread dippers with this sauce.
5. Enjoy!

Nutrition Values: calories 200, fat 1, fiber 0, carbs 6, protein 6

508. CINNAMON ROLLS AND CREAM CHEESE DIP

Preparation time: 2 hours
Cooking time: 15 minutes
Servings: 8

Ingredients:

- 1 pound bread dough
- ¾ cup brown sugar
- 1 and ½ tablespoons cinnamon, ground
- ¼ cup butter, melted
- For the cream cheese dip:
- 2 tablespoons butter
- 4 ounces cream cheese
- 1 and ¼ cups sugar
- ½ teaspoon vanilla

Directions:

1. Roll dough on a floured working surface, shape a rectangle and brush with ¼ cup butter.
2. In a bowl, mix cinnamon with sugar, stir, sprinkle this over dough, roll dough into a log, seal well and cut into 8 pieces.
3. Leave rolls to rise for 2 hours, place them

in your air fryer's basket, cook at 350 degrees F for 5 minutes, flip them, cook for 4 minutes more and transfer to a platter.
4. In a bowl, mix cream cheese with butter, sugar and vanilla and whisk really well.
5. Serve your cinnamon rolls with this cream cheese dip.
6. Enjoy!

Nutrition Values: calories 200, fat 1, fiber 0, carbs 5, protein 6

509. PUMPKIN PIE

Preparation time: 10 minutes
Cooking time: 15 minutes
Servings: 9

Ingredients:

- 1 tablespoon sugar
- 2 tablespoons flour
- 1 tablespoon butter
- 2 tablespoons water

For the pumpkin pie filling:

- ounces pumpkin flesh, chopped
- 1 teaspoon mixed spice
- 1 teaspoon nutmeg
- 3 ounces water
- 1 egg, whisked
- 1 tablespoon sugar

Directions:

1. Put 3 ounces water in a pot, bring to a boil over medium high heat, add pumpkin, egg, 1 tablespoon sugar, spice and nutmeg, stir, boil for 20 minutes, take off heat and blend using an immersion blender.
2. In a bowl, mix flour with butter, 1 tablespoon sugar and 2 tablespoons water and knead your dough well.
3. Grease a pie pan that fits your air fryer with butter, press dough into the pan, fill with pumpkin pie filling, place in your air fryer's basket and cook at 360 degrees F for 15 minutes.
4. Slice and serve warm.
5. Enjoy!

Nutrition Values: calories 200, fat 5, fiber 2, carbs 5, protein 6

510. WRAPPED PEARS

Preparation time: 10 minutes
Cooking time: 15 minutes
Servings: 4

Ingredients:

- 4 puff pastry sheets
- 14 ounces vanilla custard
- 2 pears, halved
- 1 egg, whisked
- ½ teaspoon cinnamon powder
- 2 tablespoons sugar

Directions:

1. Place puff pastry slices on a working surface, add spoonfuls of vanilla custard in the center of each, top with pear halves and wrap.
2. Brush pears with egg, sprinkle sugar and cinnamon, place them in your air fryer's basket and cook at 320 degrees F for 15 minutes.
3. Divide parcels on plates and serve.
4. Enjoy!

Nutrition Values: calories 200, fat 2, fiber 1, carbs 14, protein 3

511. STRAWBERRY DONUTS

Preparation time: 10 minutes
Cooking time: 15 minutes
Servings: 4

Ingredients:

- 8 ounces flour
- 1 tablespoon brown sugar
- 1 tablespoon white sugar
- 1 egg
- 2 and ½ tablespoons butter
- 4 ounces whole milk
- 1 teaspoon baking powder
- For the strawberry icing:
- 2 tablespoons butter
- ounces icing sugar
- ½ teaspoon pink coloring
- ¼ cup strawberries, chopped
- 1 tablespoon whipped cream

Directions:

1. In a bowl, mix butter, 1 tablespoon brown sugar, 1 tablespoon white sugar and flour and stir.
2. In a second bowl, mix egg with 1 and ½ tablespoons butter and milk and stir well.
3. Combine the 2 mixtures, stir, shape donuts from this mix, place them in your air fryer's basket and cook at 360 degrees F for 15 minutes.
4. Put 1 tablespoon butter, icing sugar, food coloring, whipped cream and strawberry puree and whisk well.
5. Arrange donuts on a platter and serve with strawberry icing on top.
6. Enjoy!

Nutrition Values: calories 250, fat 12, fiber 1, carbs 32, protein 4

512. AIR FRIED BANANAS

Preparation time: 10 minutes
Cooking time: 15 minutes
Servings: 4

Ingredients:

- 3 tablespoons butter
- 2 eggs
- 8 bananas, peeled and halved
- ½ cup corn flour
- 3 tablespoons cinnamon sugar
- 1 cup panko

Directions:

1. Heat up a pan with the butter over medium high heat, add panko, stir and cook for 4 minutes and then transfer to a bowl.
2. Roll each in flour, eggs and panko mix, arrange them in your air fryer's basket, dust with cinnamon sugar and cook at 280 degrees F for 10 minutes.
3. Serve right away.
4. Enjoy!

Nutrition Values: calories 164, fat 1, fiber 4, carbs 32, protein 4

513. COCOA CAKE

Preparation time: 10 minutes
Cooking time: 17 minutes
Servings: 6

Ingredients:

- ounces butter, melted
- 3 eggs
- 3 ounces sugar
- 1 teaspoon cocoa powder
- 3 ounces flour
- ½ teaspoon lemon juice

Directions:

1. In a bowl, mix 1 tablespoon butter with cocoa powder and whisk.
2. In another bowl, mix the rest of the butter with sugar, eggs, flour and lemon juice, whisk well and pour half into a cake pan that fits your air fryer.
3. Add half of the cocoa mix, spread, add the rest of the butter layer and top with the rest of cocoa.
4. Introduce in your air fryer and cook at 360 degrees F for 17 minutes.
5. Cool cake down before slicing and serving.
6. Enjoy!

Nutrition Values: calories 340, fat 11, fiber 3, carbs 25, protein 5

514. CHOCOLATE CAKE

Preparation time: 10 minutes
Cooking time: 30 minutes
Servings: 12

Ingredients:

- ¾ cup white flour
- ¾ cup whole wheat flour
- 1 teaspoon baking soda
- ¾ teaspoon pumpkin pie spice
- ¾ cup sugar
- 1 banana, mashed
- ½ teaspoon baking powder
- 2 tablespoons canola oil
- ½ cup Greek yogurt
- 8 ounces canned pumpkin puree
- Cooking spray
- 1 egg
- ½ teaspoon vanilla extract
- 2/3 cup chocolate chips

Directions:

1. In a bowl, mix white flour with whole wheat flour, salt, baking soda and powder and pumpkin spice and stir.
2. In another bowl, mix sugar with oil, banana, yogurt, pumpkin puree, vanilla and egg and stir using a mixer.
3. Combine the 2 mixtures, add chocolate chips, stir, pour this into a greased Bundt pan that fits your air fryer.
4. Introduce in your air fryer and cook at 330 degrees F for 30 minutes.
5. Leave the cake to cool down, before cutting and serving it.
6. Enjoy!

Nutrition Values: calories 232, fat 7, fiber 7, carbs 29, protein 4

515. APPLE BREAD

Preparation time: 10 minutes
Cooking time: 40 minutes
Servings: 6

Ingredients:

- 3 cups apples, cored and cubed
- 1 cup sugar
- 1 tablespoon vanilla
- 2 eggs
- 1 tablespoon apple pie spice
- 2 cups white flour
- 1 tablespoon baking powder
- 1 stick butter
- 1 cup water

Directions:

1. In a bowl mix egg with 1 butter stick, apple pie spice and sugar and stir using your mixer.
2. Add apples and stir again well.
3. In another bowl, mix baking powder with flour and stir.
4. Combine the 2 mixtures, stir and pour into a spring form pan.
5. Put spring form pan in your air fryer and cook at 320 degrees F for 40 minutes
6. Slice and serve.
7. Enjoy!

Nutrition Values: calories 192, fat 6, fiber 7, carbs 14, protein 7

516. BANANA BREAD

Preparation time: 10 minutes
Cooking time: 40 minutes
Servings: 6

Ingredients:

- ¾ cup sugar
- 1/3 cup butter
- 1 teaspoon vanilla extract
- 1 egg
- 2 bananas, mashed
- 1 teaspoon baking powder
- 1 and ½ cups flour
- ½ teaspoons baking soda
- 1/3 cup milk
- 1 and ½ teaspoons cream of tartar
- Cooking spray

Directions:

1. In a bowl, mix milk with cream of tartar, sugar, butter, egg, vanilla and bananas and stir everything.
2. In another bowl, mix flour with baking powder and baking soda.
3. Combine the 2 mixtures, stir well, pour this into a cake pan greased with some cooking spray, introduce in your air fryer and cook at 320 degrees F for 40 minutes.
4. Take bread out, leave aside to cool down, slice and serve it.
5. Enjoy!

Nutrition Values: calories 292, fat 7, fiber 8, carbs 28, protein 4

517. MINI LAVA CAKES

Preparation time: 10 minutes
Cooking time: 20 minutes
Servings: 3

Ingredients:

- 1 egg
- 4 tablespoons sugar
- 2 tablespoons olive oil
- 4 tablespoons milk
- 4 tablespoons flour
- 1 tablespoon cocoa powder
- ½ teaspoon baking powder

- ½ teaspoon orange zest

Directions:

1. In a bowl, mix egg with sugar, oil, milk, flour, salt, cocoa powder, baking powder and orange zest, stir very well and pour this into greased ramekins.
2. Add ramekins to your air fryer and cook at 320 degrees F for 20 minutes.
3. Serve lava cakes warm.
4. Enjoy!

Nutrition Values: calories 201, fat 7, fiber 8, carbs 23, protein 4

518. MINI STRAWBERRY PIES WITH SUGAR CRUST

Preparation Time: 15 minutes
Servings 8

Nutrition Values:237 Calories; 12.8g Fat; 28.2g Carbs; 2.7g Protein; 8.9g Sugars

Ingredients

- 1/2 cup powdered sugar
- 1/4 teaspoon ground cloves
- 1/8 teaspoon cinnamon powder
- 1 teaspoon vanilla extract
- 1 -12-ouncecan biscuit dough
- 12 ounces strawberry pie filling
- 1/4 cup butter, melted

Directions

1. Thoroughly combine the sugar, cloves, cinnamon, and vanilla.
2. Then, stretch and flatten each piece of the biscuit dough into a round circle using a rolling pin.
3. Divide the strawberry pie filling among the biscuits. Roll up tightly and dip each biscuit piece into the melted butter; cover them with the spiced sugar mixture.
4. Brush with a non-stick cooking oil on all sides. Air-bake them at 340 degrees F for approximately 10 minutes or until they're golden brown. Let them cool for 5 minutes before serving.

519. FUDGY COCONUT BROWNIES

Preparation Time: 15 minutes
Servings 8

Nutrition Values:267 Calories; 15.4g Fat; 34.0g Carbs; 1.0g Protein; 27.5g Sugars

Ingredients

- 1/2 cup coconut oil
- 2 ounces dark chocolate
- 1 cup sugar
- 2 ½ tablespoons water
- 4 whisked eggs
- 1/4 teaspoon ground cinnamon
- 1/2 teaspoon ground anise star
- 1/4 teaspoon coconut extract
- 1/2 teaspoon vanilla extract
- 1 tablespoon honey
- 1/2 cup cake flour
- 1/2 cup desiccated coconut
- Icing sugar, to dust

Directions

1. Microwave the coconut oil along with dark chocolate. Stir in sugar, water, eggs, cinnamon, anise, coconut extract, vanilla, and honey.
2. After that, stir in the flour and coconut; mix to combine thoroughly.
3. Press the mixture into a lightly buttered baking dish. Air-bake at 355 degrees F for 15 minutes.
4. Let your brownie cool slightly; then, carefully remove from the baking dish and cut into squares. Dust with icing sugar. Bon appétit!

519. EASIEST CHOCOLATE LAVA CAKE EVER

Preparation Time: 20 minutes
Servings 4

Nutrition Values:549 Calories; 37.7g Fat; 47.5g Carbs; 7.1g Protein; 38.2g Sugars

Ingredients

- 1 cup dark cocoa candy melts
- 1 stick butter
- 2 eggs
- 4 tablespoons superfine sugar

- 1 tablespoon honey
- 4 tablespoons self-rising flour
- A pinch of kosher salt
- A pinch of ground cloves
- 1/4 teaspoon grated nutmeg
- 1/4 teaspoon cinnamon powder

Directions

1. Firstly, spray four custard cups with non-stick cooking oil.
2. Put the cocoa candy melts and butter into a small microwave-safe bowl; microwave on high for 30 seconds to 1 minute.
3. In a mixing bowl, whisk the eggs along with sugar and honey until frothy. Add it to the chocolate mix.
4. After that, add the remaining ingredients and mix to combine well. You can whisk the mixture with an electric mixer.
5. Spoon the mixture into the prepared custard cups. Air-bake at 350 degrees F for 12 minutes. Take the cups out of the Air Fryer and let them rest for 5 to 6 minutes.
6. Lastly, flip each cup upside-down onto a dessert plate and serve with some fruits and chocolate syrup. Bon appétit!

521. CHOCOLATE BANANA CAKE

Preparation Time: 30 minutes
Servings 10

Nutrition Values:263 Calories; 10.6g Fat; 41.0g Carbs; 4.3g Protein; 16.6g Sugars

Ingredients

- 1 stick softened butter
- 1/2 cup caster sugar
- 1 egg
- 2 bananas, mashed
- 3 tablespoons maple syrup
- 2 cups self-rising flour
- 1/4 teaspoon anise star, ground
- 1/4 teaspoon ground mace
- 1/4 teaspoon ground cinnamon
- 1/4 teaspoon crystallized ginger
- 1/2 teaspoon vanilla paste
- A pinch of kosher salt
- 1/2 cup cocoa powder

Directions

1. Firstly, beat the softened butter and sugar until well combined.
2. Then, whisk the egg, mashed banana and maple syrup. Now, add this mixture to the butter mixture; mix until pale and creamy.
3. Add in the flour, anise star, mace, cinnamon, crystallized ginger, vanilla paste, and the salt; now, add the cocoa powder and mix to combine.
4. Then, treat two cake pans with a non-stick cooking spray. Press the batter into the cake pans.
5. Air-bake at 330 degrees F for 30 minutes. To serve, frost with chocolate butter glaze.

522. BUTTER SUGAR FRITTERS

Preparation Time: 30 minutes
Servings 16

Nutrition Values:231 Calories; 8.2g Fat; 36.6g Carbs; 3.3g Protein; 12.8g Sugars

Ingredients

For the dough:

- 4 cups fine cake flour
- 1 teaspoon kosher salt
- 1 teaspoon brown sugar
- 3 tablespoons butter, at room temperature
- 1 packet instant yeast
- 1 ¼ cups lukewarm water

For the Cakes:

- 1 cup caster sugar
- A pinch of cardamom
- 1 teaspoon cinnamon powder
- 1 stick butter, melted

Directions

1. Mix all the dry ingredients in a large-sized bowl; add the butter and yeast and mix to combine well.
2. Pour lukewarm water and stir to form soft and elastic dough.
3. Lay the dough on a lightly floured surface, loosely cover with greased foil and chill for 5 to 10 minutes.
4. Take the dough out of the refrigerator and shape it into two logs; cut them into 20 slices.
5. In a shallow bowl, mix caster sugar with

cardamom and cinnamon.
6. Now, brush with melted butter and coat the entire slice with sugar mix; repeat with the remaining ingredients.
7. Treat the Air Fryer basket with a non-stick cooking spray. Air-fry at 360 degrees F for about 10 minutes, flipping once during the baking time. To serve, dust with icing sugar and enjoy!

523. FATHER'S DAY FRIED PINEAPPLE RINGS

Preparation Time: 10 minutes
Servings 6

Nutrition Values:180 Calories; 1.8g Fat; 39.4g Carbs; 2.5g Protein; 14.9g Sugars

Ingredients

- 2/3 cup all-purpose flour
- 1/3 cup rice flour
- 1/2 teaspoon baking powder
- 1/2 teaspoon baking soda
- A pinch of kosher salt
- 1/2 cup water
- 1 cup rice milk
- 1/2 teaspoon ground cinnamon
- 1/4 teaspoon ground anise star
- 1/2 teaspoon vanilla essence
- 4 tablespoons caster sugar
- 1/4 cup unsweetened flaked coconut
- 1 medium-sized pineapple, peeled and sliced

Directions

1. Mix all of the above ingredients, except the pineapple. Then, coat the pineapple slices with the batter mix, covering well.
2. Air-fry them at 380 degrees F for 6 to 8 minutes. Drizzle with maple syrup, garnish with a dollop of vanilla ice cream, and serve.

524. OATY PLUM AND APPLE CRUMBLE

Preparation Time: 20 minutes
Servings 6

Nutrition Values:190 Calories; 7.9g Fat; 28.7g

Carbs; 1.6g Protein; 16.7g Sugars

Ingredients

- 1/4 pound plums, pitted and chopped
- 1/4 pound Braeburn apples, cored and chopped
- 1 tablespoon fresh lemon juice
- 2 ½ ounces golden caster sugar
- 1 tablespoon honey
- 1/2 teaspoon ground mace
- 1/2 teaspoon vanilla paste
- 1 cup fresh cranberries
- 1/3 cup oats
- 2/3 cup flour
- 1/2 stick butter, chilled
- 1 tablespoon cold water

Directions

1. Thoroughly combine the plums and apples with lemon juice, sugar, honey, and ground mace.
2. Spread the fruit mixture onto the bottom of a cake pan that is previously greased with non-stick cooking oil.
3. In a mixing dish, combine the other ingredients until everything is well incorporated. Spread this mixture evenly over the fruit mixture.
4. Air-bake at 390 degrees F for 20 minutes or until done.

525. BUTTER LEMON POUND CAKE

Preparation Time: 2 hours 20 minutes
Servings 8

Nutrition Values:227 Calories; 9.2g Fat; 34.3g Carbs; 4.2g Protein; 16.6g Sugars

Ingredients

- 1 stick softened butter
- 1/3 cup muscovado sugar
- 1 medium-sized egg
- 1 ¼ cups cake flour
- 1 teaspoon butter flavoring
- 1 teaspoon vanilla essence
- A pinch of salt
- 3/4 cup milk

- Grated zest of 1 medium-sized lemon
- For the Glaze:
- 1 cup powdered sugar
- 2 tablespoons fresh squeezed lemon juice

Directions

1. In a mixing bowl, cream the butter and sugar. Now, fold in the egg and beat again.
2. Add the flour, butter flavoring, vanilla essence, and salt; mix to combine well. Afterward, add the milk and lemon zest and mix on low until everything's incorporated.
3. Evenly spread a thin layer of melted butter all around the cake pan using a pastry brush. Now, press the batter into the cake pan.
4. Bake at 350 degrees F for 15 minutes. After that, take the cake out of the Air Fryer and carefully run a small knife around the edges; invert the cake onto a serving platter. Allow it to cool completely.
5. To make the glaze, mix powdered sugar with lemon juice. Drizzle over the top of your cake and allow hardening for about 2 hours.

526. FESTIVE DOUBLE-CHOCOLATE CAKE

Preparation Time: 45 minutes
Servings 8

Nutrition Values:227 Calories; 12.7g Fat; 39.5g Carbs; 3.6g Protein; 24.3g Sugars

Ingredients

- 1/2 cup caster sugar
- 1 ¼ cups cake flour
- 1 teaspoon baking powder
- 1/3 cup cocoa powder
- 1/4 teaspoon ground cloves
- 1/8 teaspoon freshly grated nutmeg
- A pinch of table salt
- 1 egg
- 1/4 cup soda
- 1/4 cup milk
- 1/2 stick butter, melted
- 2 ounces bittersweet chocolate, melted

- 1/2 cup hot water

Directions

1. Take two mixing bowls. Thoroughly combine the dry ingredients in the first bowl. In the second bowl, mix the egg, soda, milk, butter, and chocolate.
2. Add the wet mix to the dry mix; pour in the water and mix well. Butter a cake pan that fits into your Air Fryer. Pour the mixture into the baking pan.
3. Loosely cover with foil; bake at 320 degrees F for 35 minutes. Now, remove foil and bake for further 10 minutes. Frost the cake with buttercream if desired. Bon appétit!

527. APPLE AND PEAR CRISP WITH WALNUTS

Preparation Time: 25 minutes
Servings 6

Nutrition Values:190 Calories; 5.3g Fat; 33.1g Carbs; 3.6g Protein; 13.7g Sugars

Ingredients

- 1/2 pound apples, cored and chopped
- 1/2 pound pears, cored and chopped
- 1 cup all-purpose flour
- 1/3 cup muscovado sugar
- 1/3 cup brown sugar
- 1 tablespoon butter
- 1 teaspoon ground cinnamon
- 1/4 teaspoon ground cloves
- 1 teaspoon vanilla extract
- 1/4 cup chopped walnuts
- Whipped cream, to serve

Directions

1. Arrange the apples and pears on the bottom of a lightly greased baking dish.
2. Mix the remaining ingredients, without the walnuts and the whipped cream, until the mixture resembles the coarse crumbs.
3. Spread the topping onto the fruits. Scatter chopped walnuts over all.
4. Air-bake at 340 degrees F for 20 minutes or until the topping is golden brown. Check for doneness using a toothpick and

serve at room temperature topped with whipped cream.

528. FAMILY COCONUT BANANA TREAT

Preparation Time: 20 minutes
Servings 6

Nutrition Values:271 Calories; 6.6g Fat; 51.3g Carbs; 4.8g Protein; 19.3g Sugars

Ingredients

- 2 tablespoons coconut oil
- 3/4 cup breadcrumbs
- 2 tablespoons coconut sugar
- 1/2 teaspoon cinnamon powder
- 1/4 teaspoon ground cloves
- 6 ripe bananas, peeled and halved
- 1/3 cup rice flour
- 1 large-sized well-beaten egg

Directions

1. Preheat a non-stick skillet over a moderate heat; stir the coconut oil and the breadcrumbs for about 4 minutes. Remove from the heat, add coconut sugar, cinnamon, and cloves; set it aside.
2. Coat the banana halves with the rice flour, covering on all sides. Then, dip them in beaten egg. Finally, roll them over the crumb mix.
3. Cook in a single layer in the Air Fryer basket at 290 degrees F for 10 minutes. Work in batches as needed.
4. Serve warm or at room temperature sprinkled with flaked coconut if desired. Bon appétit!

529. OLD-FASHIONED SWIRLED GERMAN CAKE

Preparation Time: 25 minutes
Servings 8

Nutrition Values:278 Calories; 13.1g Fat; 38.7g Carbs; 3.6g Protein; 25.6g Sugars

Ingredients

- 1 cup flour
- 1 teaspoon baking powder

- 1 cup white sugar
- 1/8 teaspoon kosher salt
- 1/4 teaspoon ground cinnamon
- 1/4 teaspoon grated nutmeg
- 1 teaspoon orange zest
- 1 stick butter, melted
- 2 eggs
- 1 teaspoon pure vanilla extract
- 1/4 cup milk
- 2 tablespoons unsweetened cocoa powder

Directions

1. Lightly grease a round pan that fits into your Air Fryer.
2. Combine the flour, baking powder, sugar, salt, cinnamon, nutmeg, and orange zest using an electric mixer. Then, fold in the butter, eggs, vanilla, and milk.
3. Add 1/4 cup of the batter to the baking pan; leave the remaining batter and stir the cocoa into it. Drop by spoonful over the top of white batter. Then, swirl the cocoa batter into the white batter with a knife.
4. Bake at 360 degrees F approximately 15 minutes. Let it cool for about 10 minutes.
5. Finally, turn the cake out onto a wire rack.

530. VANILLA AND BANANA PASTRY PUFFS

Preparation Time: 15 minutes
Servings 8

Nutrition Values:308 Calories; 17.1g Fat; 34.6g Carbs; 5.2g Protein; 18.4g Sugars

Ingredients

- 1 package -8-ouncecrescent dinner rolls, refrigerated
- 1 cup of milk
- 4 ounces instant vanilla pudding
- 4 ounces cream cheese, softened
- 2 bananas, peeled and sliced
- 1 egg, lightly beaten

Directions

1. Unroll crescent dinner rolls; cut into 8 squares.
2. Combine the milk and the pudding; whisk in the cream cheese. Divide the pudding

mixture among the pastry squares. Top with the slices of banana.
3. Now, fold the dough over the filling, pressing the edges to help them seal well. Brush each pastry puff with the whisked egg.
4. Air-bake at 355 degrees F for 10 minutes. Bon appétit!

531. PARTY HAZELNUT BROWNIE CUPS

Preparation Time: 30 minutes
Servings 12

Nutrition Values:246 Calories; 14.5g Fat; 27.5g Carbs; 2.4g Protein; 18.6g Sugars

Ingredients

- 6 ounces semisweet chocolate chips
- 1 stick butter, at room temperature
- 1/2 cup caster sugar
- 1/4 cup brown sugar
- 2 large-sized eggs
- 1/4 cup red wine
- 1/4 teaspoon hazelnut extract
- 1 teaspoon pure vanilla extract
- 3/4 cup all-purpose flour
- 2 tablespoons cocoa powder
- 1/2 cup ground hazelnuts
- A pinch of kosher salt

Directions

1. Microwave the chocolate chips with butter.
2. Then, whisk the sugars, eggs, red wine, hazelnut and vanilla extract. Add to the chocolate mix.
3. Stir in the flour, cocoa powder, ground hazelnuts, and a pinch of kosher salt. Mix until the batter is creamy and smooth. Divide the batter among muffin cups that are coated with cupcake liners.
4. Air-bake at 360 degrees F for 28 to 30 minutes. Bake in batches and serve topped with ganache if desired.

532. SULTANA CUPCAKES WITH BUTTERCREAM ICING

Preparation Time: 25 minutes
Servings 6

Nutrition Values:366 Calories; 19.1g Fat; 47.4g Carbs; 2.8g Protein; 38.3g Sugars

Ingredients

For the Cupcakes:

- 1/2 cup all-purpose flour
- 1/2 teaspoon baking soda
- 1 baking powder
- 1/8 teaspoon salt
- 1/4 teaspoon ground anise star
- 1/4 teaspoon grated nutmeg
- 1 teaspoon cinnamon
- 3 tablespoons caster sugar
- 1/2 teaspoon pure vanilla extract
- 1 egg
- 1/4 cup plain milk
- 1/2 stick melted butter
- 1/2 cup Sultanas

For the Buttercream Icing:

- 1/3 cup butter, softened
- 1 ½ cups powdered sugar
- 1 teaspoon vanilla extract
- 1/8 teaspoon salt
- 2 tablespoons milk
- A few drop food coloring

Directions

1. Take two mixing bowls. Thoroughly combine the dry ingredients for the cupcakes into the first bowl. In another bowl, whisk the vanilla extract, egg, milk, and melted butter.
2. To form a batter, add the wet milk mixture to the dry flour mixture. Fold in Sultanas and gently stir to combine. Ladle the batter into the prepared muffin pans.
3. Air-bake at 390 degrees F for 15 minutes.
4. Meanwhile, to make the Buttercream Icing, beat the butter until creamy and fluffy. Gradually add the sugar and beat well.
5. Then, add the vanilla, salt, and milk, and mix until creamy. Afterward, gently stir in food coloring. Frost your cupcakes and enjoy!

533. BANANA & VANILLA PASTRY PUFFS

Preparation Time: 15 minutes
Smart Points: 4
Servings: 8

Ingredients

- 1 package [8-oz.] crescent dinner rolls, refrigerated
- 1 cup milk
- 4 oz. instant vanilla pudding
- 4 oz. cream cheese, softened
- 2 bananas, peeled and sliced
- 1 egg, lightly beaten

Directions:

1. Roll out the crescent dinner rolls and slice each one into 8 squares.
2. Mix together the milk, pudding, and cream cheese using a whisk.
3. Scoop equal amounts of the mixture into the pastry squares. Add the banana slices on top.
4. Fold the squares around the filling, pressing down on the edges to seal them.
5. Apply a light brushing of the egg to each pastry puff before placing them in the Air Fryer.
6. Air bake at 355°F for 10 minutes.

534. DOUBLE CHOCOLATE CAKE

Preparation Time: 45 minutes
Smart Points: 4
Servings: 8

Ingredients

- ½ cup stevia
- 1 ¼ cups keto almond flour
- 1 tsp. baking powder
- ⅓ cup cocoa powder
- ¼ tsp. ground cloves
- 1/8 tsp. freshly grated nutmeg
- Pinch of table salt
- 1 egg
- ¼ cup soda of your choice
- ¼ cup milk
- ½ stick butter, melted

- 2 oz. bittersweet chocolate, melted
- ½ cup hot water

Directions:

1. In a bowl, thoroughly combine the dry ingredients.
2. In another bowl, mix together the egg, soda, milk, butter, and chocolate.
3. Combine the two mixtures. Add in the water and stir well.
4. Take a cake pan that is small enough to fit inside your Air Fryer and transfer the mixture to the pan.
5. Place a sheet of foil on top and bake at 320°F for 35 minutes.
6. Take off the foil and bake for further 10 minutes.
7. Frost the cake with buttercream if desired before serving.

535. BANANA OATMEAL COOKIES

Preparation Time: 20 minutes
Smart Points: 3
Servings: 6

Ingredients

- 2 cups quick oats
- ¼ cup milk
- 4 ripe bananas, mashed
- ¼ cup coconut, shredded

Directions:

1. Pre-heat the Air Fryer to 350°F.
2. Combine all of the ingredients in a bowl.
3. Scoop equal amounts of the cookie dough onto a baking sheet and put it in the Air Fryer basket.
4. Bake the cookies for 15 minutes.

536. KETO SUGAR BUTTER FRITTERS

Preparation Time: 30 minutes
Smart Points: 4
Servings: 16

Ingredients

For the dough:

- 4 cups keto almond flour

- 1 tsp. kosher salt
- 1 tsp. stevia
- 3 tbsp. butter, at room temperature
- 1 packet instant yeast
- 1 ¼ cups lukewarm water

For the Cakes

- 1 cup stevia
- Pinch of cardamom
- 1 tsp. cinnamon powder
- 1 stick butter, melted

Directions:

1. Place all of the ingredients in a large bowl and combine well.
2. Add in the lukewarm water and mix until a soft, elastic dough forms.
3. Place the dough on a lightly floured surface and lay a greased sheet of aluminum foil on top of the dough. Refrigerate for 5 to 10 minutes.
4. Remove it from the refrigerator and divide it in two. Mold each half into a log and slice it into 20 pieces.
5. In a shallow bowl, combine the stevia, cardamom and cinnamon.
6. Coat the slices with a light brushing of melted butter and the stevia.
7. Spritz Air Fryer basket with cooking spray.
8. Transfer the slices to the fryer and air fry at 360°F for roughly 10 minutes. Turn each slice once during the baking time.
9. Dust each slice with the stevia before serving.

537. PEAR & APPLE CRISP WITH WALNUTS

Preparation Time: 25 minutes
Smart Points: 2
Servings: 6

Ingredients

- ½ lb. apples, cored and chopped
- ½ lb. pears, cored and chopped
- 1 cup keto almond flour
- 1 cup stevia
- 1 tbsp. butter
- 1 tsp. ground cinnamon

- ¼ tsp. ground cloves
- 1 tsp. vanilla extract
- ¼ cup chopped walnuts
- Whipped cream, to serve

Directions:

1. Lightly grease a baking dish and place the apples and pears inside.
2. Combine the rest of the ingredients, minus the walnuts and the whipped cream, until a coarse, crumbly texture is achieved.
3. Pour the mixture over the fruits and spread it evenly. Top with the chopped walnuts.
4. Air bake at 340°F for 20 minutes or until the top turns golden brown.
5. When cooked through, serve at room temperature with whipped cream.

538. SWEET & CRISP BANANAS

Preparation Time: 20 minutes
Smart Points: 3
Servings: 4

Ingredients

1. 4 ripe bananas, peeled and halved
2. 1 tbsp. almond meal
3. 1 tbsp. cashew, crushed
4. 1 egg, beaten
5. 1 ½ tbsp. coconut oil
6. ¼ cup keto almond flour
7. 1 ½ tbsp. stevia
8. ½ cup keto friendly bread crumbs

Directions:

1. Put the coconut oil in a saucepan and heat over a medium heat. Stir in the keto bread crumbs and cook, stirring continuously, for 4 minutes.
2. Transfer the keto bread crumbs to a bowl.
3. Add in the almond meal and crushed cashew. Mix well.
4. Coat each of the banana halves in the corn flour, before dipping it in the beaten egg and lastly coating it with the bread crumbs.
5. Put the coated banana halves in the Air Fryer basket. Season with the stevia.
6. Air fry at 350°F for 10 minutes.

539. KETO SHORTBREAD FINGERS

Preparation Time: 20 minutes
Smart Points: 4
Servings: 10

Ingredients

- 1 ½ cups butter
- 1 cup keto almond flour
- ¾ cup stevia
- Cooking spray

Directions:

1. Pre-heat your Air Fryer to 350°F.
2. In a bowl. combine the flour and stevia.
3. Cut each stick of butter into small chunks. Add the chunks into the flour and the stevia.
4. Blend the butter into the mixture to combine everything well.
5. Use your hands to knead the mixture, forming a smooth consistency.
6. Shape the mixture into 10 equal-sized finger shapes, marking them with the tines of a fork for decoration if desired.
7. Lightly spritz the Air Fryer basket with the cooking spray. Place the cookies inside, spacing them out well.
8. Bake the cookies for 12 minutes.
9. Let cool slightly before serving. Alternatively, you can store the cookies in an airtight container for up to 3 days.

540. COCONUT & BANANA CAKE

Preparation Time: 1 hour 15 minutes
Smart Points: 4
Servings: 5

Ingredients

- 2/3 cup stevia, shaved
- 2/3 cup unsalted butter
- 3 eggs
- 1 ¼ cup keto almond flour
- 1 ripe banana, mashed
- ½ tsp. vanilla extract
- 1/8 tsp. baking soda
- Sea salt to taste

Topping Ingredients

- stevia to taste, shaved
- Walnuts to taste, roughly chopped
- Bananas to taste, sliced

Directions:

1. Pre-heat the Air Fryer to 360°F.
2. Mix together the flour, baking soda, and a pinch of sea salt.
3. In a separate bowl, combine the butter, vanilla extract and stevia using an electrical mixer or a blender, to achieve a fluffy consistency. Beat in the eggs one at a time.
4. Throw in half of the flour mixture and stir thoroughly. Add in the mashed banana and continue to mix. Lastly, throw in the remaining half of the flour mixture and combine until a smooth batter is formed.
5. Transfer the batter to a baking tray and top with the banana slices.
6. Scatter the chopped walnuts on top before dusting with the stevia
7. Place a sheet of foil over the tray and pierce several holes in it.
8. Put the covered tray in the Air Fryer. Cook for 48 minutes.
9. Decrease the temperature to 320°F, take off the foil, and allow to cook for an additional 10 minutes until golden brown.
10. Insert a skewer or toothpick in the center of the cake. If it comes out clean, the cake is ready.

541. ROASTED PUMPKIN SEEDS & CINNAMON

Preparation Time: 35 minutes
Smart Points: 3
Servings: 2

Ingredients

- 1 cup pumpkin raw seeds
- 1 tbsp. ground cinnamon
- 2 tbsp. stevia
- 1 cup water
- 1 tbsp. olive oil

Directions:

1. In a frying pan, combine the pumpkin seeds, cinnamon and water.
2. Boil the mixture over a high heat for 2 - 3

minutes.

3. Pour out the water and place the seeds on a clean kitchen towel, allowing them to dry for 20 - 30 minutes.
4. In a bowl, mix together the stevia, dried seeds, a pinch of cinnamon and one tablespoon of olive oil.
5. Pre-heat the Air Fryer to 340°F.
6. Place the seed mixture in the fryer basket and allow to cook for 15 minutes, shaking the basket periodically throughout.

542. PINEAPPLE STICKS

Preparation Time: 20 minutes
Smart Points:
Servings: 4

Ingredients

- ½ fresh pineapple, cut into sticks
- ¼ cup desiccated coconut

Directions:

1. Pre-heat the Air Fryer to 400°F.
2. Coat the pineapple sticks in the desiccated coconut and put each one in the Air Fryer basket.
3. Air fry for 10 minutes.

543. SPONGE CAKE

Preparation Time: 50 minutes
Smart Points: 5
Servings: 8

Ingredients

For the Cake:

- 9 oz. stevia
- 9 oz. butter
- 3 eggs
- 9 oz. keto almond flour
- 1 tsp. vanilla extract
- Zest of 1 lemon
- 1 tsp. baking powder

For the Frosting

- Juice of 1 lemon
- Zest of 1 lemon
- 1 tsp. yellow food coloring
- 7 oz. stevia
- 4 egg whites

Directions:

1. Pre-heat your Air Fryer to 320°F.
2. Use an electric mixer to combine all of the cake ingredients.
3. Grease the insides of two round cake pans.
4. Pour an equal amount of the batter into each pan.
5. Place one pan in the fryer and cook for 15 minutes, before repeating with the second pan.
6. In the meantime, mix together all of the frosting ingredients.
7. Allow the cakes to cool. Spread the frosting on top of one cake and stack the other cake on top.

544. APPLE WEDGES

Preparation Time: 25 minutes
Smart Points: 4
Servings: 4

Ingredients

- 4 large apples
- 2 tbsp. olive oil
- ½ cup dried apricots, chopped
- 1 – 2 tbsp. stevia
- ½ tsp. ground cinnamon

Directions:

1. Peel the apples and slice them into eight wedges. Throw away the cores.
2. Coat the apple wedges with the oil.
3. Place each wedge in the Air Fryer and cook for 12 - 15 minutes at 350°F.
4. Add in the apricots and allow to cook for a further 3 minutes.
5. Stir together the stevia and cinnamon. Sprinkle this mixture over the cooked apples before serving.

545. CHOCOLATE LAVA CAKE

Preparation Time: 20 minutes
Smart Points: 3
Servings: 4

Ingredients

- 1 cup dark cocoa candy melts
- 1 stick butter

- 2 eggs
- 4 tbsp. stevia
- 1 tbsp. honey
- 4 tbsp. keto almond flour
- Pinch of kosher salt
- Pinch of ground cloves
- ¼ tsp. grated nutmeg
- ¼ tsp. cinnamon powder

Directions:

1. Spritz the insides of four custard cups with cooking spray.
2. Melt the cocoa candy melts and butter in the microwave for 30 seconds to 1 minute.
3. In a large bowl, combine the eggs, stevia and honey with a whisk until frothy. Pour in the melted chocolate mix.
4. Throw in the rest of the ingredients and combine well with an electric mixer or a manual whisk.
5. Transfer equal portions of the mixture into the prepared custard cups.
6. Place in the Air Fryer and air bake at 350°F for 12 minutes.
7. Remove from the Air Fryer and allow to cool for 5 to 6 minutes.
8. Place each cup upside-down on a dessert plate and let the cake slide out. Serve with fruits and chocolate syrup if desired.

546. ENGLISH LEMON TARTS

Preparation Time: 30 minutes
Smart Points: 4
Servings: 4

Ingredients

- ½ cup butter
- ½ lb. keto almond flour
- 2 tbsp. stevia
- 1 large lemon, juiced and zested
- 2 tbsp. lemon curd
- Pinch of nutmeg

Directions:

1. In a large bowl, combine the butter, keto almond flour and stevia until a crumbly consistency is achieved.
2. Add in the lemon zest and juice, followed

by a pinch of nutmeg. Continue to combine. If necessary, add a couple tablespoons of water to soften the dough.

3. Sprinkle the insides of a few small pastry tins with flour. Pour equal portions of the dough into each one and add stevia or lemon zest on top.
4. Pre-heat the Air Fryer to 360°F.
5. Place the lemon tarts inside the fryer and allow to cook for 15 minutes.

547. BLUEBERRY PANCAKES

Preparation Time: 20 minutes
Smart Points: 3
Servings: 4

Ingredients

- ½ tsp. vanilla extract
- 2 tbsp. honey
- ½ cup blueberries
- ½ cup stevia
- 2 cups + 2 tbsp. keto almond flour
- 3 eggs, beaten
- 1 cup milk
- 1 tsp. baking powder
- Pinch of salt

Directions:

1. Pre-heat the Air Fryer to 390°F.
2. In a bowl, mix together all of the dry ingredients.
3. Pour in the wet ingredients and combine with a whisk, ensuring the mixture becomes smooth.
4. Roll each blueberry in some flour to lightly coat it before folding it into the mixture. This is to ensure they do not change the color of the batter.
5. Coat the inside of a baking dish with a little oil or butter.
6. Spoon several equal amounts of the batter onto the baking dish, spreading them into pancake-shapes and ensuring to space them out well. This may have to be completed in two batches.
7. Place the dish in the fryer and bake for about 10 minutes.

548. NEW ENGLAND PUMPKIN

CAKE

Preparation Time: 50 minutes
Smart Points: 3
Servings: 4

Ingredients

- 1 large egg
- ½ cup skimmed milk
- 7 oz. keto almond flour
- 2 tbsp. stevia
- 5 oz. pumpkin puree
- Pinch of salt
- Pinch of cinnamon [if desired]
- Cooking spray

Directions:

1. Stir together the pumpkin puree and stevia in a bowl. Crack in the egg and combine using a whisk until smooth.
2. Add in the flour and salt, stirring constantly. Pour in the milk, ensuring to combine everything well.
3. Spritz a baking tin with cooking spray.
4. Transfer the batter to the baking tin.
5. Pre-heat the Air Fryer to 350°F.
6. Put the tin in the Air Fryer basket and bake for 15 minutes.

549. MIXED BERRY PUFFED PASTRY

Preparation Time: 20 minutes
Smart Points: 3
Servings: 3

Ingredients

- 3 pastry dough sheets
- ½ cup mixed berries, mashed
- 1 tbsp. honey
- 2 tbsp. cream cheese
- 3 tbsp. chopped walnuts
- ¼ tsp. vanilla extract

Directions:

1. Pre-heat your Air Fryer to 375°F.
2. Roll out the pastry sheets and spread the cream cheese over each one.
3. In a bowl, combine the berries, vanilla extract and honey.

4. Cover a baking sheet with parchment paper.
5. Spoon equal amounts of the berry mixture into the center of each sheet of pastry. Scatter the chopped walnuts on top.
6. Fold up the pastry around the filling and press down the edges with the back of a fork to seal them.
7. Transfer the baking sheet to the Air Fryer and cook for approximately 15 minutes.

550. CHERRY PIE

Preparation Time: 35 minutes
Smart Points: 3
Servings: 8

Ingredients

- 1 tbsp. milk
- 2 ready-made pie crusts
- 21 oz. cherry pie filling
- 1 egg yolk

Directions:

1. Pre-heat the Air Fryer to 310°F.
2. Coat the inside of a pie pan with a little oil or butter and lay one of the pie crusts inside. Use a fork to pierce a few holes in the pastry.
3. Spread the pie filling evenly over the crust.
4. Slice the other crust into strips and place them on top of the pie filling to make the pie look more homemade.
5. Place in the Air Fryer and cook for 15 minutes.

365-DAY MEAL PLAN

DAY	BREAKFAST	MAIN MEAL	DINNER
1	Easy Egg Muffins	Cheering Chicken Sandwiches	Easy Cheesecake Recipe
2	Breakfast Potatoes	Chicken Pie Recipe	Macaroons Recipe
3	Breakfast Ham Dish	Dill and Scallops	Orange Cake Recipe
4	Banana Oatmeal Casserole	Cheesy Ravioli and Marinara Sauce	Bread Dough and Amaretto Dessert Recipe
5	Tasty Polenta Bites	Cheese and Macaroni	Carrot Cake Recipe
6	Eggs and Tomatoes	Zucchini and Tuna Tortillas	Banana Bread Recipe
7	Breakfast Casserole	Beef Meatballs	Easy Granola Recipe
8	Fried Sandwich	Fish And Kettle Chips	Pears and Espresso Cream Recipe
9	Cheese Fried Bake	Egg Rolls	Banana Cake Recipe
10	Delightful Eggs Casserole	Special Pancake	Fried Bananas Recipe
11	Morning Egg Bowls	Turkish Style Koftas	Coffee Cheesecakes Recipe
12	Thyme Potato Breakfast Mix	Chicken Wings	Tomato Cake Recipe
13	Chicken and Spinach Breakfast Casserole	Summer Squash Fritters	Chocolate Cake Recipe
14	Breakfast Chicken Burrito	Fresh Style Chicken	White Filling Coconut and Oat Cookies
15	Fried Mushroom	Chinese Lunch	White Chocolate Chip Cookies
16	Simple Scrambled Eggs	Greek Bar B Q Sandwiches	Simple Cheesecake
17	Creamy Mushroom Pie	Unique Pie	Bread Pudding
18	Carrots and Cauliflower Breakfast Mix	Pizza Like Rolls	Bread Dough and Amaretto Dessert
19	Blackberries and Cornflakes	Wings in Old Bay Style	Cinnamon Rolls and Cream Cheese Dip
20	Delicious Doughnuts	Stew-Potato & Beef	Pumpkin Pie
21	Chicken Burrito	Simple Kale and Mushroom Chicken Mix	Wrapped Pears
22	Smoked Bacon and Bread	Lunch of Coconut Zucchini	Strawberry Donuts
23	Carrot Oatmeal	Pudding With Veggies	Chocolate Cake
24	Artichoke Omelet	Chinese Cabbage & Beef Bowls	Banana Bread
25	Cod Tortilla	Creamy Potatoes Meal	Apple Bread
26	Ham and Cheese Patties	Special Casserole For Lunch	Mini Strawberry Pies with Sugar Crust
27	Pear Oatmeal	Curry Made With Cod	Mini Lava Cakes
28	Creamy Mushroom Pie	Ravioli Lunch Meal	Fudgy Coconut Brownies
29	Cheesy Hash Brown	Pasta With Shrimp	Easiest Chocolate Lava Cake Ever
30	Peppers and Lettuce Salad	Cod Balls Lunch	Chocolate Banana Cake
31	Easy Egg Muffins	Cheering Chicken Sandwiches	Easy Cheesecake Recipe
32	Breakfast Potatoes	Chicken Pie Recipe	Macaroons Recipe
33	Breakfast Ham Dish	Dill and Scallops	Orange Cake Recipe
34	Banana Oatmeal Casserole	Cheesy Ravioli and Marinara Sauce	Bread Dough and Amaretto Dessert Recipe
35	Tasty Polenta Bites	Cheese and Macaroni	Carrot Cake Recipe
36	Eggs and Tomatoes	Zucchini and Tuna Tortillas	Banana Bread Recipe
37	Breakfast Casserole	Beef Meatballs	Easy Granola Recipe
38	Fried Sandwich	Fish And Kettle Chips	Pears and Espresso Cream Recipe

39	Cheese Fried Bake	Egg Rolls	Banana Cake Recipe
40	Delightful Eggs Casserole	Special Pancake	Fried Bananas Recipe
41	Morning Egg Bowls	Turkish Style Koftas	Coffee Cheesecakes Recipe
42	Thyme Potato Breakfast Mix	Chicken Wings	Tomato Cake Recipe
43	Chicken and Spinach Breakfast Casserole	Summer Squash Fritters	Chocolate Cake Recipe
44	Breakfast Chicken Burrito	Fresh Style Chicken	White Filling Coconut and Oat Cookies
45	Fried Mushroom	Chinese Lunch	White Chocolate Chip Cookies
46	Simple Scrambled Eggs	Greek Bar B Q Sandwiches	Simple Cheesecake
47	Creamy Mushroom Pie	Unique Pie	Bread Pudding
48	Carrots and Cauliflower Breakfast Mix	Pizza Like Rolls	Bread Dough and Amaretto Dessert
49	Blackberries and Cornflakes	Wings in Old Bay Style	Cinnamon Rolls and Cream Cheese Dip
50	Delicious Doughnuts	Stew-Potato & Beef	Pumpkin Pie
51	Chicken Burrito	Simple Kale and Mushroom Chicken Mix	Wrapped Pears
52	Smoked Bacon and Bread	Lunch of Coconut Zucchini	Strawberry Donuts
53	Carrot Oatmeal	Pudding With Veggies	Chocolate Cake
54	Artichoke Omelet	Chinese Cabbage & Beef Bowls	Banana Bread
55	Cod Tortilla	Creamy Potatoes Meal	Apple Bread
56	Ham and Cheese Patties	Special Casserole For Lunch	Mini Strawberry Pies with Sugar Crust
57	Pear Oatmeal	Curry Made With Cod	Mini Lava Cakes
58	Creamy Mushroom Pie	Ravioli Lunch Meal	Fudgy Coconut Brownies
59	Cheesy Hash Brown	Pasta With Shrimp	Easiest Chocolate Lava Cake Ever
60	Peppers and Lettuce Salad	Cod Balls Lunch	Chocolate Banana Cake
61	Easy Egg Muffins	Cheering Chicken Sandwiches	Easy Cheesecake Recipe
62	Breakfast Potatoes	Chicken Pie Recipe	Macaroons Recipe
63	Breakfast Ham Dish	Dill and Scallops	Orange Cake Recipe
64	Banana Oatmeal Casserole	Cheesy Ravioli and Marinara Sauce	Bread Dough and Amaretto Dessert Recipe
65	Tasty Polenta Bites	Cheese and Macaroni	Carrot Cake Recipe
66	Eggs and Tomatoes	Zucchini and Tuna Tortillas	Banana Bread Recipe
67	Breakfast Casserole	Beef Meatballs	Easy Granola Recipe
68	Fried Sandwich	Fish And Kettle Chips	Pears and Espresso Cream Recipe
69	Cheese Fried Bake	Egg Rolls	Banana Cake Recipe
70	Delightful Eggs Casserole	Special Pancake	Fried Bananas Recipe
71	Morning Egg Bowls	Turkish Style Koftas	Coffee Cheesecakes Recipe
72	Thyme Potato Breakfast Mix	Chicken Wings	Tomato Cake Recipe
73	Chicken and Spinach Breakfast Casserole	Summer Squash Fritters	Chocolate Cake Recipe
74	Breakfast Chicken Burrito	Fresh Style Chicken	White Filling Coconut and Oat Cookies
75	Fried Mushroom	Chinese Lunch	White Chocolate Chip Cookies
76	Simple Scrambled Eggs	Greek Bar B Q Sandwiches	Simple Cheesecake
77	Creamy Mushroom Pie	Unique Pie	Bread Pudding
78	Carrots and Cauliflower Breakfast Mix	Pizza Like Rolls	Bread Dough and Amaretto Dessert
79	Blackberries and Cornflakes	Wings in Old Bay Style	Cinnamon Rolls and Cream Cheese Dip

80	Delicious Doughnuts	Stew-Potato & Beef	Pumpkin Pie
81	Chicken Burrito	Simple Kale and Mushroom Chicken Mix	Wrapped Pears
82	Smoked Bacon and Bread	Lunch of Coconut Zucchini	Strawberry Donuts
83	Carrot Oatmeal	Pudding With Veggies	Chocolate Cake
84	Artichoke Omelet	Chinese Cabbage & Beef Bowls	Banana Bread
85	Cod Tortilla	Creamy Potatoes Meal	Apple Bread
86	Ham and Cheese Patties	Special Casserole For Lunch	Mini Strawberry Pies with Sugar Crust
87	Pear Oatmeal	Curry Made With Cod	Mini Lava Cakes
88	Creamy Mushroom Pie	Ravioli Lunch Meal	Fudgy Coconut Brownies
89	Cheesy Hash Brown	Pasta With Shrimp	Easiest Chocolate Lava Cake Ever
90	Peppers and Lettuce Salad	Cod Balls Lunch	Chocolate Banana Cake
91	Easy Egg Muffins	Cheering Chicken Sandwiches	Easy Cheesecake Recipe
92	Breakfast Potatoes	Chicken Pie Recipe	Macaroons Recipe
93	Breakfast Ham Dish	Dill and Scallops	Orange Cake Recipe
94	Banana Oatmeal Casserole	Cheesy Ravioli and Marinara Sauce	Bread Dough and Amaretto Dessert Recipe
95	Tasty Polenta Bites	Cheese and Macaroni	Carrot Cake Recipe
96	Eggs and Tomatoes	Zucchini and Tuna Tortillas	Banana Bread Recipe
97	Breakfast Casserole	Beef Meatballs	Easy Granola Recipe
98	Fried Sandwich	Fish And Kettle Chips	Pears and Espresso Cream Recipe
99	Cheese Fried Bake	Egg Rolls	Banana Cake Recipe
100	Delightful Eggs Casserole	Special Pancake	Fried Bananas Recipe
101	Morning Egg Bowls	Turkish Style Koftas	Coffee Cheesecakes Recipe
102	Thyme Potato Breakfast Mix	Chicken Wings	Tomato Cake Recipe
103	Chicken and Spinach Breakfast Casserole	Summer Squash Fritters	Chocolate Cake Recipe
104	Breakfast Chicken Burrito	Fresh Style Chicken	White Filling Coconut and Oat Cookies
105	Fried Mushroom	Chinese Lunch	White Chocolate Chip Cookies
106	Simple Scrambled Eggs	Greek Bar B Q Sandwiches	Simple Cheesecake
107	Creamy Mushroom Pie	Unique Pie	Bread Pudding
108	Carrots and Cauliflower Breakfast Mix	Pizza Like Rolls	Bread Dough and Amaretto Dessert
109	Blackberries and Cornflakes	Wings in Old Bay Style	Cinnamon Rolls and Cream Cheese Dip
110	Delicious Doughnuts	Stew-Potato & Beef	Pumpkin Pie
111	Chicken Burrito	Simple Kale and Mushroom Chicken Mix	Wrapped Pears
112	Smoked Bacon and Bread	Lunch of Coconut Zucchini	Strawberry Donuts
113	Carrot Oatmeal	Pudding With Veggies	Chocolate Cake
114	Artichoke Omelet	Chinese Cabbage & Beef Bowls	Banana Bread
115	Cod Tortilla	Creamy Potatoes Meal	Apple Bread
116	Ham and Cheese Patties	Special Casserole For Lunch	Mini Strawberry Pies with Sugar Crust
117	Pear Oatmeal	Curry Made With Cod	Mini Lava Cakes
118	Creamy Mushroom Pie	Ravioli Lunch Meal	Fudgy Coconut Brownies
119	Cheesy Hash Brown	Pasta With Shrimp	Easiest Chocolate Lava Cake Ever
120	Peppers and Lettuce Salad	Cod Balls Lunch	Chocolate Banana Cake

121	Easy Egg Muffins	Cheering Chicken Sandwiches	Easy Cheesecake Recipe
122	Breakfast Potatoes	Chicken Pie Recipe	Macaroons Recipe
123	Breakfast Ham Dish	Dill and Scallops	Orange Cake Recipe
124	Banana Oatmeal Casserole	Cheesy Ravioli and Marinara Sauce	Bread Dough and Amaretto Dessert Recipe
125	Tasty Polenta Bites	Cheese and Macaroni	Carrot Cake Recipe
126	Eggs and Tomatoes	Zucchini and Tuna Tortillas	Banana Bread Recipe
127	Breakfast Casserole	Beef Meatballs	Easy Granola Recipe
128	Fried Sandwich	Fish And Kettle Chips	Pears and Espresso Cream Recipe
129	Cheese Fried Bake	Egg Rolls	Banana Cake Recipe
130	Delightful Eggs Casserole	Special Pancake	Fried Bananas Recipe
131	Morning Egg Bowls	Turkish Style Koftas	Coffee Cheesecakes Recipe
132	Thyme Potato Breakfast Mix	Chicken Wings	Tomato Cake Recipe
133	Chicken and Spinach Breakfast Casserole	Summer Squash Fritters	Chocolate Cake Recipe
134	Breakfast Chicken Burrito	Fresh Style Chicken	White Filling Coconut and Oat Cookies
135	Fried Mushroom	Chinese Lunch	White Chocolate Chip Cookies
136	Simple Scrambled Eggs	Greek Bar B Q Sandwiches	Simple Cheesecake
137	Creamy Mushroom Pie	Unique Pie	Bread Pudding
138	Carrots and Cauliflower Breakfast Mix	Pizza Like Rolls	Bread Dough and Amaretto Dessert
139	Blackberries and Cornflakes	Wings in Old Bay Style	Cinnamon Rolls and Cream Cheese Dip
140	Delicious Doughnuts	Stew-Potato & Beef	Pumpkin Pie
141	Chicken Burrito	Simple Kale and Mushroom Chicken Mix	Wrapped Pears
142	Smoked Bacon and Bread	Lunch of Coconut Zucchini	Strawberry Donuts
143	Carrot Oatmeal	Pudding With Veggies	Chocolate Cake
144	Artichoke Omelet	Chinese Cabbage & Beef Bowls	Banana Bread
145	Cod Tortilla	Creamy Potatoes Meal	Apple Bread
146	Ham and Cheese Patties	Special Casserole For Lunch	Mini Strawberry Pies with Sugar Crust
147	Pear Oatmeal	Curry Made With Cod	Mini Lava Cakes
148	Creamy Mushroom Pie	Ravioli Lunch Meal	Fudgy Coconut Brownies
149	Cheesy Hash Brown	Pasta With Shrimp	Easiest Chocolate Lava Cake Ever
150	Peppers and Lettuce Salad	Cod Balls Lunch	Chocolate Banana Cake
151	Easy Egg Muffins	Cheering Chicken Sandwiches	Easy Cheesecake Recipe
152	Breakfast Potatoes	Chicken Pie Recipe	Macaroons Recipe
153	Breakfast Ham Dish	Dill and Scallops	Orange Cake Recipe
154	Banana Oatmeal Casserole	Cheesy Ravioli and Marinara Sauce	Bread Dough and Amaretto Dessert Recipe
155	Tasty Polenta Bites	Cheese and Macaroni	Carrot Cake Recipe
156	Eggs and Tomatoes	Zucchini and Tuna Tortillas	Banana Bread Recipe
157	Breakfast Casserole	Beef Meatballs	Easy Granola Recipe
158	Fried Sandwich	Fish And Kettle Chips	Pears and Espresso Cream Recipe
159	Cheese Fried Bake	Egg Rolls	Banana Cake Recipe
160	Delightful Eggs Casserole	Special Pancake	Fried Bananas Recipe
161	Morning Egg Bowls	Turkish Style Koftas	Coffee Cheesecakes Recipe
162	Thyme Potato Breakfast Mix	Chicken Wings	Tomato Cake Recipe

163	Chicken and Spinach Breakfast Casserole	Summer Squash Fritters	Chocolate Cake Recipe
164	Breakfast Chicken Burrito	Fresh Style Chicken	White Filling Coconut and Oat Cookies
165	Fried Mushroom	Chinese Lunch	White Chocolate Chip Cookies
166	Simple Scrambled Eggs	Greek Bar B Q Sandwiches	Simple Cheesecake
167	Creamy Mushroom Pie	Unique Pie	Bread Pudding
168	Carrots and Cauliflower Breakfast Mix	Pizza Like Rolls	Bread Dough and Amaretto Dessert
169	Blackberries and Cornflakes	Wings in Old Bay Style	Cinnamon Rolls and Cream Cheese Dip
170	Delicious Doughnuts	Stew-Potato & Beef	Pumpkin Pie
171	Chicken Burrito	Simple Kale and Mushroom Chicken Mix	Wrapped Pears
172	Smoked Bacon and Bread	Lunch of Coconut Zucchini	Strawberry Donuts
173	Carrot Oatmeal	Pudding With Veggies	Chocolate Cake
174	Artichoke Omelet	Chinese Cabbage & Beef Bowls	Banana Bread
175	Cod Tortilla	Creamy Potatoes Meal	Apple Bread
176	Ham and Cheese Patties	Special Casserole For Lunch	Mini Strawberry Pies with Sugar Crust
177	Pear Oatmeal	Curry Made With Cod	Mini Lava Cakes
178	Creamy Mushroom Pie	Ravioli Lunch Meal	Fudgy Coconut Brownies
179	Cheesy Hash Brown	Pasta With Shrimp	Easiest Chocolate Lava Cake Ever
180	Peppers and Lettuce Salad	Cod Balls Lunch	Chocolate Banana Cake
181	Easy Egg Muffins	Cheering Chicken Sandwiches	Easy Cheesecake Recipe
182	Breakfast Potatoes	Chicken Pie Recipe	Macaroons Recipe
183	Breakfast Ham Dish	Dill and Scallops	Orange Cake Recipe
184	Banana Oatmeal Casserole	Cheesy Ravioli and Marinara Sauce	Bread Dough and Amaretto Dessert Recipe
185	Tasty Polenta Bites	Cheese and Macaroni	Carrot Cake Recipe
186	Eggs and Tomatoes	Zucchini and Tuna Tortillas	Banana Bread Recipe
187	Breakfast Casserole	Beef Meatballs	Easy Granola Recipe
188	Fried Sandwich	Fish And Kettle Chips	Pears and Espresso Cream Recipe
189	Cheese Fried Bake	Egg Rolls	Banana Cake Recipe
190	Delightful Eggs Casserole	Special Pancake	Fried Bananas Recipe
191	Morning Egg Bowls	Turkish Style Koftas	Coffee Cheesecakes Recipe
192	Thyme Potato Breakfast Mix	Chicken Wings	Tomato Cake Recipe
193	Chicken and Spinach Breakfast Casserole	Summer Squash Fritters	Chocolate Cake Recipe
194	Breakfast Chicken Burrito	Fresh Style Chicken	White Filling Coconut and Oat Cookies
195	Fried Mushroom	Chinese Lunch	White Chocolate Chip Cookies
196	Simple Scrambled Eggs	Greek Bar B Q Sandwiches	Simple Cheesecake
197	Creamy Mushroom Pie	Unique Pie	Bread Pudding
198	Carrots and Cauliflower Breakfast Mix	Pizza Like Rolls	Bread Dough and Amaretto Dessert
199	Blackberries and Cornflakes	Wings in Old Bay Style	Cinnamon Rolls and Cream Cheese Dip
200	Delicious Doughnuts	Stew-Potato & Beef	Pumpkin Pie
201	Chicken Burrito	Simple Kale and Mushroom Chicken Mix	Wrapped Pears
202	Smoked Bacon and Bread	Lunch of Coconut Zucchini	Strawberry Donuts

203	Carrot Oatmeal	Pudding With Veggies	Chocolate Cake
204	Artichoke Omelet	Chinese Cabbage & Beef Bowls	Banana Bread
205	Cod Tortilla	Creamy Potatoes Meal	Apple Bread
206	Ham and Cheese Patties	Special Casserole For Lunch	Mini Strawberry Pies with Sugar Crust
207	Pear Oatmeal	Curry Made With Cod	Mini Lava Cakes
208	Creamy Mushroom Pie	Ravioli Lunch Meal	Fudgy Coconut Brownies
209	Cheesy Hash Brown	Pasta With Shrimp	Easiest Chocolate Lava Cake Ever
210	Peppers and Lettuce Salad	Cod Balls Lunch	Chocolate Banana Cake
211	Easy Egg Muffins	Cheering Chicken Sandwiches	Easy Cheesecake Recipe
212	Breakfast Potatoes	Chicken Pie Recipe	Macaroons Recipe
213	Breakfast Ham Dish	Dill and Scallops	Orange Cake Recipe
214	Banana Oatmeal Casserole	Cheesy Ravioli and Marinara Sauce	Bread Dough and Amaretto Dessert Recipe
215	Tasty Polenta Bites	Cheese and Macaroni	Carrot Cake Recipe
216	Eggs and Tomatoes	Zucchini and Tuna Tortillas	Banana Bread Recipe
217	Breakfast Casserole	Beef Meatballs	Easy Granola Recipe
218	Fried Sandwich	Fish And Kettle Chips	Pears and Espresso Cream Recipe
219	Cheese Fried Bake	Egg Rolls	Banana Cake Recipe
220	Delightful Eggs Casserole	Special Pancake	Fried Bananas Recipe
221	Morning Egg Bowls	Turkish Style Koftas	Coffee Cheesecakes Recipe
222	Thyme Potato Breakfast Mix	Chicken Wings	Tomato Cake Recipe
223	Chicken and Spinach Breakfast Casserole	Summer Squash Fritters	Chocolate Cake Recipe
224	Breakfast Chicken Burrito	Fresh Style Chicken	White Filling Coconut and Oat Cookies
225	Fried Mushroom	Chinese Lunch	White Chocolate Chip Cookies
226	Simple Scrambled Eggs	Greek Bar B Q Sandwiches	Simple Cheesecake
227	Creamy Mushroom Pie	Unique Pie	Bread Pudding
228	Carrots and Cauliflower Breakfast Mix	Pizza Like Rolls	Bread Dough and Amaretto Dessert
229	Blackberries and Cornflakes	Wings in Old Bay Style	Cinnamon Rolls and Cream Cheese Dip
230	Delicious Doughnuts	Stew-Potato & Beef	Pumpkin Pie
231	Chicken Burrito	Simple Kale and Mushroom Chicken Mix	Wrapped Pears
232	Smoked Bacon and Bread	Lunch of Coconut Zucchini	Strawberry Donuts
233	Carrot Oatmeal	Pudding With Veggies	Chocolate Cake
234	Artichoke Omelet	Chinese Cabbage & Beef Bowls	Banana Bread
235	Cod Tortilla	Creamy Potatoes Meal	Apple Bread
236	Ham and Cheese Patties	Special Casserole For Lunch	Mini Strawberry Pies with Sugar Crust
237	Pear Oatmeal	Curry Made With Cod	Mini Lava Cakes
238	Creamy Mushroom Pie	Ravioli Lunch Meal	Fudgy Coconut Brownies
239	Cheesy Hash Brown	Pasta With Shrimp	Easiest Chocolate Lava Cake Ever
240	Peppers and Lettuce Salad	Cod Balls Lunch	Chocolate Banana Cake
241	Easy Egg Muffins	Cheering Chicken Sandwiches	Easy Cheesecake Recipe
242	Breakfast Potatoes	Chicken Pie Recipe	Macaroons Recipe
243	Breakfast Ham Dish	Dill and Scallops	Orange Cake Recipe
244	Banana Oatmeal Casserole	Cheesy Ravioli and Marinara Sauce	Bread Dough and Amaretto Dessert Recipe

245	Tasty Polenta Bites	Cheese and Macaroni	Carrot Cake Recipe
246	Eggs and Tomatoes	Zucchini and Tuna Tortillas	Banana Bread Recipe
247	Breakfast Casserole	Beef Meatballs	Easy Granola Recipe
248	Fried Sandwich	Fish And Kettle Chips	Pears and Espresso Cream Recipe
249	Cheese Fried Bake	Egg Rolls	Banana Cake Recipe
250	Delightful Eggs Casserole	Special Pancake	Fried Bananas Recipe
251	Morning Egg Bowls	Turkish Style Koftas	Coffee Cheesecakes Recipe
252	Thyme Potato Breakfast Mix	Chicken Wings	Tomato Cake Recipe
253	Chicken and Spinach Breakfast Casserole	Summer Squash Fritters	Chocolate Cake Recipe
254	Breakfast Chicken Burrito	Fresh Style Chicken	White Filling Coconut and Oat Cookies
255	Fried Mushroom	Chinese Lunch	White Chocolate Chip Cookies
256	Simple Scrambled Eggs	Greek Bar B Q Sandwiches	Simple Cheesecake
257	Creamy Mushroom Pie	Unique Pie	Bread Pudding
258	Carrots and Cauliflower Breakfast Mix	Pizza Like Rolls	Bread Dough and Amaretto Dessert
259	Blackberries and Cornflakes	Wings in Old Bay Style	Cinnamon Rolls and Cream Cheese Dip
260	Delicious Doughnuts	Stew-Potato & Beef	Pumpkin Pie
261	Chicken Burrito	Simple Kale and Mushroom Chicken Mix	Wrapped Pears
262	Smoked Bacon and Bread	Lunch of Coconut Zucchini	Strawberry Donuts
263	Carrot Oatmeal	Pudding With Veggies	Chocolate Cake
264	Artichoke Omelet	Chinese Cabbage & Beef Bowls	Banana Bread
265	Cod Tortilla	Creamy Potatoes Meal	Apple Bread
266	Ham and Cheese Patties	Special Casserole For Lunch	Mini Strawberry Pies with Sugar Crust
267	Pear Oatmeal	Curry Made With Cod	Mini Lava Cakes
268	Creamy Mushroom Pie	Ravioli Lunch Meal	Fudgy Coconut Brownies
269	Cheesy Hash Brown	Pasta With Shrimp	Easiest Chocolate Lava Cake Ever
270	Peppers and Lettuce Salad	Cod Balls Lunch	Chocolate Banana Cake
271	Easy Egg Muffins	Cheering Chicken Sandwiches	Easy Cheesecake Recipe
272	Breakfast Potatoes	Chicken Pie Recipe	Macaroons Recipe
273	Breakfast Ham Dish	Dill and Scallops	Orange Cake Recipe
274	Banana Oatmeal Casserole	Cheesy Ravioli and Marinara Sauce	Bread Dough and Amaretto Dessert Recipe
275	Tasty Polenta Bites	Cheese and Macaroni	Carrot Cake Recipe
276	Eggs and Tomatoes	Zucchini and Tuna Tortillas	Banana Bread Recipe
277	Breakfast Casserole	Beef Meatballs	Easy Granola Recipe
278	Fried Sandwich	Fish And Kettle Chips	Pears and Espresso Cream Recipe
279	Cheese Fried Bake	Egg Rolls	Banana Cake Recipe
280	Delightful Eggs Casserole	Special Pancake	Fried Bananas Recipe
281	Morning Egg Bowls	Turkish Style Koftas	Coffee Cheesecakes Recipe
282	Thyme Potato Breakfast Mix	Chicken Wings	Tomato Cake Recipe
283	Chicken and Spinach Breakfast Casserole	Summer Squash Fritters	Chocolate Cake Recipe
284	Breakfast Chicken Burrito	Fresh Style Chicken	White Filling Coconut and Oat Cookies
285	Fried Mushroom	Chinese Lunch	White Chocolate Chip Cookies

286	Simple Scrambled Eggs	Greek Bar B Q Sandwiches	Simple Cheesecake
287	Creamy Mushroom Pie	Unique Pie	Bread Pudding
288	Carrots and Cauliflower Breakfast Mix	Pizza Like Rolls	Bread Dough and Amaretto Dessert
289	Blackberries and Cornflakes	Wings in Old Bay Style	Cinnamon Rolls and Cream Cheese Dip
290	Delicious Doughnuts	Stew-Potato & Beef	Pumpkin Pie
291	Chicken Burrito	Simple Kale and Mushroom Chicken Mix	Wrapped Pears
292	Smoked Bacon and Bread	Lunch of Coconut Zucchini	Strawberry Donuts
293	Carrot Oatmeal	Pudding With Veggies	Chocolate Cake
294	Artichoke Omelet	Chinese Cabbage & Beef Bowls	Banana Bread
295	Cod Tortilla	Creamy Potatoes Meal	Apple Bread
296	Ham and Cheese Patties	Special Casserole For Lunch	Mini Strawberry Pies with Sugar Crust
297	Pear Oatmeal	Curry Made With Cod	Mini Lava Cakes
298	Creamy Mushroom Pie	Ravioli Lunch Meal	Fudgy Coconut Brownies
299	Cheesy Hash Brown	Pasta With Shrimp	Easiest Chocolate Lava Cake Ever
300	Peppers and Lettuce Salad	Cod Balls Lunch	Chocolate Banana Cake
301	Easy Egg Muffins	Cheering Chicken Sandwiches	Easy Cheesecake Recipe
302	Breakfast Potatoes	Chicken Pie Recipe	Macaroons Recipe
303	Breakfast Ham Dish	Dill and Scallops	Orange Cake Recipe
304	Banana Oatmeal Casserole	Cheesy Ravioli and Marinara Sauce	Bread Dough and Amaretto Dessert Recipe
305	Tasty Polenta Bites	Cheese and Macaroni	Carrot Cake Recipe
306	Eggs and Tomatoes	Zucchini and Tuna Tortillas	Banana Bread Recipe
307	Breakfast Casserole	Beef Meatballs	Easy Granola Recipe
308	Fried Sandwich	Fish And Kettle Chips	Pears and Espresso Cream Recipe
309	Cheese Fried Bake	Egg Rolls	Banana Cake Recipe
310	Delightful Eggs Casserole	Special Pancake	Fried Bananas Recipe
311	Morning Egg Bowls	Turkish Style Koftas	Coffee Cheesecakes Recipe
312	Thyme Potato Breakfast Mix	Chicken Wings	Tomato Cake Recipe
313	Chicken and Spinach Breakfast Casserole	Summer Squash Fritters	Chocolate Cake Recipe
314	Breakfast Chicken Burrito	Fresh Style Chicken	White Filling Coconut and Oat Cookies
315	Fried Mushroom	Chinese Lunch	White Chocolate Chip Cookies
316	Simple Scrambled Eggs	Greek Bar B Q Sandwiches	Simple Cheesecake
317	Creamy Mushroom Pie	Unique Pie	Bread Pudding
318	Carrots and Cauliflower Breakfast Mix	Pizza Like Rolls	Bread Dough and Amaretto Dessert
319	Blackberries and Cornflakes	Wings in Old Bay Style	Cinnamon Rolls and Cream Cheese Dip
320	Delicious Doughnuts	Stew-Potato & Beef	Pumpkin Pie
321	Chicken Burrito	Simple Kale and Mushroom Chicken Mix	Wrapped Pears
322	Smoked Bacon and Bread	Lunch of Coconut Zucchini	Strawberry Donuts
323	Carrot Oatmeal	Pudding With Veggies	Chocolate Cake
324	Artichoke Omelet	Chinese Cabbage & Beef Bowls	Banana Bread
325	Cod Tortilla	Creamy Potatoes Meal	Apple Bread
326	Ham and Cheese Patties	Special Casserole For Lunch	Mini Strawberry Pies with Sugar Crust

327	Pear Oatmeal	Curry Made With Cod	Mini Lava Cakes
328	Creamy Mushroom Pie	Ravioli Lunch Meal	Fudgy Coconut Brownies
329	Cheesy Hash Brown	Pasta With Shrimp	Easiest Chocolate Lava Cake Ever
330	Peppers and Lettuce Salad	Cod Balls Lunch	Chocolate Banana Cake
331	Easy Egg Muffins	Cheering Chicken Sandwiches	Easy Cheesecake Recipe
332	Breakfast Potatoes	Chicken Pie Recipe	Macaroons Recipe
333	Breakfast Ham Dish	Dill and Scallops	Orange Cake Recipe
334	Banana Oatmeal Casserole	Cheesy Ravioli and Marinara Sauce	Bread Dough and Amaretto Dessert Recipe
335	Tasty Polenta Bites	Cheese and Macaroni	Carrot Cake Recipe
336	Eggs and Tomatoes	Zucchini and Tuna Tortillas	Banana Bread Recipe
337	Breakfast Casserole	Beef Meatballs	Easy Granola Recipe
338	Fried Sandwich	Fish And Kettle Chips	Pears and Espresso Cream Recipe
339	Cheese Fried Bake	Egg Rolls	Banana Cake Recipe
340	Delightful Eggs Casserole	Special Pancake	Fried Bananas Recipe
341	Morning Egg Bowls	Turkish Style Koftas	Coffee Cheesecakes Recipe
342	Thyme Potato Breakfast Mix	Chicken Wings	Tomato Cake Recipe
343	Chicken and Spinach Breakfast Casserole	Summer Squash Fritters	Chocolate Cake Recipe
344	Breakfast Chicken Burrito	Fresh Style Chicken	White Filling Coconut and Oat Cookies
345	Fried Mushroom	Chinese Lunch	White Chocolate Chip Cookies
346	Simple Scrambled Eggs	Greek Bar B Q Sandwiches	Simple Cheesecake
347	Creamy Mushroom Pie	Unique Pie	Bread Pudding
348	Carrots and Cauliflower Breakfast Mix	Pizza Like Rolls	Bread Dough and Amaretto Dessert
349	Blackberries and Cornflakes	Wings in Old Bay Style	Cinnamon Rolls and Cream Cheese Dip
350	Delicious Doughnuts	Stew-Potato & Beef	Pumpkin Pie
351	Chicken Burrito	Simple Kale and Mushroom Chicken Mix	Wrapped Pears
352	Smoked Bacon and Bread	Lunch of Coconut Zucchini	Strawberry Donuts
353	Carrot Oatmeal	Pudding With Veggies	Chocolate Cake
354	Artichoke Omelet	Chinese Cabbage & Beef Bowls	Banana Bread
355	Cod Tortilla	Creamy Potatoes Meal	Apple Bread
356	Ham and Cheese Patties	Special Casserole For Lunch	Mini Strawberry Pies with Sugar Crust
357	Pear Oatmeal	Curry Made With Cod	Mini Lava Cakes
358	Creamy Mushroom Pie	Ravioli Lunch Meal	Fudgy Coconut Brownies
359	Cheesy Hash Brown	Pasta With Shrimp	Easiest Chocolate Lava Cake Ever
360	Peppers and Lettuce Salad	Cod Balls Lunch	Chocolate Banana Cake
361	Easy Egg Muffins	Cheering Chicken Sandwiches	Easy Cheesecake Recipe
362	Breakfast Potatoes	Chicken Pie Recipe	Macaroons Recipe
363	Breakfast Ham Dish	Dill and Scallops	Orange Cake Recipe
364	Banana Oatmeal Casserole	Cheesy Ravioli and Marinara Sauce	Bread Dough and Amaretto Dessert Recipe
365	Tasty Polenta Bites	Cheese and Macaroni	Carrot Cake Recipe

CONCLUSION

Thanks for getting this book. Let's hope it was informative and provided you with all of the valuable information you need to achieve your goals whether you are seeking a way to lose weight or any just want to live a healthier lifestyle. Life cannot be much simpler than this.

The next step is to decide which recipe you want to test out first. Do you remember these?

- Easy Cheesecake Recipe

- Macaroons Recipe

- Orange Cake Recipe

- Bread Dough and Amaretto Dessert Recipe

- Carrot Cake Recipe

- Banana Bread Recipe

- Easy Granola Recipe

Does any of that strike your fancy for this evening?

Enjoy!!!

Made in the USA
Middletown, DE
29 January 2020